PLANNING URBAN EDUCATION

New Ideas and Techniques
to Transform Learning in the City

PLANNING URBAN EDUCATION

New Ideas and Techniques to Transform Learning in the City

Dennis L. Roberts, II
Editor

Educational Technology Publications
Englewood Cliffs, New Jersey 07632

PREFACE

It is now painfully evident that our urban schools are caught in an accelerating cycle of decline. Since urban schools will constitute the vast majority of American schools by the end of the 1970's, we are talking about a decline in American education.

The true measure of a structure of formal public education goes well beyond its effects on individual children. Cities are paying a heavy toll for the decline in educational quality—the economic, political, cultural and social life is being directly affected. Thus, we hear about the exodus of business and industry from the cities, and learn that one of the chief reasons given for this movement is the poor quality of education received by the graduates of urban schools.

The decline has begun to trigger a national loss in public confidence in our public schools. Yet, the most evident and tragic failures are occurring in those quarters of the city that need education most desperately—the low-income neighborhoods.

Whether the reaction is vocal protest or quiet frustration, the result throughout our cities is disillusionment with an institution that should be stimulating hope and promise. No citizen, no business or industry, no parent, no teacher, no school administrator, or no student should rest easy while this spiral of decline continues.

As an urbanized society, we are increasingly dependent on a modern educational system for the development of sophisticated manpower. Yet America's educational system is not urban-oriented; it is operationally still rooted in agrarian thinking. The updating of our public schools represents one of the most serious domestic problems facing America in the decade ahead.

The caliber of urban schools has a direct relationship to the economic, political, cultural and social life of the city itself. As the quality of schooling declines, the effects on both the producer and consumer are critical. In an age of education, consumers need quality education to survive. If they are denied the kind of education required, they are compelled to seek alternatives. For some who can afford it, there is the option of private schools. For many more, the option is to move to the suburbs, where both the quality of life and schooling are viewed as superior. For those who do not have the economic means for pursuing these alternatives, the option is to increase one's voice in the improvement of local schools. This latter option—largely relegated to the poor—is taking the form of decentralization and community control.

But what is indeed urban about urban schools? First, the urban context is one in which there is persistent stress imposed by intensely concentrated social realities. Although, of course, all schools operate in such a context, there are basic differences for those in urban centers. Schools in smaller, more homogeneous, communities have much less tension, because the schools reflect a reality that is more congruent to that of the surrounding community. Futhermore, there is not the intense consequence and concentration of so many varied slices of life. The urban school finds itself located in the center of great density and diversity, which affects very basically man's natural search for human satisfaction. Urban man must work through a whole intricate maze to satisfy both his physical and psycho-social needs. The consequences of urbanization to the individual—his dignity, his sense of "self" worth and his aspirations—are at the core of the problems under review here.

Density, one of the key urban characteristics, systematically results in a gradual loss of identity. Is the city dweller being lost in the massive shuffle of big city life? Urban society makes the individual feel like a mass man—depersonalized man. We hear from our instant-replay mass media about mass deaths from floods, from holiday tolls on the highways, from war and from the daily screams of the fire engines; and the individual soon learns that he is not as valuable as all that.

Further, modern urban centers, in order to deal with masses of people, create large organizations—bureaucracies. Bureaucratization continues the dehumanization process by communicating a sense of *powerlessness* to the individual. We are all familiar with, "You can't fight City Hall," or "What can one man do?" It is virtually impossible for an individual parent or citizen to know how to deal with a large, centralized school system.

Cities are also the places where the pluralistic nature of our society is most visible. We know that there is a Black section of the city, a Jewish, an Italian, a Puerto Rican and an Oriental section. When election returns are described, they reveal ethnic or religious voting trends. In short, cities are diverse. This diversity further affects the individual by pointing out his disconnection from others. How do I as a Black person connect with whites? How can I as a Jew connect with gentiles? Further, how do these sub-groups continue their own culture while connecting to the mainstream? What do they have to give up? Why?

The urban environment has become negative to human growth and development. Public schools have been unable to adapt themselves quickly enough to serve as instruments for human renewal. Public schools do deal with the next generation. They *could* have profound effects on our children's behavior. Public schools could prepare the next generation to use political and economic power differently—for rebuilding negative environments such as ghettos, for cleaning up our polluted water and air, and for combating disease, poverty and ignorance.

In short, public schools are the only social institution left which can influence an entire generation in humane ways. The next generation will assume roles as citizen, worker, parent and consumer. How and where will they learn these roles? Will the next generation perform these roles in essentially the same manner as previous generations?

Public schools can become the renewal instruments of modern society—but not as they are presently structured. Since urban schools are the most visible problems, we must start there. But the reader must realize that the urban crisis in education is itself a symptom of a broader problem with American education.

American education is in need of reform, and it must begin with our urban centers. How well we deal with urban education will, to a great extent, determine whether we can indeed reform American education swiftly enough to reverse the dehumanizing effects of the other forces which are shaping us all.

We have learned some things from our initial attempts at urban school improvement, e.g., compensatory education, decentralization and alternative subsystems. For example, we have learned about the nature of the educational problem. We had assumed that the problem was with the student, not the school; with the client, rather than the institution. With such a diagnosis, it made sense to mount programs of compensatory education, i.e., concentrated remediation of the "disadvantaged" learner with the aim of rehabilitating him to fit the existing school. Most of our federal programs of intervention—most notably Title I of the Elementary and Secondary Education Act—were compensatory in nature, attempting to have learners adjust to schools, rather than the other way around.

It was not until the latter part of the sixties that we began to raise questions about compensatory education. Reports from the field began to indicate that the results were not encouraging.

Consequently, any appropriate assumption for the seventies shifts the problem from the learner to the institution. The problem is *institutional obsolescence.* We are asking the standard school, which was forged in the nineteenth century, to solve twentieth and twenty-first century problems. The schools as presently standardized cannot meet the challenge which universal public education demands. The schools as major social institutions simply do not have the capacity to deal with diversity. We are asking public schools to become the major instrumentation for solving many of our social ills—poverty, racism, alienation, powerlessness—while also responding to the manpower needs of an advanced technological society. In short, we have given public education a mission for which it presently is not prepared. Faced with these growing demands, schoolmen have responded the only way they could, through an add-on strategy, i.e., building layers onto the standard educational structure, while at the same time keeping the present system running. Thus, we have added vocational education, special education, adult education, early childhood education, etc., but each has remained separated from the other.

The result over the years is that the total educational system has become ponderous and unresponsive to the growing aspirations of those who use schools. The basic charge for the seventies, therefore, is institutional reform.

The second major assumption of the sixties was that more money was needed for public school improvement. While on the surface this does not appear to be a fallacious assumption, it becomes so when more money is used to do more of the same thing. When, for example, more money is used for more reading teachers, more counselors and more psychologists who try to rehabilitate the learner to adjust to the conventional school, then *new* money is used in old ways. Federal money made available to public education in the sixties was *new* money which could have been used in *new* ways, thereby providing guidance for a better usage of the old money.

We have been pouring money into an outdated system, and if it continues, we will end up with an improved, outdated educational system. Putting more money into the present system is like putting money into an old car—after a point, diminishing returns set in. We are well into this stage.

In New York City, for example, the school system doubled its educational budget in less than a decade. Taking into account inflation and rising costs, the doubling of expenses has produced no significant difference in results. We assume, for instance, that we should continue to build schoolhouses. The Parkway Program in Philadelphia—the "School Without Walls"—used the elm as a campus and saved the school district $15 million on construction costs alone.

The question for the seventies must be, "More money for what?" Assumptions undergirding the fiscal policies for the decade of the seventies must center on the effects or results of various conceptions of education; i.e., given the same per-pupil cost, what are the results of different educational approaches?

A third assumption of the last decade had to do with the notion that the only legitimate party of interest in education was the professional educator—an administrator. It was his responsibility to decide how the money was to be spent. However, the sixties also saw the rise of the parties closest to the teaching front—teachers, students and parents. The seventies will see an increased voice of these major parties of interest in educational decision-making. Consequently, the assumption for the seventies must emphasize the consumer of schools— parents and students as well as teachers and administrators. An integral part of this assumption is that the *process* is as important as the *product*. The parties of interest must be connected in a *search* for quality education. Ideas, however sound, cannot be superimposed on others. Doing something *for* or *to* others must be replaced by doing something *with* others.

There have been and will continue to be books written on selected aspects of this subject. We are just beginning the long, hard journey toward urban reform. This volume, however, deals with the urban crisis in education from a scientific, technological and *total systems* frame of reference. Urban education is viewed within the context of a total urban community system. This makes the book both unique and useful. Most of the other books treat the issue from the perspective of various disciplines: history, sociology, anthropology, psychology and political science. This book deals with the management, planning, cost-effectiveness, systems analysis and communications approaches to urban school reform. This is not to say that the other, more human, dimensions are not treated—only that they are viewed from an overall framework which is total systems-oriented. The tapping and coordination of a wide range of available resources—not only those commonly used in education—as a means for improving our ability to effectively respond to human needs is the central theme of this collection.

This book is substantive. It introduces its readers, especially those in education, to new concepts: *ekistics, city of man, systems approach, forecasting, cost-effectiveness analysis, sense of community, urban simulation, urban service, information system design, cybernetic-ontogenetic approach, urban metapolicy, service delivery system, urban education marketplace* and the *turnkey approach,* to mention a few.

A word needs to be said about the contributors to this volume. What impressed me was the list of *new* names, representing fields of expertise not normally utilized in educational reports dealing with the urban school crisis. The authors are not detached, scholastic observers of the urban scene. They are involved practitioners and researchers, who have been in the action, and who are currently spearheading a wave of innovations on the urban education and urban planning scenes. Each views the problem from his own, unique vantage point.

There are, to be sure, some old pro's, like Robert J. Havighurst, whose vast experience and unique understanding of educational and organizational development help to make the volume useful.

This volume provides all those interested in renewing urban environments—especially our public schools—into humane centers serving human needs, with new insights and new analytic tools to grapple with the enormously difficult, but necessary, tasks ahead. It should be read by students and teachers, parents and administrators, researchers and practitioners, businessmen and governmental officials, and by all of those who are genuinely searching for *new* ways to make our schools more effective and our cities more livable places.

Mario D. Fantini
State University College
New Paltz, New York

CONTENTS

PLANNING URBAN EDUCATION

*New Ideas and Techniques
to Transform Learning in the City*

URBAN METAPOLICY
AND URBAN EDUCATION

Yehezkel Dror

The main thesis of this paper is that innovative changes in both urban metapolicy and in urban education are needed to meet present and future urban problems. Metapolicy deals with policies on policymaking, including the characteristics of the policymaking system and basic policy frameworks and postures. Unless urban metapolicy is improved, no meaningful improvements are possible in concrete policies on specific issues. Required changes in urban metapolicy include: (1) development of urban policy sciences knowledge; (2) invention of new urban policy tools; (3) explicit strategy determination; (4) new policy-contributing institutions and/or policy research organizations; (5) improvements of urban policymaking personnel; (6) advancement of citizen participation. This analysis has important implications for urban educators. On one hand, similar improvements in the urban education policymaking subsystem are needed for better urban educational policies. On the other hand, some radical changes in urban education are needed to meet the needs of better urban metapolicies. These include: (1) education of adults for more active roles in urban policymaking; (2) preparation of children for even more active future roles in urban policymaking; (3) training and retraining of urban policy practitioners for new patterns of urban policymaking; (4) training of new types of urban policy professionals; and (5) development of policy scientists. The proposed improvements in urban metapolicy and urban education are interrelated; therefore multidimensional reforms are necessary to meet the urban challenge.

Yehezkel Dror, on leave from The Hebrew University of Jerusalem, is with The Rand Corporation, Santa Monica, California.

3

A Short Appraisal of Urban Policymaking[1]
"Urban problems"—however ill-defined this concept may be[2] —are one of the main concerns of modern society. The transition to a "saturated society" in which many of the material and service necessities of life become free goods, the population growth, anticipated innovations in technology, and many of the possible (though unpredictable) transformations in culture and values—all will result in urban configurations and urban problems even more difficult to manage and resolve than the contemporary ones. Therefore, when we compare our incapacities to handle present urban issues with the problems of urban conglomerates of tomorrow, which will be more difficult by several orders of magnitude, one cannot but be somewhat afraid about the future. The extrapolated shape of urban issues seems clearly to bear out what I like to call aphoristically the Dror Law:

> *While the difficulties and dangers of problems tend to increase at a geometric rate, the knowledge and manpower qualified to deal with these problems tend to increase at an arithmetic rate.*

Two typical reactions to present and expected problems are: (1) to try to deal with them by pushing harder for solutions which are supposed to have worked in the past (e.g., more police in the streets to control crime); and (2) to look for new ideas in respect to concrete and acute problems faced today. But very little is done to improve urban policymaking and decision-making capabilities, so as to be better able to handle dynamic problems and changing situations.

The search for better solutions to present problems is both essential and useful, and much more needs to be done to move from

1. This section is based in part on comments I made at the round table on "Long-Range Urban Planning" at the American Orthopsychiatric Association 47th Annual Meeting—March 23-26, 1970, San Francisco.

2. My impression is that the term "urban problems" is used as referring to a vague cluster of social problems, with different emphasis on various issues—depending on the interests of the users. Even in its narrower uses, the term "urban problems" is significantly broader than the term "city problems," though there is much overlapping between them. For the purposes of this paper, I will use the term "urban problems" without further definitions. My main justification for doing so is that my analysis and conclusions are quite insensitive to various uses and meanings of that term.

"muddling through" to explicit policy innovations. But I think that efforts limited to resolving defined problems are doomed unless they are accompanied by far-reaching attempts to improve the urban policymaking system (which includes components in all levels of government—federal, state and local—as well as special interest groups, the universities, etc.). The case for this rests mainly on three reasons:

1. Innovative policy proposals have little chance of being carefully considered, adopted, implemented and revised unless the urban policymaking system develops new capacities for creativity, policy analysis, implementation and feedback. Also required are significant relaxations of present constraints on policies, including, in particular, political and organizational constraints. New patterns of decision-making are needed which in turn require changes in most of the elements of the urban policymaking system—including personnel, structure, "rules of the game," equipment and, perhaps most important of all, "policymaking culture."
2. Many problems can be better resolved before they are made visible by assuming crisis dimensions. Therefore, prediction of problems and allocation of resources to treatment of future problems are needed, requiring in turn changes in urban policymaking so as to make it more future-sensitive.
3. For many present and expected problems, no useful policies can be identified through contemporary policymaking knowledge. What are required, therefore, are new types of policy knowledge, policy research, policy invention and policy professionals.

Urban planning does little to change the picture. To be more exact: there exists no urban planning, but only city planning—which is something quite different. Not only is city planning constrained by the above-mentioned limitations of contemporary urban policymaking as a whole, but it suffers from a number of additional inadequacies of its own, such as:

1. Strong orientation to the physical features of cities, despite much lip service to more comprehensive approaches. Social problems in particular are ignored in most real-life city planning.

2. Poorness in policy instruments. Thus, despite recognized

extreme weaknesses, "master plans" and zoning continue to be regarded as major policy instruments of city planning.

3. Fargoing isolation from most facets of urban policymaking, including nearly all acute problems, the treatment of which in fact significantly shapes urban futures. Attempts to tie in city planning with ongoing decision-making through PPBS have as yet achieved very little.

4. Value-loadedness. Most city planners not only prefer one image of "ideal city"[3] over all others, but regard their preference as science-based and avoid all explicit value-sensitivity testing. The recent undermining of many "ideal city" images causes much bewilderment and heartsearching, but as yet has contributed little to a clearer conception of the roles of city planning in relation to urban policymaking and in respect to value judgments.

Most, if not all, of these weaknesses are recognized by the more advanced city planning scholars and practitioners, who slowly move toward a conception of urban planning in the full sense of that term. But, as yet, actual city planning is little influenced by the newer ideas and it is hard to see how even a sophisticated urban planning approach could have significant impact within the present urban policymaking system.

To sum up my short appraisal of contemporary urban policy-making, I see the main problem not as one of weaknesses of present urban policies alone. I think the problem is a more fundamental one: the present urban policymaking system is incapable of handling present and future urban issues. Not only do we not have an urban policy,[4] but a good urban policy cannot be formulated and implemented without redesign of the urban policymaking system.

In short, my main thesis is that in order successfully to face urban problems, we must innovate metapolicies, that is, policies on how to make policies.

3. For an illuminating discussion of "ideal cities," see C.A.O. van Nieuwenhuijze, The Ideal City or the Varieties of Metasocial Experience: A Typology. In C.A.O. van Nieuwenhuijze (Ed.) *The Nation and the Ideal City.* The Hague: Mouton, 1966, pp. 74-148.

4. Compare Daniel P. Moynihan. Toward a National Urban Policy. *The Public Interest*, No. 17, Fall 1969, pp. 3-20.

Approaches to Urban Metapolicy

Governmental reform is not a new idea, and there has been quite some talk in the United States on required adjustments in public institutions to meet urban problems[5] and even some action in this direction.[6] But the idea of metapolicy goes beyond individual reform proposals. Its basic framework is a systems view of policy-making:[7] Policymaking is regarded as an aggregative process in which a large number of different units interact in a variety of partially stabilized but open-ended modes. In other words, urban policy is made by a system, the urban policymaking system (which is very closely related to the public policymaking system, as urban policy is related to public policy).

This system is in a dynamic, open, non-steady state, and includes a large variety of different and changing multi-role components inter-connected in different degrees and through a multiplicity of channels; it is closely interwoven and overlapping with other policymaking systems and with social macro-systems (e.g., the productive system, the demographic-ecological system, the technological and knowledge system and the cultural system), and it behaves in ways which defy detailed modeling.

Even such a very simple systems perspective of public policy-making leads to three important improvement-relevant conclusions:

A. As urban policy is a product of complex interactions among a large number of various types of components, similar changes in the output (or similar "equifinal stages") can be achieved through many alternative variations in the components. This means, for our purposes, that different combinations of a variety of improvements may be equally useful in achieving equivalent changes in the quality of policymaking. This is a very helpful conclusion, because it permits us to

---

5. E.g., see Theodore J. Lowi. *The End of Liberalism: Ideology, Policy and the Crisis of Public Authority.* N.Y.: Norton, 1969; and Robert Wood. When Government Works. *The Public Interest*, No. 18, Winter 1970, pp. 39-51.

6. For instance, establishment of the Urban Institute and of the National Goals Research Staff in the White House.

7. See Yehezkel Dror. Some Normative Implications of a Systems View of Policymaking. In Milton D. Rubin (Ed.) *Man in Systems.* N.Y.: Gordon and Breach, 1970. (Earlier version, Rand Paper P-3991-1, February 1969.)

pick out of a large repertoire of potentially effective improvements those which are more feasible under changing political and social conditions. This view also emphasizes the open-ended (or, to be more exact, "open-sided") nature of any search for improvement-suggestions: there is, in principle, unlimited scope for adventurous thinking and invention.

B. A less optimistic implication of a systems view of urban policymaking is that improvements must reach a critical mass in order to influence the aggregative outputs of the system. Improvements which do not reach the relevant impact thresholds will, at best, be neutralized by countervailing adjustments of other components (e.g., a new urban planning method may be reacted to in a way that makes it an empty ritual), or, at worst, may in fact reduce the quality of overall urban policy (e.g., through possible boomerang effect, reducing belief in capacity of human intelligence, with possible retreat to some types of mysticism, leader-ideology, etc., or by implementing wrong policies more "efficiently," and thus reducing an important social protective mechanism—inefficiency as diminishing the dangers of implementation of wrong decisions and as permitting slow and tacit learning).

C. The third, and again optimistic, implication of a systems view of urban policymaking is that, thanks to the interactions between different system components, it may be possible to achieve the threshold of overall system output effects through a combination of strategic changes in controlling subcomponents, each one which by itself is incremental. In other words, a set of incremental changes can in the aggregate result in fargoing system output changes. Furthermore, because we are speaking about changes in the urban policymaking system, there may be a good chance that a set of relatively minor and quite incremental changes in the urban policymaking system will permit—through multiplier effects—fargoing innovations in the specific policies made by that system. This possibility is of much practical importance, because of the greater feasibility of incremental change than of radical change in United States urban politics. (Though, I think, the readiness to innovate is increasing by step-level functions, as a result of shock effects of highly perceived crisis symptoms.)

The systematic design, analysis and evaluation of policymaking system improvements is the main subject of metapolicy. Urban metapolicy is therefore concerned with improving the urban policy-making system. Such improvements involve all dimensions of the urban policymaking system, including environment, inputs, policy knowledge, personnel, structure, process patterns and stipulated output.[8] Also included in the concept of urban metapolicy are frameworks and directives for the substantive policies made by the urban policymaking system, in respect to basic assumptions, problem perceptions, value hierarchy, strategies and so on.

Let me make concrete the idea of innovative urban metapolicy with a number of illustrative interrelated ideas:

1. Encouragement of innovative policy research on urban problems, as a part of emerging policy sciences.[9] This involves novel research methods (such as social experimentation), novel research tools (e.g., acceptance of tacit knowledge of politicians and senior executives as an important source of knowledge) and novel research structures (e.g., interdisciplinary policy-oriented teams). Also necessary are study and utilization of experience with urban problems in other countries. Especially relevant are European and Japanese experiences, about which very little is known in the United States. A main aim of such urban policy research should be development of an overall conception of "urban policy," which can be of much help, initially, by operationalizing the meaning of "urban problems" and then by providing heuristic search patterns of possible resolutions.[10]

8. For a detailed discussion within a general policy sciences orientation, see Yehezkel Dror. *Public Policymaking Reexamined*. San Francisco: Chandler, 1968, esp. Part V.

9. On the nature and characteristics of policy sciences, see Harold D. Lasswell. The Emerging Conception of Policy Sciences. *Policy Sciences,* Spring 1970, *1* (1); and Yehezkel Dror. Prolegomena to Policy Sciences. *Policy Sciences, 1* (1).

10. The absence of any integrated conception of "urban policy" in the United States is not surprising, but is very disturbing. This omission is well demonstrated by the differences between foreign affairs and urban affairs. Foreign affairs are heterogenous and multidimensional; nevertheless, some integrating conceptions exist, as is well illustrated in President Nixon's First Annual Foreign Affairs Message, *United States Foreign Policy for the 1970's: A New Strategy for Peace.* But were one to decide to put together an Annual Social State of the Nation, it would have to be either very eclectic or very abstract—because there exists not even a usable concept package for urban affairs. Also, relatively simple issues, such as the relation between the "urban problems" cluster and the emerging "environmental problems" cluster, are quite unexplored.

2. Invention and development of new urban policy tools, ranging from monitoring and information processing to new policy instruments. Such tools may include, for instance: urban indicator systems, to permit early identification of problems and to encourage feedback on policy results; cable TV, to provide multiple communication channels with citizens; home computer consoles, for systematic contingency opinion polling; differential scheduling of work hours, weekend days and holidays, to deal with rush-hour and rush-day traffic; and so on.

3. Explicit strategy decisions (including mixed strategies) are needed on the following issues, among others: degrees and locations of acceptable innovations in policies; extent of risk to be accepted in policies and choice between a maximax posture and/or maximin posture and/or minimin-avoidance posture;[11] preferable mix between comprehensive policies, narrow-issue oriented policies and shock-policies (which aim at breakthroughs accompanied by temporary disequilibration); and preferable mix between policies oriented towards concrete goals, towards a number of defined future options, and/or towards building up resources better to achieve as yet undefined goals in the future. Such strategy decisions in turn require a variety of methodological innovations, such as construction of alternative comprehensive urban futures and policy analysis networks.[12]

4. New institutions must be designed and established as influential components of the urban policymaking system. Especially urgent is the need for "think tank" research institutes to work specifically on urban

11. I use the term "minimin-avoidance" to refer to policies directed at avoiding the worst of all possible situations. One important advantage of such a strategy concerns support recruitment: it is often much easier to achieve agreement on ills to be avoided than on operational positive formulations of "good life" to be realized.

Some success in minimin-avoidance would constitute a significant improvement over reality. However simple this may sound, human capacities to approximate minimin is amazing. Still well worth reading in this connection is Walter B. Pitkin. *A Short Introduction to the History of Human Stupidity*. N.Y.: Simon and Schuster, 1932. Urban policies could fill a long chapter in a modern version of such a history.

12. On this concept see Yehezkel Dror. *Policy Analysis: A Theoretic Framework and Some Basic Concepts*. Rand Paper P-4156, July 1969; and *A Policy Sciences View of Future Studies: Alternative Futures and Present Action*. Rand Paper P-4305, February 1970.

policy issues. The short experience of the New York-Rand Institute demonstrates the importance of such services for urban government. Establishment of The Urban Institute is another important step in this direction. But a whole set of such institutes to serve all centers of urban policymaking is required. Other possible institutional innovations include Look Out Institutes for early identification of emerging problems, and allocation of urban policymaking roles to universities.

5. Urban policymaking personnel must be improved. This includes, for instance, intense efforts to improve qualifications of urban politicians. Thus, urban politicians should be encouraged to participate in courses and seminars in policy sciences, to be designed for this purpose. Also needed is reform of urban senior civil service policy, including requirements for better qualifications, encouragement of rotation with other governments and with business, and incentives to draw top-quality candidates. More important are activities to train presently non-existing urban policy scientists and urban policy professionals. All this involves the relations between urban metapolicy and urban education, to which I will return soon.

6. Also closely related to urban education is another main direction of urban metapolicy improvement, namely advancement of citizen participation in urban policymaking. Here, modern technology may be very helpful, by providing tools for much better presentation of urban issues on TV and citizen education through active participation in urban games through cable TV, and for more intense involvement of the public in decision-making (e.g., as already mentioned, systematic opinion polling with the help of computer home consoles).

Having clarified the concept of metapolicy, we are now ready to take up our next and final subject, which I already touched upon in the last two metapolicy directives—namely, some relations between urban education and urban metapolicy.

Urban Education and Urban Metapolicy

One rather obvious application of our general analysis to education concerns the necessity for reform of the urban educational policymaking subsystem as a requisite for improving urban educational policies. All our analysis on the dependency of better policies on improved metapolicy applies to education, as do the various illustrations of needed metapolicy directions. Some adjustments are necessary to meet the special characteristics of educational policymaking.[13] But the general conclusion is I think quite clear without further details: The urban educational policymaking subsystem must be improved through innovative metapolicy, as a condition for design, evaluation, adoption and implementation of urban educational policies that can meet contemporary and future needs.

One point that should be emphasized is that improvement of the urban educational policymaking subsystem cannot take place in isolation. Because of the strong interconnections and overlappings between the urban educational policymaking subsystem and the urban policymaking system as a whole, the first cannot be changed without changes in the latter. Furthermore, because of the diffuse nature of education and the multiple forms of educational institutions,[14] any sharp distinction between "education" and other policy issues is a doubtful one. Education constitutes a main policy instrument for achievement of nearly all urban policy goals, and the states of nearly all aspects of urban life influence urban education. Therefore, educational policies must be closely fused with urban policies as a whole; and the educational policymaking subsystem must be considered and improved as an integral part of the urban policymaking system.

Less obvious are the implications of our analysis for the functions of urban education as an essential instrument of metapolicy innovations. This is still a very neglected subject. Let me therefore point out a few main directions of changes in urban education required in order to reform the urban policymaking system. Such changes are needed on at least five levels:

1. Education of adults for more active roles in urban policymaking.
2. Preparation of children for even more active future roles in urban policymaking.
3. Training and retraining of urban policy practitioners for new patterns of urban policymaking.
4. Training of new types of urban policy professionals.
5. Development of urban policy scientists.

13. See Rachel Elboim-Dror. Some Characteristics of the Education Policy Formation System. *Policy Sciences,* Summer 1970, *1* (2).

14. See Michael Marien. *The Education Complex: Emergence and Future of a Macro-System.* N.Y.: Free Press, 1970.

I will discuss these five levels one by one.

1. Education of adults for more active roles in urban policymaking. I already mentioned the intensification of citizen particpation in urban policymaking as one of the directions of urban metapolicy improvement. But in order for increasing citizen participation to constitute in fact an improvement, changes in the quality of that participation are needed. At the very least, needed are: more knowledge on urban problems; better understanding of interrelations between different issues and various resolutions; and fuller realization of longer range consequences of different alternatives. Also highly desirable are better value explication and sensitivity to value trade-offs; increased propensities to innovate; and capacities to face uncertainty.

The slogan of "enlightened citizen" as a requisite of democracy has been with us for too long to be taken seriously. Nevertheless, increasing demands for citizen participation based both on ideological reasons and functional needs do combine and make "citizen enlightenment" a hard necessity. Indeed, because of the growing complexity of urban issues, increased quality of citizen contributions to urban policies is essential in order to preserve the present level of citizen participation in urban policymaking. In other words: If the quality of citizen inputs into urban policymaking remains as it is now, meritocracy may well become the only chance for survival. Therefore, building up the policy contribution capacity of the citizen is essential for the continuous viability of urban democracy.

This is the challenge facing adult education from the point of view of urban metapolicy. When we add the many other reasons making adult education into an increasingly important social and individual activity (such as learning as a main leisure-time activity), then we arrive at a really first class challenge for adult education. To meet this challenge, radical novadesign of urban adult education is required.

To illustrate, let me mention these main plausible directions of novadesign of urban adult education:

a. The mass media of communication must develop new formats for presenting and analyzing public issues in ways conducive to informed individual opinions formation. For instance, policy issues should be presented in the form of policy analysis networks, with clear alternatives, explicit sensitivity analysis, uncertainty explication and assumption visibility. Present techniques are adequate for presentation of such programs on TV in ways which combine audience appeal with

14 - Planning Urban Education

improvement of citizen comprehension of complex issues.

b. Training tools which are simultaneously interesting and beneficial must be developed. Such tools include, for instance, cases, projects, urban games and individual policy exploration programs. In particular, urban games and individual policy exploration programs are very promising. Based on computers and brought to each house through cable TV and home computer consoles, suitable games and policy exploration programs can combine education for better urban policymaking with inputs into urban policymaking[15] —while also providing fascinating leisure-time activities. (The same equipment can serve other multiple purposes in respect to broad educational goals, urban metapolicy improvements, leisure-time use, communications, etc., thus justifying their costs.)

c. Incentives for participation in policy-oriented educational activities must be provided. Hopefully, increased opportunities to participate in urban policymaking together with availability of clearly relevant learning opportunities will provide basic motivation. This may be the case all the more because of the possibility—illustrated by the proposed techniques—to combine the useful with the attractive. But additional incentives may be necessary. Competitive games and exercises may provide one set of incentives; public attention and dramatization may provide a second set of incentives. If this does not work out, reservation of some special opportunities to participate in urban policymaking (other than the basic rights of voting, expression of opinion, etc., reserved of course for all) for those who do undergo a set of learning activities might prove necessary in some circumstances in the longer run. But adoption of suitable programs in schools—as soon discussed—should make such distasteful distinctions unnecessary.

These are only some illustrations which do point out possibility for redesign of urban education to serve, *inter alia*, the needs of increasing citizen participation in urban policymaking. This is a problem in need of much research and creativity.

2. *Preparation of children for even more active future roles in urban policymaking.* On a more fundamental level, preparation for increased participation in urban policymaking must take place before

15. E.g., see Stuart Umpleby. Citizen Sampling Simulation: A Method for Involving the Public in Social Planning. Paper presented at the International Future Conference, Kyoto, Japan, April 10-16, 1970.

maturation. The best location to prepare the citizen for increased policymaking roles is in school, when the necessary knowledge and capacities should be developed as a basic part of the equipment needed by every citizen in a modern urban democratic society.

The necessary knowledge and capacities to be conveyed and developed at school do include, among others: some knowledge and understanding of the urban system and of urban dynamics; a feel for alternative urban futures; abilities to handle uncertainty and probabilities; basic skills in logic and semantics; understanding of the elements of policy analysis and capacity to handle problems with the help of policy analysis networks; tolerance of ambiguity; appreciation of the main concepts of social sciences, economics and decision theory and their application to urban issues; and ability to search for information on new problems and issues and absorb that information within one's frame of appreciation.

This is a formidable list which may look prohibitive, unless we bear in mind that no technical skills and professional knowledge are aimed at. Some familiarity with fundamental concepts, some appreciation of their use and—most important of all—some skill in application of the knowledge and concepts to concrete issues as a main mode for making up one's mind, this is all that is aimed at.

Even so, this is an ambitious program, which can only be approximated through fargoing changes in school teaching. Much of the required knowledge and capacity should be developed through new approaches and novel teaching methods in traditional subjects. Thus, the study of history should include the history of urban life, should be problem oriented, and should be supplemented by treatment of alternative futures. To add another illustration: mathematics should be taught as a problem-solving approach, with emphasis on probability theory, Boolean algebra and theory of games. Some new subjects also have to be added, devoted explicitly to urban problems and policy analyses. In the new subjects and in the new contents of the traditional subjects, new teaching methods play a major role. Such new teaching methods include, for instance, gaming, computer interaction and internships. Existing methods such as projects and essays can also be very useful, if suitably adjusted.

These few pointers provide no solution to the nearly insurmountable difficulties of reforming school education—which are beyond both my competence and the scope of this paper. But I do want to emphasize that preparation of the future citizen for his future roles in urban policymaking while still in school is essential for managing the urban clusters of tomorrow democratically. This is only one of many demands upon school education resulting from the changing patterns of urbanism; but it is a demand deeply rooted in the requisites of improved urban metapolicy.

3. Training and retraining of urban policy practitioners. The need to train and retrain urban policy practitioners for the changing requirements of urban policymaking is a clear and straightforward one, which would not require much elaboration were it not for the taboos surrounding parts of it.

The need to reequip urban civil servants is more and more recognized. With changes in the main functions of urban management from administrative efficiency to urban problem solution and directed social change, the classic contents and skills of public administration become relatively less important (though they should not be forgotten). Instead, urban policy sciences, applied social sciences and modern organization theory must be the foundations for urban management. Even though it is a hard and slow process, suitable changes do go on at universities, at new schools of urban affairs, at redesigned schools of public administration and at schools of management. These changes can be expected to take care of training and retraining urban civil servants, though this trend should be accelerated.

The situation is completely different in respect to the most important component of urban policy practitioners and of the urban policymaking system as a whole, namely urban politicians. As a result of naive misunderstandings of democratic theory and of institutional carry-over from simpler periods, the idea that elected politicians *ipso facto* their election are qualified (as distinct from legitimized) to fulfill crucial roles in policymaking is usually accepted without questioning. This is a wrong conclusion, ideologically as well as factually.

Ideologically, democracy does imply that candidates do not have to pass any educational qualification test and that every person duly elected is legitimately entitled to exercise all the prerogatives of office. But there is no reason in democratic ideology for ignoring the need that politicians be suitably qualified and for abstaining from establishing institutions to encourage politicians to develop the necessary knowledge and capacities. Factually, the dangers of politicians either overrelying on experts and meritocrats or of underutilizing modern knowledge, as a result of lacking sufficient knowledge and capacities to correctly utilize systematic knowledge and structure rationally, are obvious today. These dangers will be aggravated in the future when both relevant knowledge and problems are even more complex and difficult to handle.

My conclusion, therefore, is that improvement of politicians through learning is essential (though, by itself, insufficient) for qualifying them to handle present and future urban problems. The need can be handled within the tenets of democracy, if we are innovative enough in designing suitable institutions. In particular, needed are special courses, seminars and curricula for politicians, ranging from one week to a year, devoted to conveying to politicians appreciation, knowledge and skills in urban policy sciences.[16] While politicians cannot and should not be forced to participate, better politicians will welcome short and well-designed seminars which may help them in fulfilling their duties. At the same time, sabbatical leave for politicians to engage in longer courses of study paid for by the public should become universal. Hopefully, participation in courses and training will be recognized by the electorate as desirable, thus providing a powerful incentive for politicians who are looking, as they should, for votes.

Here, some synergetic relations between different proposals become visible, namely the interdependence between adult education for better urban policymaking, preparation of pupils for future participation in urban policymaking and popular support for policy relevant studies by politicians. But let me wait with further emphasis of the mutually reinforcing bonds between various policy-oriented changes in urban education till we examine the training of new types of urban policy professionals and the development of urban policy scientists.

4. and 5. Training of new types of urban policy professionals and development of urban policy scientists. Development of reliable urban policy sciences knowledge is a precondition for all other proposed improvements both of urban metapolicy and of urban policy relevant to education. Only reliable urban policy sciences knowledge can serve as a basis for better urban metapolicies and for urban policy relevant teaching material. In order to develop urban policy sciences systematically and on a massive scale, a new generation of scholars and

16. Special institutes providing short courses to elected urban politicians exist in some countries. The *Kommunskolan* in Sweden is a good illustration.

researchers is needed who avoid the trained incapacities of existing disciplines and are able to work out the innovative paradigms of policy sciences. And in order to apply urban policy sciences to concrete urban metapolicy and policy problems, a new profession of urban policy analysts is necessary to fill new roles in the urban policymaking system.

It is convenient to discuss education of policy sciences scholars and of policy analysis professionals together, because: (a) there should be no clear distinction between these two roles, as movement between and fusion of abstract research and concrete applications is among the specific characteristics of policy sciences; and (b) similar innovative academic arrangements are necessary for both of them. What are required are teaching programs on the post-graduate level which are characterized by the following features:[17] (1) interdisciplinary basis, with special emphasis on decision theories on one hand and behavioral sciences on the other; (2) strong emphasis on training through applied work, so as to develop capacity to transform abstract knowledge into concrete recommendations and to develop abstract knowledge on the basis of real life applications; (3) encouragement of creative innovation, together with strict analysis; (4) strong emphasis on methodology, combined with extensive problem area knowledge; (5) sensitization to involved values, with education for a "clinic rational" approach; (6) very demanding programs, which only limited groups of carefully selected students can successfully undertake.

Such programs need new locations at universities; it may even be the case that such programs have a better chance to succeed not at established universities, but at policy research organizations which can combine applied policy sciences work, production of new policy sciences knowledge, and advanced teaching in policy sciences.

Additional variations come easily to mind. For instance, some elements of urban policy sciences should be included in all university curricula—to broaden preparation for citizen participation (under-graduate programs), prepare different professions for urban policy relevant work (e.g., medicine, social work, social science and engineering) and to initiate future urban politicians (e.g., law). But, as in all other sections, my intention here is not to exhaust the subject, only to indicate some guidelines for thought, research and action.

17. For a detailed discussion, see Yehezkel Dror. Teaching of Policy Sciences: Design for a Doctorate University Program. *Social Science Information* (1970); (earlier version Rand Paper P-4128-1, November 1969).

It is important to recognize the interdependence of the different analyses and proposals. Not only are different metapolicy proposals interdependent, and different urban education proposals interdependent, but better urban metapolicy depends on improvement of urban education, and improvement of urban education depends on better urban metapolicy. This does not imply that everything can or should be done simultaneously. But it is correct to draw the conclusion that *isolated incremental changes here or there will make no worthwhile contributions.* A massive and multidimensional effort is needed to improve urban metapolicy and urban education, so as to meet the urban challenges of the present and of the foreseeable future.

THE FUTURE OF
THE CITY OF MAN

Constantinos A. Doxiadis

Nowadays we like to talk about the "City of Man"; apparently that reinforces our pride and encourages us in facing our problems. But isn't this reminiscent of aging people who like to speak about their strength when it is beginning to fade away, and their successes when no more are in prospect?

If we look at our city from the air we will see it covered by buildings of all sorts and large areas with moving or idle cars in thousands; if we look at it from the street level we will find it controlled by machines which have pushed people against the buildings. Why do we call it the "City of Man," when that poor creature is hiding deep inside the buildings or way out in five-acre suburban homes?

In fact, I do not believe that we are entitled to speak about the "City of Man" as a reality of the present anymore, even though certainly such a city should become our goal once again. Our city of today consists—as it always has—of five elements. A more poetic expression is the "five-star city."

These five elements—Nature, in which we live; Man who, as we like to believe, initiates the urban process; Society, which is formed by Man; the Shells or buildings, which are built by him; and the Networks of roads, railways, water-pipes, power lines, and others, which he

Constantinos A. Doxiadis is president of Doxiadis Associates, consultants on development and ekistics, Athens, Greece.

creates—are interwoven to form systems of increasing complexity (see Figure 1). When we try to understand them we become confused, and no wonder, since they can be seen in many different ways—from the economic point of view, the social, the political or administrative, the technological or the cultural. When a merchant says that he likes his city, what he means is that business has been very good during the past few years; when his wife says she does not, what she means is that social life is declining and she feels lonelier; his daughter might have to abandon it because it has no artistic activity; his young son might be delighted because of a new sports-ground built in the neighborhood, while his mother-in-law calls it uncivilized because the age-old elm trees along the street had to be cut down to make room for more traffic.

Each citizen has his views, and the mayor cannot satisfy all the needs of any one person. The city consists of five elements, which can be seen in five different ways; and it is wrong to assume therefore that there are 25 ways of looking at them. In fact the five elements seen in five different ways can lead to more than 33 million combinations, and if considered at different levels of community organization they lead to many billions (see Figure 2). The result is the utmost confusion concerning our cities and their problems, and very often despair leading to a passive attitude.

In order to face our problem, a critical re-examination of it is necessary. This is what I will attempt by making six points, namely:

1. The City of Man is becoming inhuman.
2. Such a process is leading to a three-element or three-star city.
3. We must change our course.
4. The frame has been set for the Universal City of Man.
5. Our task is to make it human.
6. Our cities have well defined roles.

1. The City of Man Is Becoming Inhuman

If we examine all five elements of our cities we can understand our failure to make them human.

The natural container on which our life depends is becoming gradually worse for Man. We are polluting the water, and as a consequence somebody else further downstream must suffer. We are contaminating the atmosphere (of course we purify the air inside our buildings, but we throw the contaminated air outside to breathe when

Figure 1
The Five Elements of Human Settlements

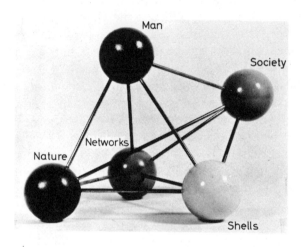

Figure 2
The Ekistic Elements and Their Forces

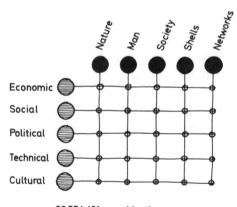

33,554,431 combinations

we go out "for some fresh air"). A cartoon shows two children in a dirty road in the smog; the one is saying to the other: "When my Ma tells me to go out an' get some fresh air, I never know whether she's rewardin' or punishin' me."

We are eliminating the beautiful landscapes near our cities, and we are decreasing the area of parks per capita; we are making contact between Man and Nature more difficult. We are wasting the one commodity which is irreplaceable: our land resources.

Man himself is losing most of his battles inside his city; for the first time in his history, since he came down from the trees, he is losing the right to walk inside his cities—the cars have deprived him of his public squares, and the downtown areas of his trees; the traffic lights have deprived him even of the right to cross the streets when he reaches the crossings; his children cannot run free, he himself cannot walk. As a result of all this, Man develops all sorts of phobias and psychoses.

His own Society is operating very poorly. We are making the grave mistake of believing that we are living at higher densities; this is completely wrong. The urban dweller is living at continually decreasing densities; all our studies point to that. In a recent study carried out for the urban Detroit area, which contains 7 million people, it was proved that the land used by each person has increased during the last 40 years by 200 percent. As a result of these trends, people are now living further apart. It is wrong to believe that, because of motorcars and TV, people have come closer together. The children, the aged, the infirm and the destitute—that is, probably more than 50 percent of the population—do not drive, while TV works only in one direction—we cannot hold a conversation with the TV announcer. The operation of our Society is becoming more impersonal.

The buildings are becoming larger and the highways wider but people are living further apart. In multi-story buildings we do not get to know our neighbors, since there can be no head-to-feet contact between people. The highways have not decreased our distances—we travel at higher speeds on them, but we spend more time on the road than at any time before.

Social and racial tensions are increasing—whether they are made apparent by demonstrations or not—and we are unable to cope with them. We are now less safe than before inside cities.

Whereas national development is taking place on the basis of more or less rational laws and people are moving to the areas most suitable for them, and whereas the architecture of the single building is becoming more and more satisfactory once we are inside the building, in the scale of the city we have become confused, we are losing our perspective and our goals, and we are turning out progressively inhuman cities.

2.   Towards a Three-Element City

There is no indication at all that these trends are going to change, that we are going to save the city for the sake of Man. On the contrary, we have every reason to believe that the situation is getting worse with every day that passes. I have not yet met any mayor or city official who can claim that the situation in his city is going to become better in the future in terms of human values. If there is any official who can make such a claim, we must learn about it and study the case carefully, so as not to spoil the conditions of that unique city which is becoming more human.

The average city is facing graver problems with every day that passes and has fewer means of avoiding them. In this way the "City of Man" is losing two of its five elements, since the two protagonists who initiated the process, Nature and Man, are fading. The expanding city is eliminating Nature, and when it does not eliminate it, it contributes to its degradation, crushing Man in the process.

Increasingly complex networks of roads and facilities are going to turn Man into an animal completely dependent on the machine. Increasingly elaborate multi-story structures are going to isolate Man and gradually turn him into a nomad within his city, a troglodyte within his buildings.

Society will cease to operate for Man's benefit; the small units of neighborhood and community, which provide a human surrounding for him, will be replaced by a large inhuman Society which will not be based on a dialogue but on instructions issued from the peak of the pyramid.

The city fathers will look upon the situation unable to face the new problems since in many cases they will not have enough authority and in all cases they will not have the financial means of providing the necessary degree of services for citizens, who, with every right, demand better services—while living at lower densities. How can a mayor provide proper services for the development of roads and other facilities, their maintenance, and the operation of the city, when people are living further and further apart? The system is getting out of control.

Present trends show that the three-star city will necessarily lead to an anarchistic society which will lead to an autocratic system of complex networks, big buildings and fascist administration with the human values increasingly forgotten.

Present trends are leading to disaster, and we are still suffering from three great diseases which do not allow us to escape the danger: the lack of understanding of the crisis, the absence of goals, and the lack of courage to work toward acquiring any. Consequently we are allowing our cities to decline while we seek escape to visionary utopias—avoiding the realization of the fact that we will have even greater problems tomorrow; and to physical ones—small new isolated cities, leaving the others to struggle in the downtown areas which manifest the coming crisis.

3.   Changing the Course

There is an imperative need that the course we are following be changed. In order to effect this change we must understand the crisis, we must set goals, and we must have the courage to implement their attainment. To the grim picture that I have drawn, I can now add the first bright color. Although we are as yet unable to set goals and develop the necessary courage, I can definitely report progress in the first of the three indispensable steps—the understanding of the crisis. Only a few years ago it was unthought of to speak about a crisis in our cities. This year it has become the national slogan in the United States, and this is a very encouraging step indicative of the fact that we are beginning to change our course.

But this is not enough; we must learn more about the crisis by studying the anatomy and the physiology of our cities, and then we must proceed to set our goals—before planning—before preparing programs and budgets. If I go to a businessman and recommend changes in his industrial plant without telling him what the direct benefits resulting from the new investment program are going to be, he will throw me out. When, however, we are working for our cities, we fail to define the benefits to be expected for Man.

We have to set human goals expressed in terms of human values; in terms of the time that we spend commuting and the time that we are free to spend with our families at home, in the park, or at the library; and in terms of the satisfaction which we derive and the good health which we guarantee for ourselves. We must acquire the courage to dream about happiness and safety and to work towards making the dream come true in our city, as the average man does for the happiness and safety of his children.

We must then understand that we can attain our goals by way of proper programs and plans based on sound economic policies. We cannot hope to save our cities and the downtown areas with their business functions by continuous surgery through urban renewal. This process has become indispensable today because of the crisis, in the same way as surgery is imperative for a patient who is critically ill. But no man can survive continuous surgical operations. We can save cities as we do people, by curative policies, and, even better, by preventive ones.

Why do we have the courage to protect our people by legislation from unfit food and drugs, and not from unfit and dangerous living conditions in unfit cities? We must acquire the courage to create the real "City of Man" and protect him from the city which is leading him to disaster.

In order to achieve this, we must overcome the fallacious tendency of respecting the present trends, on which most of our planning is based. We must study and understand the present trends and respect them as long as they work for our benefit—on this point we must be extremely conservative—but change them when they start working against the interest of Man. In this we must be extremely radical, since the well-being of Man is our only concern.

4.   The Universal City

A proper study of the present trends shows that we are heading toward much larger cities, which will develop under the influence of three basic forces: the attraction of major existing urban complexes, the attraction of the transportation networks, and the attraction of the areas which are most interesting because of natural beauty or of climate or both. As a result of these forces we must expect our cities to merge gradually into one continuous system of cities which will cover our countries from one end to the other and spread with the corresponding systems of neighboring countries to form a universal city or Ecumenopolis (see Figure 3).

Figure 3
The Universal City of Ecumenopolis

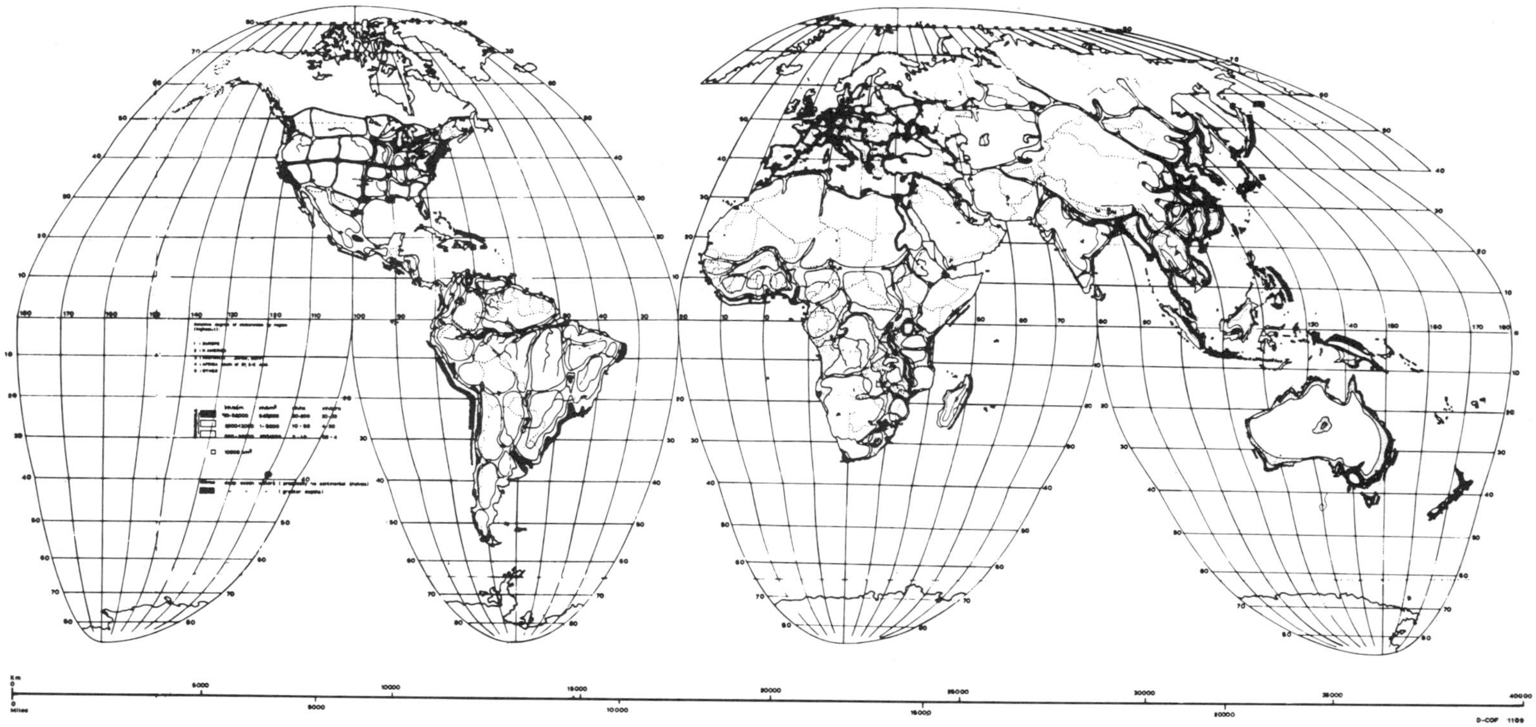

This is not imagination. This is the realistic view of the future. Any careful study of the real forces surrounding our cities shows that within one generation's time we are going to witness the emergence of major continuous systems of metropolises and megalopolises, such as the one connecting Milwaukee with Chicago with Detroit, Toledo, Cleveland and Pittsburgh—more than 600 miles long—and that in two generations' time many more such complexes will exist with heavy concentrations in their central areas and thin urban ribbons between them.

Of the forces that will shape the universal city of the future we are quite certain, since no new invention can change the major trends as of tomorrow—it will need decades to have any practical impact. Actually, even when we speak of the present, we mean, in terms of development, five and ten years from now. The present in cities is already past. It will be five years before one mayor can lay the foundation stone of projects conceived today, and 10 years before he can see the results. The *future* of cities is the present for which we must work. If we understand these truths we will be able to work for the universal city which is coming; we must be certain about that, as certain as we can be about any aspect of human affairs.

The fact that we are realistically certain of the future merging of our cities to form a system even more complex than the present one, and the fact that this is unavoidable, should not allow us to forget that this universal city is tending to be inhuman. This is the grave danger: we cannot escape the universal city, and this is necessarily a city inhuman in dimensions, tending to be inhuman in content and to crush Man.

What can we do?

5.   Towards the "City of Man"

Our only course is not to try to escape the universal city and its inhuman dimensions; the type of our civilization makes such a city an imperative necessity, resulting from the population growth, the increasing productivity, and the increasing demands for production and services. Our only course is to transform the inhuman nature of this city, to create ideal human conditions within the realistic inhuman frame.

This is the course that we must follow in order to create the "City of Man" once again. You can ask me whether this is not merely a literary way of expression: human conditions within an inhuman frame; I will answer that it is definitely not. As an example I will mention the modern airplane which provides Man with a human scale; he can sit, walk, breathe within an inhuman frame, since if he moves outside of it he cannot survive. This is how we must look at our cities: downtown shopping centers where people can walk freely, can be properly interrelated, can enjoy a quiet surrounding and create and admire art. These human communities should become the cells which will be interconnected by mechanical means of transportation and communications to form major systems and major cities.

You can ask me at this stage whether such communities can exist and can be created. On this my answer can be very positive. Humanity, working for thousands of years in the great laboratory in which Man is both the guinea pig and the research director, has created thousands of human communities which were so successful that we make pilgrimages to visit them—Athens and Florence, the city of London, earlier Paris and cities like Williamsburg in the United States. Today, once again, in spite of the machine, we are coming to recognize the ways in which human conditions can be created within inhuman frames.

Such cities are going to be not only more human but also much more economic to build and to operate than the cities of the present. The American citizen is not deprived of the ability to recognize the proper solutions which will work for his own good, and he cannot overlook the economic aspects, since no matter who finances the projects, ultimately it is he who will pay for their creation and operation, and he who will live in them and be forced to walk or drive the unreasonably long roads of the city, if we fail to make it human.

The question of how we can attain our goals can now be raised. I think that proper studies show the course; we must concentrate on them much more and demonstrate not what we like and dislike in a subjective, often unreasonable way, but what can and should be done on the basis of what mankind has learned in its long history, facts that can be demonstrated in an objective, measurable way, facts expressed in terms of human commodities like time, satisfaction and money.

6.   The Role of Our Cities

We now have to face one major question about the role of every one of our cities. Statements about the forthcoming universal city may frighten every citizen and confuse each leader about the role of his own city—is it going to be forgotten out in the wilderness, or absorbed by the growing cancer of the megalopolitan areas?

The answer is that anything may happen, depending on the location and the forces in and around the city, but that in no case should this mean a disaster—on the contrary, in all cases the role of each city may be very important for its own citizens and for those who become their neighbors. The reason is that we need all types of cities, and no matter how large complexes we will form, we will need all cities to preserve their values and contribute to the Universal City of Man.

In practice we will have three major categories of cities. The first consists of those cities which are or are becoming the central ones for the whole system. These are the ones in which Man and his values are threatened because of great pressures. They can be saved if we recognize in time that we should relieve them of pressures for which they are not fit. Our wisdom is going to be shown by decisions to divert major new pressures.

The second category consists of the existing or new cities which are situated in the outskirts of major urban areas; they usually suffer from very low densities, which isolate people from each other, and often provide fewer services than they need (police force, for example) or else increase the cost of their operation. They can create better conditions for their citizens when they recognize the need for proper densities, if proper services are to be had at lower cost.

Finally we have the category of cities which are situated far from centers and appear to be isolated from the growing system. These can become the cities in which the human scale can be more easily saved or re-established, in which more human ways of living can be demonstrated more easily at lower cost and in a shorter time. Not only can the process start from them, but, if the major ones fail, it is in these small cities that our civilization might be saved.

A CONJECTURE ABOUT
THE FUTURE OF THE SCHOOL

Perry E. Rosove

. . . it is clear that what we mean by "education" is changing, and we
will soon educate very differently than we do now.

> "Planning Education for the Future,"
> *American Behavioral Scientist,*
> March 1967

In the future, we may have to admit to the younger generation that we
do not know what they need to know, and this is a frightening idea.

> Robert Bickner, quoted in
> "Planning Education for the Future"

. . . the long-range forecaster trying to guess, let us say, the state of
engineering in 2020 is in a predicament. He cannot predict the state of
scientific knowledge in 2020, but he can be sure that by the standards
of that era, his 1968-style knowledge will be laughably antique.

> Jay Mendell, *The Futurist,*
> October 1968

The purpose of this chapter is to present a provocative conjecture about
the future of a traditional educational institution—the school. I shall
use the shock treatment to make my point. Let me conjecture that by
the year 2000 the school as we know it today will have disappeared.

Perry E. Rosove is with Computer Sciences Institute, El Segundo, California.

Its two major functions—(1) the transmission of culture and (2) the socialization of the individual—will have been taken over by other institutions.

This conjecture about the future of the school gives rise to two questions:

(1)   what evidence is there to support it and, assuming it may prove to be valid,

(2)   what institutions will replace the traditional school?

Emergence of a New Historical Period

It is commonplace to note that we are living in an age of change. But what is the extent and depth of this change? The scientific, economic, technological, political, military and sociocultural changes that are occurring, I submit, represent not merely additive changes but, rather, the transition from one historical epoch to another.

Writing in the *American Anthropologist* in 1961, Charles E. Gray[1] states that:

> Even the most cautious, prudent thinkers must admit that in these recent years (the 1950's) we seem to have commenced the leap to a new and higher civilization with the advent of atomic power, ballistic warfare and space exploration, automation, electronics and computing machines, and so forth.

The rapid emergence of these astonishing capabilities within a single decade makes pale by contrast the gradual evolution of industrialism out of an agrarian society.

It is the rapidity and depth of change today that is difficult to comprehend. Writing about trends in communications, H.S. Kleiman writes:[2]

> No less than 150 years ago, communication was practiced as it had been for centuries before. In 1832 Morse's telegraph and in 1876 Bell's telephone allowed instant communication over wires. Marconi disposed of the wires about the turn of the century, and television later added a picture. Now the prospects appear more likely that we will utilize existing technology in new ways rather than seeking new forms. The communications satellite, the marriage between computers and communication media, and the laser innovation might alter our means of information sensing and gathering in the next 30 years as much as the notable inventions cited did in the past 130 years.

A growing number of scholars, scientists and social commentators are coming to share the view that the present period of history, beginning about the midpoint of the century, constitutes a major transformation in human history comparable in magnitude only to the Neolithic Period, when the domestication of plants and animals made permanent, man-made settlements possible for the first time. I shall refer to the work of three writers, each in a different area of specialization, to make my point. The three are Kenneth E. Boulding,[3] an economist, Bernard J. Muller-Thym,[4] visiting professor of industrial management at the Massachusetts Institute of Technology, and Alvin Toffler,[5] whose recent book, *Future Shock,* is receiving considerable publicity.

Boulding, Muller-Thym and Toffler divide the history of mankind into three distinctive phases. Boulding refers to the three phases as (1) pre-civilization, (2) civilization and (3) post-Neolithic. Toffler refers to them in terms of types of people: (1) people of the past, (2) people of the present and (3) people of the future. Toffler's divisions differ from the other two in that he groups together both food gatherers and agrarian societies as the people of the past. Despite these differences, the important point is that all three writers agree with Gray that the tempo of change in the decade of the 1950's was sufficiently extensive to warrant the conclusion that a new civilizational style, or a new historical epoch, is emerging. Our concern here is with the consensus of these three writers on the fact of an emerging historical epoch, rather than with their minor differences. Table 1 lists their basic concepts concerning the current period. I have emphasized the educational features in the table.

Table 1
Major Trends

Boulding	Muller-Thym	Toffler
5-10 percent of population are farmers	the wheel disappearing	"future shock" as the disease of accelerating change
world-wide communication and transportation	the transient nuclear family	

Table 1 (continued)

a world-style in art, architecture, music, literature	organized invention (R&D)	transience of everything: things, places, people, organizations, information
disintegration of the city	the business as wealth creator	novelty—the newness of almost everything
obsolescence of the nation-state system	economy of abundance	diversity—negation of standardization in things and social groups
an affluent society	competence as a value (as distinct from things)	
a universal middle class	world-wide culture	world-wide super-industrial society
quasi-automatic factories and offices	electronics (instantaneity, totality, random access)	SCHOOLS FACE BACK-WARD BUT MUST PREPARE PEOPLE FOR THE FUTURE
nuclear weapons	action-communication organization (as distinct from hierarchical organization)	
deterrence		
progressive accelerations of the rate of change	nuclear bombs	
disappearance of poverty and inequality	missiles	
LEARNING FROM CHANGING SYSTEMS	space exploration	
	generalized machines	
	systems concept	
	automatic factories	
	OBSOLESCENCE OF UNIVERSITY CURRICULA	

Technological Changes

I shall briefly summarize here the major technological developments in the fields of computers and communications which have occurred since the early 1950's and which, I believe, will ultimately have a profound impact on the manner in which culture is transmitted, how people will interact with one another and how education will be conducted. Table 2 lists the major developments.

Table 2
Major Technological Developments
in Computers and Communications

Transformation of computer-driven digital data into visual images.

Direct interaction between a user and a computer via a cathode ray tube screen, console switches and a light gun.

Development of on-line, real-time computerized systems for air defense, airline seat reservations and other applications.

Data retrieval from a computer data bank (memory) by a remote user using standard descriptors.

User capability to design, restructure and update a file or data base stored in a remote computer.

User interaction with a computer using natural English.

Construction of very large disk and drum data storage capabilities (one billion bits) with random access capabilities.

Transmission of digital data over telephone lines via acoustic couplers.

Telephone, telegraph, television, and data and facsimile transmission via satellites.

Transmission of visual images over telephone lines (the Picturephone).

Development of facsimile and copying machines via electronic process.

National and international time-sharing computerized systems simultaneously used by approximately 100 subscribers.[6]

Typing via electronic keyboard onto magnetic tape cassettes for batch processing of digital data (by-passes keypunch operations).

Development of the minicomputer (priced under $10,000).

Hierarchically structured computer systems linked into a computer network composed of computers of different sizes and capabilities.

Use of the laser beam in communications.

Computer assisted instruction, counseling, testing and record keeping.

The use of computers to create new art forms in design, graphics, music, poetry and sculpture.

It is incredible but true that the applications of these developments occurred during the 15-year period from 1955 to 1970. Individually, these are remarkable technological achievements. Taken as a whole, their impact is overwhelming.

The significance of the revolution in technology within the area of communications was recently summed up by a speaker at a meeting sponsored by the American Bar Association's Committee on Law and Technology.[7] He notes that one very important result

is the abolition of the distinctions that have separated the various forms of communication by sight, sound and signal . . . The technical unity of services is becoming general. The telephone line that links us with a friend or relative or client can now carry our images as well as our voices. Over the same line we may interrogate and receive data stored in the tape file of a distant computer. The wideband cable which now brings television into many homes can just as easily link us tomorrow in two-way exchange with stores, banks, offices or computerized reference libraries.

Current Trends and the Traditional School

What will be the impact of the sociocultural and technological trends identified above upon the traditional concept and structure of the school?

It is easy to forget that the public school, as we know it today, is a relatively new institution. In the United States the public school is little more than a century old. The two major functions of the school—the transmission of culture and the socialization of the individual—have been conducted for thousands of years without the benefit of the school as we know it. What reason is there to believe that it will last much longer? Can educators justify the continuance of the public school? Is it really necessary? If it is, will it be necessary ten years from today? Thirty years from today?

If we had the opportunity to look back upon the history of this century and its educational forms from, say, the mid-point of the next century, we might perceive that the public school was a transitory phenomenon that served the purpose of mass production of educated people for a very brief period of time and then disappeared to be replaced by other institutions better adapted to the diverse and less standardized requirements of the latter part of the twentieth century.

The reasons why the public school came into prominence and received wide support in the first half of the twentieth century are well known. The public school was the institutional device whereby the children of the immigrants of Europe were mixed in the melting pot and "Americanized." Industrialization in the United States had progressed to the point around 1900 where a literate population was required to man the thousands of standardized posts available in the burgeoning, hierarchically organized factories and plants, gradually replacing what once was an agrarian society. Subsequently, those same schools produced in mass numbers the white-collar workers required for the emerging service and knowledge industries. The public school was the ideal institution for a nation of social strivers in an open and growing industrial society. It produced an army of interchangeable blue- and white-collar workers at the precise moment in history when that army was needed. And as historians of education have noted, the *school itself was modeled after the factory assembly line.*

In the first half of the twentieth century, the means available to transmit the culture to the army of immigrant children was the teacher, chalk and pointer in hand, only sufficiently more literate than his charges so that the basic skills of reading, writing and arithmetic could be passed on. Supplementing the teacher was the textbook. The school, conceived as an "egg-crate," was the place where teacher, students and textbooks were brought together so that the process of cultural transmission could occur. Little else was required until a rapidly growing population, at a later date, caused the creation of an expensive administrative superstructure.

The school has persisted in its original form with only minor modifications down to the present time and in a bureaucratic, administrative context. But a major revolution in technology has occurred since 1950. There are now dozens of devices which are more efficient as cultural transmitters than the traditional teacher; and today knowledge is generated so rapidly that a textbook is obsolete by the time it is published. Table 2 lists some of the new mechanisms whereby information about any subject from the aardvark to the zygote could be transmitted if we desired to do so. There are many reasons why the development and use of these new mechanisms in educational institutions are not much more advanced than they are today. Bureaucratic inertia is only one. There are also financial problems, public ignorance of what is feasible, the low priority of educational research and development in government circles, etc.

The school not only is a clumsy institutional device to educate the young, but it also fails to educate the adults in the community who, in a changing world, have as great a need for education as their children. Ralph Tyler[8] points out, for example, the irony that:

the majority of the states in the country right now, through statutes or constitutional provisions, prohibit the expenditure of funds for the education of persons over 21 years of age.

The traditional school has not yet been adapted to the new social requirements for life-long, continuing education.

Current Trends and the Future of the School

In a study of forecasting for education done a few years ago,[9] I stated that education for today and tomorrow should occur in "real time," rather than in the current non-real time mode. As Table 2 indicates, the technology to do it is already within the state of the art. We can no longer afford the luxury of teaching young people knowledge that was created 30 years ago. The exponential growth of new knowledge and the rate of obsolescence of existing knowledge is such that those who seek knowledge must be linked on an individual basis directly to the sources that generate new knowledge.

I believe that Alvin Toffler is correct in his book, *Future Shock*, when he states that modern society is breaking up into myriads of subcultures based on age, marital status, vocations and other interests.[10] The "masses" and "classes" of traditional sociology are giving way to smaller, culturally distinctive groupings, each with its own life-style and educational requirements. Thus mass education in which everyone receives doses of the same curricula is becoming a relic of the past. Educators recognize this fact in the concept of individualized instruction and the "open-concept" school. But the application of these concepts is hampered by the persistence of traditional concepts—the "egg-crate" local school facility, the fixed classroom and the teacher as the dispenser of knowledge. Of course, I am not proposing a complete and immediate break with traditional approaches. What I am suggesting is that the rate of innovation within the educational establishment is too slow to meet pressing needs.[11]

It is evident that an educational revolution outside of normal educational channels is already occurring. The demand for knowledge both vocational and avocational is such that the traditional schools simply cannot meet the demand. On all sides we see new educational institutions emerging—"Sesame Street" on television, Head Start, street academies, tutorial programs, VISTA and many others. Private industry is moving strongly into the educational field.

Let us give credit to the great public school system of the United States for its incredible achievements of the first half of the twentieth century. But it would be unfortunate if we allowed those achievements to blind us to the increasing obsolescence and, yes, evils of that system.[12] The culture must be transmitted or our society will die. One of the tasks of educational planners should be to explore all the mechanisms that are available to insure that that culture is transmittable. The list provided in Table 2 is a point of departure.

To make my presentation more concrete, let me give one illustration of the type of computerized system that I believe in the long run will revolutionize education.[13] There now exists a Uniform Migrant Student Record Transfer System. This computer-based system can retrieve the educational and medical records of any registered child in the migratory agricultural working community. There are 300,000 children whose school and health records are usually lost as they migrate from one farming community to another. Starting in the fall of 1970 the records of such children in many states have been fed into a central data bank. This computerized record system was financed under Title I of the Elementary and Secondary Education Act. The system was developed under contract to the Arkansas State Department of Education with participating states contributing funds from 1969 Title I sources. States participating in the system on a pilot basis are Arkansas, Colorado, Kansas, Missouri, New Mexico, Oklahoma and Texas. The pilot states are linked to the computer data center by 300 local terminals.

The system is expected to handle about 12,000 information requests per day when it is in full operation. It is anticipated that all 48 mainland states will be able to receive data on any migrant child within four hours.

This system has been financially supported because it will benefit hundreds of disadvantaged children. But a system that can help the children of migratory agricultural workers can also be used in a similar fashion to assist the children of any family that is highly mobile, a characteristic of many American families today.

As a by-product of its educational function, the school also serves as the great socializer. The school is a place where the socialization process occurs. Children meet other children in a school, and this is good. They acquire social skills, the ability to get along with others, and some understanding, sometimes, of how a democratic society operates. While these are good things, it is obvious that a school is not essential for these things to happen. Almost any other kind of institution that made it possible for young people to associate with one another would contribute equally to the socialization process. Almost any kind of residence hall or summer camp would serve the purpose better than today's school environment.

We need new institutions for socialization outside of the school environment. The current situation has produced one of the most colossal social aberrations of all time—the drug scene. If it were technically feasible to transmit the culture in the home, then the parents could retain their control over the socialization process, as parents have always done. Or if parents cannot do this, for whatever reason, day nurseries or social clubs could be established, appropriate to given age levels, where the socialization process can take place. In such social clubs, the boredom induced by mass education could be eliminated. The youngsters could still go to football games on Saturday afternoons, but let us give up the quaint notion that this is related to education.

In the education of the future it will not be necessary to isolate children from their parents in separate physical facilities. Rudimentary education can begin in the home as a natural extension of the child's inherent curiosity, through the use of television, videotapes, tape recordings, educational games and toys, etc. Available to the child as another type of plaything should be a teletype terminal equipped with a simple form of keyboard. The growing child will then be linked to computerized time-sharing systems which will respond in simple English to his questions and display, upon request, appropriate three-dimensional images on a color screen. Through such a system all the accumulated knowledge of the ages could be made available in branching sequences suitable to the educational level of the inquirer.[14]

Young adults, parents and grandparents, as well as infants, will have the same capabilities at their fingertips. The family of the future may be highly mobile, but the technology should make mobility an irrelevant factor insofar as education is concerned. The image of education portrayed here is one in which the student—whoever and wherever he may be—can plug himself at will into an educational network which is somewhere out there in space and which has attributes of instantaneity, totality and random access.

The demise of the school as a place where education occurs does not imply the end of the teacher's role or functions. As just noted, the transmission of culture can occur through media that do not require the physical school facility. But someone must still transmit the culture, regardless of the manner in which it is transmitted. Someone will have to design the information transmitting networks; someone must translate the corpus of knowledge in a specific discipline so that it can be processed electronically; someone must write and produce the educational television programs; etc. The educator will always be with us, but he may not resemble the teacher with chalk and pointer in hand who sat in front of his class in P.S. 161 in Brooklyn, circa 1927, explaining the rules of English grammar, words which all too often fell on deaf ears.[15]

Dr. J.R. Pierce, director of communications and research at Bell Laboratories, has noted that the technology of the future will make it possible to "communicate to work." Why commute to an office over clogged freeways once it becomes possible to interact with one's colleagues, customers or employees via teletype terminals or televideo devices? Reports, letters, financial reports, memoranda, etc., will be transmitted electronically, either automatically or upon request. It will then become unnecessary to commute to work except for social or other special purposes. The analogy to education is perfect. By the year 2000 the student, regardless of age or interests, should be able to *communicate to school.*

The social implications of this concept of education are staggering to the imagination. Since I am already way out on a limb, I will climb further out by conjecturing that the technology of the latter part of this century will usher in an age of democratization such as no previous age has witnessed. Education is a great social leveler; and access to education or the lack of it has in the recent past served to demarcate social classes. Scholars have noted the democratizing function of the inventions of antiquity such as paper, writing, iron and, in the Middle Ages, the printing press. The computer, time-sharing systems, new methods of communication, the capability to interchange sights, sounds and signals, and other technical achievements of today and those yet to come will contribute much more to democratization. These technologies should wipe out the residual social distinctions between rich and poor, black and white, and rural and urban. There will be cultural diversity, but it will be diversity based upon the ability to achieve and upon educated choices—not upon ascribed status or ignorance. This prospect is something worth planning for.

References

1. C.E. Gray. An Epicyclical Model for Western Civilization. *American Anthropologist*, Vol. 63, No. 5, October 1961, p. 1014.
2. H.S. Kleiman. The Business/Economic Dimensions of Automation. *Automation and Society*. (Eds.) E.L. Scott & R.W. Bolz. The Center for the Study of Automation and Society, Athens, Georgia, 1969, pp. 174-75.
3. K.E. Boulding. Where Are We Going If Anywhere? A Look at Post-Civilization. *Human Organization*, Vol. 21, Summer 1962, pp. 162-67.
4. B.J. Muller-Thym. Culture and Social Changes. *The Changing American Population*. (Ed.) H.S. Simpson. A Report of the Arden House Conference, 1962, pp. 85-96.
5. A. Toffler. *Future Shock*. Random House, New York, 1970.
6. Approximately 60 independent organizations offer a variety of time-sharing services.
7. *Datamation*, November 15, 1970, p. 118.
8. R. Tyler. Education Must Relate to a Way of Life. *Automation and Society, op. cit.,* p. 96.
9. P.E. Rosove. Toward Education in Real Time. Proceedings of the Fall Joint Computer Conference, 1968, pp. 1479-89.
10. A. Toffler, *op. cit.*
11. In his book, *Run, Computer, Run*, A.G. Oettinger states that he does not believe that computers will significantly alter the traditional teaching situation

within the next decade. There is no disagreement on that point. The question here is will computers and associated communications media alter that situation significantly in three decades?

12. The evils are well described by C.E. Silberman. *Crisis in the Classroom: The Remaking of American Education.* Random House, New York, 1970.

13. M.P. Pfeil. Computer Harvests Migrant Records. *American Education,* Vol. 6, No. 9, U.S. Department of Health, Education, and Welfare, Office of Education, November 1970, pp. 7-9.

14. For a review of this subject see R.J. Seidel. Computers in Education: The Copernican Revolution in Education Systems. *Computers and Automation,* March 1969, pp. 24-29. For an account of more recent developments in computer assisted instruction, see D. Alpert & D.L. Bitzer. Advances in Computer-Based Education. *Science,* March 20, 1970, pp. 1582-1590.

15. There remains, however, the dilemma raised by Robert Bickner, that the older generation in the future may not know what the younger generation needs to know. This is, indeed, frightening—unless we can accept the principle that young people will seek out their own knowledge and also contribute, at the same time, to its generation.

THE FAILURE OF
INNER CITY SCHOOLS:
A Crisis of Management
and Service Delivery

David Rogers

There has been a lot of recent discussion in Washington and among professional "urbanists" throughout the nation about the importance of improving the management of urban development programs. In manpower and education especially, the 1960's witnessed an outpouring of federal programs for the cities which, however inadequate they were in absolute fiscal terms, should have done a lot more for the poor populations they were designed to reach than was actually the case. As Daniel Moynihan has observed, the number of domestic programs increased from 45 in 1960 to 435 in 1968, but with depressingly little result and contributing to the declining confidence in government that we are experiencing today.[1] There were lots of bold pronouncements, and much well-meaning rhetoric about wars on poverty and illiteracy during this period, but the delivery seems in many cases to have been abominable. Serious questions are even being raised as to whether government alone can really run effective domestic programs, were the necessary funds available.

1.   Daniel P. Moynihan. Toward a National Urban Policy. *The Public Interest*, Fall 1969, *17*.

David Rogers is associate professor of sociology and management at the Graduate School of Business Administration, New York University, and the author of *110 Livingston Street,* a four-year study of the politics and bureaucracy of the New York City Schools.

As is well known, many federal programs have proliferated without taking into account what has and has not worked well in the past. Evaluations are often not done, or done poorly; and, even if done well, are not considered in program and policy decisions. And the situation may be especially bad in education, where a slew of compensatory education programs—from New York City's Higher Horizons to Title I—have not appreciably raised the reading scores, lowered the dropout rates or increased the employability of the ghetto poor.

Many liberals and some traditional fiscal conservatives are beginning to suggest that one important reason for this is bad management, using that term in the most generic sense to refer to the structure, operations and personnel of the schools, including the policies and programs that educators habitually generate. Some of these liberals, myself among them, have mixed feelings about conservative Republican arguments for holding down spending for education. We feel that much more money is certainly needed, but to spend it in the same old ways, which is to say in ways that replicate and spread past mistakes, as many Title I programs often do, seems senseless. Better to waste it on education than on wars and missiles, but why waste it at all?

The federal government is, in this regard, now establishing a National Institute of Education, analogous to the National Institutes of Health, to better evaluate the public schools. It is certainly long overdue. Such an agency might help in suggesting what works well and poorly in education, why, what to replace it with, and how to gain acceptance and legitimacy for new programs.

Diagnoses

Most major works on inner city schools—either in the guise of social science, social criticism, or journalism—have been of the exposé genre. Their apocalyptic rhetoric, replete with Cassandra-like imagery, "death at an early age," "growing up absurd," and "schools against children," reflects a widespread national concern with the inadequacies of inner city schools.[2] The failure of any reform strategy to either be

2. See, for example, Jonathan Kozol, *Death at an Early Age* (Boston: Houghton-Mifflin, 1967); Nat Hentoff, *Our Children are Dying* (New York: Viking, 1966); Paul Goodman, *Compulsory Mis-Education* (New York: Vintage, 1962), and *Growing Up Absurd* (New York: Random House, 1951); and Annette T. Rubinstein (Ed.), *Schools Against Children: The Case for Community Control* (New York: Monthly Review Press, 1970).

implemented or to work —and that includes compensatory education, desegregation, community control and competitive private schools— indicates that we may well have reached a state of considerable desperation.[3] The school crisis cries out for an adequate diagnosis and reconstruction strategy.

It is not easy to reach a consensus on the goals of the schools; but if one looks at data on reading and arithmetic scores, dropout rates, types of diplomas, school utilization, teacher and supervisory experience and curriculum and instructional methods, it becomes clear that inner city schools are in deep trouble. In New York City in 1966, for example, 12,000 pupils were suspended, 30 percent of the teachers were "permanent substitutes" without standard licenses, 89,227 pupils attended overcrowded schools, while 99,872 were in under-utilized schools; and the situation was just as grim in other inner cities throughout the nation. Teacher strikes, high school student protests and drug addiction, deteriorating community relations and increasing criticism of student unpreparedness by business are still further indications of the schools' failures.[4]

There are many diagnoses of this condition, including the need for more money; poverty and segregation; factional politics and continued unrest which force boards and educators always to mediate in crisis situations and do not give them a clear-cut mandate to move ahead with needed reforms; and the failures of inter-agency planning such as new housing, transportation and urban renewal projects which involve the settlement and relocation of tremendous numbers of families and are often not coordinated with school construction.

These are at best, however, only partial explanations for the schools' failures. They overlook such other conditions as the outdated teacher and administrator training; the lack of experience and empathy for ghetto youngsters of many people entering teaching, their racism, and low expectations; the limited knowledge about how to teach, about

3.   Marilyn Gittell and Alan G. Hevesi (Eds.) *The Politics of Urban Education* (New York: Praeger, 1969) contains numerous accounts of the failures of reform in inner city schools. See also Marilyn Gittell and T. Edward Hollander, *Six Urban School Districts* (New York: Praeger, 1968).

4.   David Rogers. *110 Livingston Street.* New York: Random House, 1968, p. 473.

what constitutes "good" and "bad" performance; and, perhaps most important of all, the strangled, rule-ridden bureaucracies of school systems themselves. Even if we had much more money, better and more relevant teacher and administrator training, more competent educators and more innovative curricula and instructional methods, it could all be for nought, given the record of how administrative rules, "bad management," and the protectionist politics of many educators have often absorbed, diluted and discredited potentially good programs.

Having spent some years looking at the management of the New York City Schools—if, indeed, they can be said to be managed at all—and having observed several other big city school systems, I would like to describe how and why they are poorly run, and to suggest some needed reforms. Many of the reforms I will discuss are not new, and are beginning to gain wider currency. As with so many others in education, however, they have had very limited implementation, suggesting the need to develop a better reform strategy. That includes, of course, a keen sensitivity to politics, both inside and outside the school Establishment.

Toward a Reconstruction Strategy

Peter Drucker writes quite convincingly in his *The Age of Discontinuity* of the fundamental sickness of big government, choked in its vested interests and inertia, and both totally unmanaged and over-administered. He was referring mainly to the federal government, but his judgments apply equally well to state and municipal bureaucracies, especially to big city school systems.[5]

Several years of research on the New York City school system have led me to the depressing conclusion that it is a "sick" bureaucracy, incapable of reforming itself from within. Its structure and day-to-day operations regularly subvert the realization of its stated goals, prevent any flexible accommodation to changing client demands, and make orderly administration little more than a pleasant fantasy.[6]

5.   Peter Drucker. *The Age of Discontinuity.* New York: Harper & Row, 1968, chaps. 8-11.

6.   What follows is a condensed discussion of the main characteristics of the "sick" bureaucracy of the New York City schools. For a detailed elaboration and documentation on each assertion, see my book, Rogers, *op. cit.,* chaps. 7-11;

Indeed, this is a system that is strangled in red tape; mired in inertia, incompetence and petty corruption; inefficient; insulated from its clients and from most outside institutions; and fragmented into power blocs (teachers, principals, district superintendents, divisions, bureaus, staff units at headquarters and districts, a Board of Examiners) that veto new ideas and prevent the efficient use of resources by failing to coordinate. It is, in addition, leaderless; it has no adequate auditing, monitoring, or information system to evaluate programs and see if policies are carried out; it faces continued subversion of headquarters directives for change by field officials; it protects mediocrity through outdated civil service standards; it is highly inbred, allowing protectionist power blocs inside to develop and solidify their baronies and vested interests against client demands for change; it is then accountable to nobody but itself; and it victimizes almost anybody who comes in contact with it, including its superintendents and lay boards, who are emasculated with regularity by the professional staff, and whose efforts are absorbed by the cumbersome workings of the system. Talk to teachers, principals and district superintendents, and you will find that they, too, are victimized.

Much, though not all, of the problem is an institutional one. There are many capable and idealistic educators in the New York City school system, but the system itself absorbs and defeats their efforts at reform. A main point of my book, and one that can be documented for most other big city school systems, is that the schools have failed to innovate on most significant questions (decentralization, civil service reforms, curriculum, staffing, budget); and to adapt and transform themselves in the face of major changes in their clientele and in the city.

This suggests, furthermore, that the "incrementalist" social change strategy of gradual, piece-meal reform simply doesn't work and in fact constitutes retrogression.[7] New programs and reform strategies within

---

my article, New York City Schools: A Sick Bureaucracy, in *Saturday Review,* July 20, 1968, pp. 47ff; and Marilyn Gittell, *Participants and Participation* (New York: Praeger, 1967). Gittell and Hevesi, *op. cit.,* and Gittell and Hollander, *op. cit.,* document some of these points in other big city school systems.

7.   For good critiques of "incrementalism" as a social change strategy, see Yehezkel Dror, Muddling Through—Science or Inertia, *Public Administration Review, 24,* 3 (September, 1964); and Amitai Etzioni, *The Active Society* (New York: The Free Press, 1968), chaps. 11-12.

an "old bureaucracy" and an "old politics" not only get absorbed but—by being inefficiently administered—get discredited along the way. Thus, New York City tried and killed many desegregation techniques before other big cities even adopted desegregation as school policy, and this probably had a negative effect on implementation elsewhere.

A more radical, "transformative" strategy, involving major institutional change, seems called for; and that is what decentralization and community control represent. Unfortunately, the coalitions necessary for such radical reforms are not yet being developed, and the educators keep prevailing in the state legislature by successfully blocking strong decentralization bills. As in the losing battle over desegregation, New York City's early failures then tend to strengthen the status quo forces in other cities and correspondingly weaken and demoralize protest groups.

Short of throwing up our hands in sheer desperation, I believe that there are many administrative reforms that could conceivably be implemented that would improve the management of inner city schools. Most involve changes in administrative structure and practice that, while not as transformative as community control, are much more so than the limited program changes and demonstrations that have failed very often in the past.

Top Management—One of the reasons for the failures of big city schools is very weak leadership from the top. Often, teachers, middle management officials and top headquarters administrators redefine the directives of the superintendent, appealing to ancient bureaucratic rules, and either subvert the directives or delay their implementation.[8] They feed him selective data, distorting in various ways what is going on. The superintendent thus needs a fairly large cadre of associates, preferably brought in from outside the system, and with no vested interests in particular inside programs, administrative units or pressure groups (for example, supervisory associations). Otherwise, it becomes very difficult for him to either have adequate "intelligence" or to have the inside power base and coalitions necessary to gain compliance for new programs. Dr. Calvin Gross came to New York City's highly politicized school system as superintendent in 1963 with only his own private secretary, and was literally engulfed by the educators there who

8.   Rogers, *op. cit.*, chaps. 7,8.

distrusted "outsiders" and wanted one of *their own* as superintendent. There was much more to his failure than that, but state and city education laws that prevented him from bringing in his own staff helped undercut him and dilute his power even before he arrived.

New York City's new decentralization law replaces the superintendent with a czar-like "chancellor," who has tremendous powers. However, unless the strong person to be recruited comes in with a cadre of associates, he will be beaten down as Gross was. Few distinguished public figures have much time for such a potentially traumatic and frustrating interlude in their careers. Judging from the experience of other big city superintendents, the job is tough everywhere.

The other top leadership change required is in lay boards. Numerous recent books and journalistic commentaries have documented the powerlessness of school boards in middle sized and small cities as well as large.[9] The problem is most acute, however, in the biggest cities with the most unmanageable school bureaucracies and the most pressing social problems. Even the so-called Lindsay-packed board, for example, that took over in 1968 in New York City, did not move the system appreciably forward. As committed to reform as some board members were, they were hampered by state education laws that prevented them from having their own large staff; and they continued to be incapable of making policy and monitoring how it was implemented.[10]

Without such basic reforms at the top, giving top management and policy-makers the resources and authority commensurate with their legal responsibilities, big city school systems will go on being leaderless and drifting from crisis to crisis with depressing regularity.[11]

9.   A recent work is Robert Bendiner's *The Politics of Schools* (New York: Harper & Row, 1969); see my review of it in *The New York Times Book Review*, December 14, 1969.

10.   Many public officials and critics of the NYC school system have come to the position that the concept of a lay board is an anachronism in New York. Since all school matters are political ones, these people have urged that the system be run by a paid commission, located in the mayor's office, responsible to him, and equipped with a staff large enough to actually manage the system, something its predecessors could not do. Instead, the 1969 state legislature passed a decentralization bill calling for an elected board of five members.

11.   For an analysis of "crisis management" in the NYC schools, see Rogers, *op. cit.*

Personnel Changes—One of the reasons that inner city schools are badly managed is that they foster much in-breeding by promoting unqualified teachers and supervisors to higher level administrative posts. The pattern in New York is, with minor variations, repeated elsewhere. There, all examinations above the principal level are fitted to the man, and it is almost exclusively people who have been in the system and have cultivated close informal relations inside who get the positions. Indeed, many key administrative and staff positions at headquarters are filled by teachers-on-assignment or by former field supervisors—with few qualifications; and administrative and technical "amateurism" are rampant throughout the headquarters' bureaucracy. Untrained teachers-on-assignment and former supervisors have important positions in zoning, human relations, demographic research, programming and data processing, and federally funded programs. Their promotions reflect a pattern of "rewards for early conformity"; and it is little wonder that the schools are so inefficiently run.

One of the more heroic efforts at inner city school reform, in this regard, was Philadelphia Superintendent Mark Shedd's action in 1968 to eliminate several hundred administrative positions and/or old-line civil service bureaucrats and bring in new managers.[12] Provisions were made to protect the equities of the insiders who were deposed—early retirement, transfers, etc.—while the new administrators brought in had considerable competence in their fields: city planning, finance, accounting and race relations. The change precipitated a tremendous political backlash from the educators, supported by Mayor Tate at City Hall; but Shedd and his board had set an important precedent.

The strategy of recruitment from outside applies to teachers and supervisors as well as administrators. By "outside" in this context I mean people who have not necessarily come through the conventional teacher training institutions. Bringing in more black, Puerto Rican and other new minority group educators, more VISTA and Peace Corps types and more college graduates generally who have not taken the largely irrelevant education courses given to teachers-in-training might help a lot. Giving teacher examinations more often in other cities, especially in the South and Puerto Rico, would be a way to get many such outsiders into inner city schools.

12.   Henry S. Resnik. The Shedd Revolution: A Philadelphia Story. *The Urban Review*, 3(3), pp. 20-25.

It is especially important to recruit more blacks and Puerto Ricans, not just to ease tensions or to be fair, but because many of them have needed skills and experience that most lower middle class whites do not have. Little learning will ever take place in ghetto schools until they stop being the "outpost" institutions they now are and become much more integrated into the communities. This means greater contact among the educator, students, parents and community leaders; and it means modifications of the curriculum to better reflect the racial and ethnic identities of the community, and to indicate much more empathy with community aspirations. Black and Puerto Rican educators can perhaps best do that.

This is not at all to embrace the concept of only black or Puerto Rican educators for black and Puerto Rican schools, and even the most militant leaders of community control groups don't want or expect that. They know that there aren't enough black and Puerto Rican educators available to fill all the posts in their schools, even were it legally possible to do so. Instead, they want people with an understanding of ghetto life as well as with traditional educational credentials.

More blacks and Puerto Ricans than whites probably fit into this category. Yet some idealistic young white educators are also trying to restore trust in the ghetto schools where they work. New York City now has increasing numbers of beginning teachers who are there to avoid the draft. Many have social attitudes and skills that fit them for work in ghetto schools much more in fact than do the vast majority of middle and lower middle class white graduates of conventional teacher training colleges.

Improved teacher training for this group is absolutely essential. The young white teacher's culture shock and incapacity to cope when first assigned to a ghetto school can be quite crippling. Many who have entered inner city schools tend to be of lower middle class origins, second generation, from families that just emerged from their own ghettoes, have had little previous contact with poor black and Puerto Rican youngsters, and they have no idea how to deal with many of the situations they encounter in the schools. Most will tell you how poorly trained they were for their experience.

Such improved training would have to include courses in Black culture and history, ghetto institutions and urban social problems. It should also require that the student have as much direct contact as possible with ghetto conditions, serving in an apprenticeship capacity in ghetto schools during undergraduate training. Those who realize that they don't have the skills and commitment to continue teaching in ghetto schools will leave, and the others will gain a valuable experience. It isn't enough just to attend seminars led by black spokesmen who "tell it like it is."

In addition, it is critical that the entire career experience and rewards of teachers be changed, so that good ones are encouraged to stay in touch with the classroom, and beginners can receive the professional help and support on the job that they now so sorely lack. Teachers now flee the classroom to administrative and supervisory positions where the rewards (salary, authority, prestige, opportunities for more colleagial contacts) are much greater. We must change all that.

One way is to develop career lines within teaching, so that more experienced and competent people become senior (master) teachers, helping and supervising younger colleagues. They may spend less time in the classroom, but the impact of their knowledge will still be felt there. They must be well-compensated, however, and inner cities should take their cues from some cities that actually pay experienced teachers as much as they do their superintendent, to keep them in the schools.

Another change that would improve the effectiveness of teachers in ghetto schools and provide more links with the youngsters and communities is the employment of more parents as teacher aides and in other para-professional positions. This will free the classroom teacher from burdensome and routine chores—discipline, clerical tasks—and even from some simple instructional duties.

Further, there is now a desperate need to improve communications between the school and community, and the use of parents in the classrooms is one of the best means available. It not only provides jobs and income for ghetto residents, but it might enable teachers to function at some level of effectiveness for the first time.

The use of streetworkers in the high schools, as mediators between teachers and alienated ghetto youth, has similar potential benefits. Communication between the teachers and the Blacks has completely broken down in many inner city high schools, and we have to devise every means possible to re-open it. One effective way is to have ghetto people do it, people who have the trust of the youngsters and the community; indeed, people who are part of the community.

Quality Control

Changes in structure and personnel, while significant, must also be supplemented by major attempts at instituting much better quality controls in the schools. Most inner city schools have very inadequate auditing, monitoring and evaluation procedures.[13] It is difficult for boards and school professionals to make decisions based on experience, since they often don't know what that experience has been. Critics of the public schools have been asking for state and nationwide performance appraisals of the schools for years, and their suggestions have met with strong resistance by the educators. Afraid that their professional autonomy will be encroached on by outside "political meddlers," educators, by resisting such evaluations, have often in effect perpetuated mediocrity and "non-professionalism" in their own ranks.

There are admittedly many problems in reaching consensus on the goals of the schools, in establishing indicators of performance and enforcing them, and status quo-oriented educators have much to gain from pointing out the complexity of these tasks. Unless we get on with that job, however, we may never appreciably improve the quality control and accountability of the schools.

Those of us who have studied inner city schools know the many ways that educators have steadfastly resisted instituting any rational system of performance appraisal that might then be used in personnel and staffing decisions. As one high-ranking New York City school official stated: "Public education is the only industry in the world that blames the failures of its product on the client and gets away with it." Promotions, pay increases, transfers and dismissals should be geared to measures of performance, and not just seniority. Though there are perfunctory ratings of teachers by principals and of principals by district superintendents, they are only that. This contributes to poor teaching and supervision, poor quality control, wasted human resources and accelerating social unrest. In most business enterprises, if people are not producing, they are held to account, and that is a reasonable goal for the public schools. In the long run, this will help protect both the community (through accountability) and the educators (through objective standards).

Of particular importance is the establishment of statistical, quality control studies of schools. Systematic information should be collected

13.   Gittell and Hollander, *op. cit.*; and Rogers, *op. cit.*, esp. chap. 9.

at least annually on (1) how much money is being spent in each school; (2) how this correlates, if at all, with variations in school performance (pupil achievement); and (3) how much other school resources (space, staff experience, books and supplies, class size) affect performance. The extent to which middle class white schools still get preferential treatment (e.g., more experienced teachers and supervisors, more space), a widespread pattern in most inner cities, should also be investigated in terms of its possible effects on performance.

One very fruitful line of analysis would be to interpret variations in performance among ghetto schools. Holding constant racial, ethnic and class composition of such schools, there may well be fairly significant differences in their quality, at least judging from reading score data. It is important to find out why, so that practices in the best schools can be emulated, and those in the worst eliminated. Interviews and activity studies of principals should be done as well, to develop profiles of "successful" and "unsuccessful" supervisory styles.

If urban social policy in the 1970's is to emphasize the improved management and service delivery of federally funded programs, as is likely, the above suggestions and many others like them should be given very serious consideration. The fact that this has not yet happened attests both to the tremendous capacity of the educators to resist change, and to the neglect of the schools by the citizenry. These administrative-institutional reform ideas are now just beginning to catch on, however, not just among militant ghetto-based groups, but in business, university, government and foundation circles that have the influence to break down resistance to change. Large employers, especially, realize that the schools are not meeting their manpower needs. They realize that they are double and triple taxed for the school's failures, and that they cannot afford to sit idly by and claim that it is neither their right nor their responsibility to intervene to reform the schools. Indeed, they no longer have that option, if they are at all attuned to long or even short run economic self-interest.

There are those social analysts and public officials who are increasingly bored with the "crisis rhetoric" of many public school critics. They argue that such rhetoric reduces some very complex issues to simplified slogans and adds little to public policy. The fact of the matter is, however, that it took such strident critics, along with the civil rights movement, to even open up this issue of the schools' viability. If we are to meet the needs of future generations, we would do well to heed the criticisms and develop some workable alternatives to our decaying schools. That can only be done through the very active involvement of large established institutions, in alliance with citizen groups. It would be a great tragedy for the entire society, and not just for the poor, if we failed to respond to this challenge. Our future as a nation may well hang in the balance.

URBAN EDUCATIONAL PLANNING
AND PROBLEMS OF IMPLEMENTATION

Corinne Rieder and Harry Davidow

Urban educational systems are in decay. Neither school systems nor planning agencies have adequately planned for their revitalization. School officials have generally concentrated on crisis management and piecemeal reform. Planning agencies, new to the task of planning for specific functional sectors (education, health, welfare, criminal justice), have either remained entirely uninvolved or limited their educational planning activities to enrollment forecasting, capital budgeting and site selection. A few venturesome agencies have formulated policy statements on desegregation or decentralization. This essay analyzes the demands and constraints on the planning process, discusses new efforts by the Educational Planning Section of the New York City Planning Department to fill the gaps in planning, and suggests guidelines and criteria for its own future planning and for that of planning agencies in other large cities.

The Educational Planning Section is attempting to go beyond basic "school planning" to become actively engaged in research and policy development in such areas as the proper trade courses for high schools, program and structural revisions to increase utilization of existing school space, and changes in administrative policy to reduce school violence. To those familiar with the planning profession, such

Corinne H. Rieder is acting chief of the Educational Planning Section of the New York City Planning Department. Harry Davidow is supervisor of research of the Educational Planning Section of the New York City Planning Department.

activities must seem at least slightly startling. Two questions then arise: first, why is the City Planning Department involved with questions touching on curricular reform, general program revision and school administration—areas traditionally left to educators—and, second, what does this involvement suggest about the evolving relationship between operating and non-operating agencies?

Background

Because planning agencies are only beginning to become involved in planning education (as opposed to planning school buildings), both prior agency experience and theoretical literature are sparse. Practicing planners and the existing literature tend to define the planning process through a set of assumptions about the environment in which planning occurs. Specifically, the literature seems to assume the following:

1. The planning agency is sanctioned to speak and be involved in the planning process and works closely with an effective planning division in an operating agency.
2. The structure of the operating agency is adequately flexible and the environment stable enough to allow planning and implementing of plans.

The following analysis of the New York experience suggests that these assumptions are inaccurate. After discussing the realities of the situation, we will present a set of guidelines that underlie the Educational Planning Section's current activities and suggest the kinds of planning appropriate to a planning agency in this situation.

Sanctions and Involvement

The major contacts between the Educational Planning Section and the New York City Board of Education* relate to the school construction budget and selection of school sites. The first contact derives from the City Planning Commission's charter responsibility to prepare a draft capital budget and five year capital improvement plan for the City annually. The second derives from the Commission

---

*The term "Board of Education" is most often used in this paper to refer to the central school system. In a few instances it is used in a more limited way to refer only to the appointed lay Board of Education. The context in which the term appears should indicate its usage.

Chairman's membership on the City's Site Selection Board and the Commission's charter responsibility to approve all zoning and street changes.

The exercise of these Commission responsibilities can be interpreted narrowly or broadly. The City Planning Department has learned from practical experience that it could not make physical analyses devoid of social components. Over the years the scope of its concern has widened. At the same time, the Planning Department has recently prepared and published its first proposed comprehensive plan for the city's development. The mandate in the 1938 City Charter to produce this plan is being interpreted to grant the Department authority to undertake ongoing comprehensive planning and to publish periodic documents reflecting the current state of planning activities in City agencies and indicating their future direction. In education, the document reflects the Board of Education's plans to decentralize the school system. It also reflects the Planning Department's recommendations regarding these plans in terms of City goals and total developmental needs as described in the comprehensive plan.

The trend toward increasing responsibilities of the Educational Planning Section has extended to its operational functions. For example, recent capital budgets submitted by the Board of Education have grown beyond the limits of the City's financial resources. For this reason, the Educational Planning Section has been forced to examine more critically the premises behind these budgets, premises involving program as well as construction issues.

For a planning agency to work effectively with an operating agency, the operating agency must have a department which has as its function the development, coordination, evaluation and implementation of plans. The Board's School Planning and Research Section, perhaps the most effective planning unit within the Board of Education, is limited to developing formulae to determine school capacity, developing programs of requirements for school design, forecasting enrollment, preparing capital budget recommendations and working on selection of school sites. A second unit, perhaps the most likely to take on a central planning role in the future, is the Planning-Programming-Budgeting Section, which is attempting to develop a PPB system and beginning to conduct cost-benefit analyses. Despite the existence of these sections, however, no section in the Board of Education has the authority to make and implement policy plans. Because no such section exists, there is no section to work effectively with an outside planning agency.

Structure and Environment

Even if the Board of Education had an effective educational planning division, its organization characteristics and environmental constraints would still seriously hinder planning and implementation efforts. Implementation requires a top level staff oriented towards planning and a bureaucratic structure flexible enough to adapt to the changes innovative planning entails. David Rogers, in an analysis of the New York school system's efforts to integrate the public schools, notes five major barriers to efficient operation that particularly influence the ability to innovate: (1) overcentralization and the upward orientation of staff; (2) vertical and horizontal fragmentation, isolating units from one another and limiting communication and coordination of functions; (3) the consequent development of chauvinism within particular units, reflected in actions to protect and expand their power; (4) the exercise of strong, informal pressure from peers within units to conform; and (5) compulsive rule following.* These barriers are to varying degrees characteristic of all bureaucracies, but are exacerbated by the sheer size of New York's educational system and the problems it faces.

If the Board were oriented more towards planning and had the staff and bureaucratic structure adequate for innovative planning and implementation, environmental factors would still seriously hamper these efforts.

All elements of educational planning in New York—goals, values and physical and social characteristics—are shifting so rapidly that planning has become extremely complex. One example is the Board's attempt to design and implement a plan to develop comprehensive high schools.

New York City now maintains separate academic and vocational high schools. In 1964 the State Commissioner of Education, James Allen, released a report criticizing New York's efforts to integrate its public schools and recommending development of comprehensive high schools to further integration. The following year the Board of Education adopted this recommendation and began to design a plan to

---

*David Rogers. *110 Livingston Street.* New York: Random House, 1968.

implement a comprehensive high school system.

Although the Board never prepared an officially adopted plan to implement this goal, the tentative proposal was put forth as a working document in December, 1968. Apart from detailed criticism of this particular plan, two major factors obviate much of the value of any such plan. First, interest in the initial goal—integration—has declined markedly. Militant groups on both sides have increased their opposition to integration as a first priority goal in achieving quality education. Second, the ethnic composition of the city's high schools is changing so much that the initial analysis underlying this policy is becoming invalid. It is unlikely that full implementation of the comprehensive high school proposal over the next few years would significantly increase integration in the high schools.

Generalizations can be drawn from this situation. Changing populations, system characteristics, values and goals make implementation over long periods of time difficult. Moreover, major innovations— especially those involving construction—take extensive time to implement.

A further constraint on effective planning and implementation is the environment of crisis that permeates the educational system. Almost half the students entering tenth grade in 1966-67 did not graduate with their class two years later. Forty-seven percent of high school students read more than one year below grade level, and more than 20 percent read more than three years below level. The average high school has a 76 percent attendance rate. The academic high schools have an average enrollment approximately 30 percent over capacity, with some schools running overlapping four-session days lasting 11 hours. Although statistics on school disturbances are extremely hard to obtain, both violence and narcotics have reached epidemic proportions. A conservative estimate indicates that the average high school calls for police help twice a month to deal with disorder. Public battles with unions and community groups further complicate the picture. As a result, most of the Board of Education's top-level administrators have little or no time to do detailed analysis or long-term planning. The school bureaucracy is of necessity oriented towards crisis management to the general exclusion of planning, a tendency most evident by examining the activities of the lay Board.

Developing the myriad of details involved in implementing a plan requires considerable staff time and effort. It also requires some

confidence that uncontrollable factors will be predictable enough to be
"planned around." The crises facing New York City schools require
almost constant attention from the staff. The uncertainties whirling
around the school system (for example, will the state legislature modify
the present decentralization law?) make prediction difficult. Thus,
under these conditions, a plan's probable success is inversely related to
its size and scope.

A final major limit to rational planning is related to the Board's
ability to control its own resources. All operating agencies have some
specific limitations on their actions and some uncontrollable commitments of funds. What is unique here is the extent to which the Board's
resources are bound by contractual obligation. Eighty-four percent of
the Board's operating budget is committed to salaries of teaching,
administrative and supportive school staff—expenses negotiated biannu-
ally with the union—in addition to being contractually committed to
policies, such as class size limitations and special programs, which
require additional funds. Once negotiations are complete, the Board has
little or no ability to shift funds. Housing planners, in comparison, have
considerable freedom to manipulate their budgets (assuming they have
budgets) and some leeway to select their clients and the government
programs they wish to use. The Board of Education has a relatively
stable budget, but little control over allocation of funds and no control
over its choice of clients.

In addition, of course, there are general political limitations on
any government system. In New York, however, the school system
must deal with a teachers' union which is undoubtedly the most
powerful in the country. Union policy includes influencing action in a
wide range of issues. In effect, the union often has veto power over
programs, limiting much of the flexibility left to the Board after
contractual obligations have been met.

The Planning Agency's Activities

The situation facing planning agencies attempting to plan with
operating agencies in such areas as education is obviously difficult. We
have chosen to focus first on demands and constraints to counter a
tendency we see in the literature to underestimate the difficulties of
practical planning. We do not suggest that such constraints make
planning impossible. Rather we have analyzed these constraints in order
to describe the kinds of planning that can and should be done by a

planning agency under these conditions. Before analyzing in detail the role appropriate to a central planning agency, we shall briefly describe the strengths and weaknesses of the New York City Planning Department and the kinds of research and planning activities in which it is engaged.

The Educational Planning Section and the Board of Education must operate under many of the same constraints—a changing environment, the City's size, shifting goals and values, the scope and complexity of the urban education crisis, and the absence of any clearly workable solutions to many of the most difficult problems. In addition to the constraints which the Section shares with the Board of Education, the Educational Planning Section has unique strengths and weaknesses. Among its strengths is a staff with different skills and backgrounds than most Board of Education staff, limited allegiance to past and present education programs, little internal pressure to conform to established educational practices and policies, and fewer time pressures than an operating agency. On the other hand, the Educational Planning Section operates under certain limitations. It has a small staff, limited access to information, and little of the intimate knowledge of the school system that comes from involvement in day-to-day operations.

From these characteristics and constraints we can generate a set of criteria which determine the Section's research and planning activities. Before discussing these criteria in detail, it is useful to examine the studies in which the Section is currently engaged.

Private and Parochial School Study

Parochial schools are reportedly in serious financial difficulty. Two factors seem responsible. First, many middle-income families, the traditional source of parish support, have moved to the suburbs. Second, the schools are employing increasing numbers of salaried lay teachers in place of low-stipend religious teachers. These have been major sources of rapidly escalating deficits.

The City faces two long range possibilities, both with important implications for public schools and the City. Government can either partially or totally subsidize the parochial system or it can plan eventually to absorb an undetermined number of parochial students into the public schools, placing a severe strain on the already overcrowded public classrooms.

At present, there is little information about the central issues surrounding possible public support of independent and parochial schools. There has been no systematic attempt to discover alternate policies the City might adopt and no estimates of either probable curtailment of private school operations if government subsidy were not available, or the impact of such curtailment on public school enrollments.

The Mayor must take a position on aid to the private and parochial schools, and he must know the options and implications of various decisions. The Board of Education and the City's budget agencies must be able to anticipate the potential impact on capital and operation requirements of various policies. Because the issue clearly requires major decisions by both the City and the Board of Education, the Planning Commission has undertaken a systematic analysis of the problem.

School Space Study

Overcrowding in the public schools is seriously impairing education, and projected increases in enrollments are expected to aggravate the situation. Moreover, the shortage of space prevents the Board of Education from implementing other needed reforms which require additional space. Capital construction is not an effective solution because costs are too high to allow construction of enough school space to relieve crowding and because the construction process is cumbersome and plagued by delays. New construction will not provide significant relief for overcrowding in the next five years.

The Board of Education has made no systematic attempt to explore alternative methods of obtaining temporary or permanent school space or of using existing space more effectively. Such a study is clearly needed.

The Educational Planning Section is examining three possible components of a new school space policy: (1) a search for educational innovations throughout the country involving more efficient use of space or use of alternate sources of space; (2) an investigation of procedures and problems involved in Board of Education efforts to rent and renovate space; and (3) sources of information on available space in the City and its adaptability for education purposes.

The Section's purpose in initiating this study is to develop policy alternatives to induce the Board to develop implementation proposals.

Manpower and Vocational Training Study

The City's economy depends heavily on the ability of its schools to provide an adequately trained labor force. The schools are responsible for providing each student with the skills to find good employment or access to post-secondary school training. Clearly, the present secondary schools do not effectively meet these needs. The Board of Education is now changing from a system of separate academic and vocational high schools to a comprehensive high school system. The plan developed to implement this goal, however, has serious flaws, including a pre-established set of trade programs to be instituted over the next 10 years without adequate consideration of changes in the City's job markets. The Educational Planning Section decided that, with a minimum of staff time, it might be able to produce information which would convince the Board of Education to reexamine its proposal and develop a program more nearly suited to the anticipated number of job openings in the City.

The present study compares trade-by-trade trends of the City's manpower needs with current and projected career oriented programs in the public high schools. It is intended to provide program guidelines so that training programs are consistent with anticipated labor force demands and to provide a basis for rational division of training responsibility among high schools, institutions of higher education and industry.

High School Disturbance Study

Disturbances in the public high schools reached epidemic proportions in the past two years. Pressures from various sources inside and outside the school system have encouraged it to respond primarily with policies oriented towards control.

The Educational Planning Section believes that it is necessary to isolate the factors underlying the upsurge in disturbances so that a broader range of policies can be pursued. Using a multiple regression analysis, the Section is determining the systems characteristics correlated with school violence. Rather than concentrating on characteristics of students involved in disturbances, the Section has focused on characteristics of the schools—school size, session structure, community participation, existence of special programs and teacher characteristics—which might be subject to policy decisions. The Section is hopeful that its conclusions will generate additional policy alternatives for the Board of Education.

Criteria

An examination of the studies in which the Educational Planning Section is engaged indicates an implied set of criteria defining the Section's roles. These criteria warrant explicit presentation to determine their applicability as guidelines for planning agencies in similar situations. Studies may be initiated in response to any of the following criteria:

1. *Studies should relate to charter concerns where the planning department's mandate is relatively well defined and should not relate to concerns which impinge on policy areas clearly within the mandated responsibilities of the operating agency.*

This criterion concerns legitimacy of activities. For example, any attempt by a planning agency to engage in curriculum development would correctly be viewed by a Board of Education as beyond the planning department's authority. Studies related to capital programming, however, would be accorded greater legitimacy.

2. *Studies should focus on areas in which policy decisions are imminent and in which it is anticipated that the operating agency will not have an adequate policy response available.*

The logic behind this criterion is obvious. Planning departments should develop policy where it is needed and not being developed elsewhere. In addition, however, there are sound strategic arguments in favor of it. It is likely that the operating agency will recognize the need for a policy decision. Such recognition should mean that the operating agency's staff is more open to policy recommendations externally developed. In contrast, if an outside agency develops a policy proposal when the need for such a proposal is less pressing, the proposal is likely to receive less serious consideration. The private school study being conducted by the Educational Planning Section exemplifies this type of focus.

3. *Studies should have policy implications beyond the immediate concerns of school systems or involve the policy of more than one public agency.*

This criterion is a logical development from the planning profession's traditional concern with the city as a whole, as well as its claim to a role as coordinator of actions of public agencies. The Educational Planning Section's manpower study includes a description of the relation between the high school vocational trade programs and similar programs in the City University system and recommends methods of coordinating the two more effectively.

> 4.   *Studies and study designs should serve as models for continuing research activities conducted directly by the operating agency.*

The planning department may initiate studies which ideally should be conducted directly by the school bureaucracy but which are not yet within its scope. Such studies may serve two purposes: first, reach the policy conclusions the study indicates; second, demonstrate to the operating agency both the value of the research technique and the method of using it. A study of procedures for testing the relative accuracy of alternate methods of forecasting enrollments would be typical of such research.

> 5.   *Studies should be consistent with the time and skill limitations of a small research staff.*

Educational planning sections will inevitably be small, and the skills available to them extremely limited. Before beginning a research project, the section should consider carefully whether its time and skill resources are sufficient to conduct the study adequately. Such considerations should be neither intuitive nor off-hand but based on careful analysis of staff limitations.

> 6.   *It should be possible to conduct studies relying exclusively on secondary sources of information.*

This criterion is partly justified by time limitations, but also by the separation of the planning agency from its prime sources of information. Lack of operational responsibility may make data collection a complicated and sensitive problem, and the planning agency must carefully consider the data needs of a study before initiating it. For example, a study requiring the evaluation of all school principals might be possible if the evaluation were already completed and in the public domain. However, if no such evaluation were available, it is unlikely that the planning agency would be able to perform it.

>   7.   *Studies should have as probable outcomes policy which is implementable with the operating agency's resources.*

In order to use this criterion effectively, the planning agency must have a fairly sophisticated understanding of the operating agency's resources. It would be pointless, for example, to conduct a study recommending alternate uses of resources not effectively under the operating agency's control. It would be equally useless to do a study leading to policy recommendations requiring long periods of time to implement.

>   8.   *Studies should lead to multiple benefits.*

For example, a study leading to a policy to alleviate school over-crowding will not only produce a direct benefit but also make it easier to develop other policies which in turn were hindered by lack of space.

The criteria are determined by the Section's view of the current educational environment in New York City and by the limits this environment places on the roles appropriate to a central planning agency. As conditions change, these criteria will undoubtedly change also. In fact, the development of a decentralized school system is already leading to a major rethinking of the planning department's role. However, the process of developing criteria will remain as indicated in this paper: (1) detailed examination of the relationships involved in the educational planning process and the constraints on the planning department's actions indicated by this analysis; (2) examination of the kinds of roles available to the department under these limitations; and (3) development of criteria indicating the maximum return obtainable within these constraints, given the department's concept of the school system and the city.

Outside of their areas of direct operations (housing, zoning, etc.) City planning departments have a history of engaging in policy research which is often disregarded. Planning agencies entering into work in the functional areas risk the same fate. The most efficient way to avoid this is for the planning agency to tailor its research activities to a role carefully rooted in its chartered responsibilities and limited by the exigencies of the environment in which implementation must take

place. Without such careful grounding and without a clear understanding of the limited role of central planning agencies in this
situation, the most sophisticated planning efforts are likely to be wasted.

IMPLICATIONS OF EDUCATIONAL CHANGES AND RESOURCE TRENDS FOR URBAN PLANNERS

Robert J. Havighurst

The educational changes that are clearly visible present a challenge to urban planners. These changes will not automatically improve education. They may simply be a blind, mechanical response to the demographic and economic evolution of our society. On the other hand, they may result in major educational improvement, provided they are understood and directed toward democratic goals, and provided the resources are adequate and are skillfully used.

Urban planning can make the difference between a wastage of money and people in a vain, unimaginative and mechanical response to social changes, or an efficient and foresighted application of education to the betterment of our society.

To demonstrate this proposition we shall first summarize the educational changes that are taking place, then analyze the resources available to support these changes, and finally discuss the functions of urban planning in relation to educational development.

Imminent Educational Changes

The educational changes of the coming decade may be summarized in terms of: demand for services, organization and administration of school systems, physical location of people and goals of education.

Robert J. Havighurst is professor of education at the University of Chicago.

The Demand for Educational Services. This is partly a matter of the *amount and kinds* of education required by various age and economic groups, and partly a matter of *physical location of the people to be served* (see next page).

It is generally agreed that enrollments in colleges and universities will be pushed up by the growing demand for college-level and adult education. Today about 38 percent of young people enter college, and about 24 percent graduate from a four-year college course. Nobody knows when these figures will quit rising. Probably a conservative estimate is that 50 percent of young people will enter college and 30 percent will complete a four-year course. Also, this increase will take place within the next 20 years, and much of it within the next 10 years. Since most colleges are now filled to capacity, this means that the higher education plant must expand about 25 percent during the next two decades.

It also appears certain the pre-school education for children at least a year before kindergarten will be established at public expense for children of low-income families. This will be an extension and consolidation of the present federal government-supported Head Start program, and will probably be made available to about one million children a year. As it becomes a regular part of the school system, this program will have to be housed in permanent quarters. This may mean that more elementary school buildings will be needed, or that a new kind of facility—a child care center—will be created.

Change in School System Organization and Administration. The present structure of school district organization is a heavy contributor to the growing difficulties of operating an educational system in large cities. There are about 230 "standard metropolitan statistical areas" in the country, with 65 percent of the population. These are natural ecological units of population, covering from one to eleven counties. But each contains many different government units, most of these being local town or townships or village or city governments, and local school districts. In these metropolitan areas there are about 5,500 school districts. Three thousand of them have a total of about 27 million pupils, with an average enrollment of more than 7,000 pupils. The other 2,500 school systems in metropolitan areas are relatively small, with less than a thousand pupils.

If there were to be a "new deal" today in local government, with the slate wiped clean of the traditional structures, our society would create a relatively small number of government units to do the work of civil government and of public education. But instead we have a chaotic jumble of governing units, some very big and some very small, with very little cooperation or coordination among them.

Physical Location of People. These metropolitan areas have come into being as the result of a vast redistribution of people and of jobs which has been going on since 1920, with the pace of change very much increased after 1950. During the process of metropolitan growth, the central cities gained in their proportion of working class residents and of Negroes, while the suburbs gained in their proportion of middle-class white residents. Thus the metropolitan areas became stratified along economic and racial lines. The inner shells of the city are populated largely by people with low incomes; the outer shells of the city contain people with middle incomes; and the outer edges of the city and the suburbs have high incomes.

In effect, schools became more homogeneous with respect to socioeconomic status. From 1920 to 1965, the segregation of children by social class (and by race in northern cities) was increasing. This means that the percent of middle-class children attending schools in which 80 percent or more of the students are middle class has increased since 1920; and the percent of working-class children attending schools in which 80 percent or more of the students are working class has increased since 1920. In the Northern cities, the percent of Negro children attending schools in which 80 percent or more of the pupils are Negroes has also increased.

The numbers of school-age children per family vary enormously from one part of the metropolitan area to another. The assessed valuation of property per school pupil varies enormously. Inequity and inefficiency are characteristic of all of the large metropolitan areas, as far as school government is concerned.

Two contrasting solutions are being tried. Small suburban school systems are being combined into larger and more efficient ones; and the big central city systems are being subdivided on the ground that their bigness causes inefficiency. The decentralization of administration in big city districts is being forced by state law in some cases—notably in New York City and Detroit—while other big city school systems are being carved into regional and district units with a considerable amount of autonomy, though they operate under one school board and one central administration.

Some critics argue that the small local school district has no value in a metropolitan area, and should be abolished. Robert Bendiner, an editor of *The New York Times,* urges a reorganization of school government parallel to one in local county government, as an alternative to the abolition of the small local units. He says:

> . . . a real alternative is emerging—slowly, with variations and difficulty, but with promise, too, because it corresponds in school government to the evolutionary change that is even more slowly and painfully emerging on the political front. I refer to that still groping movement in the country's great metropolitan areas toward some sort of internal cooperation—between suburb and suburb, between city and country, between city and suburb—a cooperation ranging from the loosest agreements on specific matters all the way to consolidation, federation and metropolitan-area government, that new political entity that has been cropping up here and there under the name *Metro.*[1]

Some sort of coordination and cooperation must come to bring together suburbs and central city, and small and large government units; the urban planner has a key role in bringing about these changes.

Changes in Goals of Education. American education has in the past been directed toward two major goals, which are now being pushed to one side in order to make way for a third goal. The traditional goals or purposes have been to make people more efficient producers of goods and services, and to extend opportunity for socioeconomic advancement to economically disadvantaged youth. These have been accomplished reasonably well, as judged by comparison with the educational systems of other countries. They will continue to be important goals, but they are being revalued and reconsidered in light of the fact that we now live in an economy of abundance, where the task of maintaining a high material standard of living is no longer regarded as the over-riding problem of the society.

This economy of abundance, with its technology, is causing a pervasive change in societal and individual values, which are now changing the emphasis we place on the various educational goals. Our

1. Robert Bendiner. The Impotent School Board. *Washington Monthly,* 1969. Adapted from *The Politics of Schools: A Crisis in Self-Government.* New York: Harper and Row, 1969.

society has become so rich that it is hardly worthwhile to produce more
material goods, unless we find some valuable new ways of disposing of
our excess production. Thus we tend to downgrade the values
associated with production, and therefore to downgrade the values of
work, saving, thrift and preparing against a hard time in the future. On
the other hand, intangible goods increase their value, e.g., educational
excellence and health. The next step is to increase the emphasis we
place on studies that are not productive of material goods—the arts and
humanities.

The old values of self-denial and saving tend to become irrelevant
in a world of economic abundance. Writing about the impact of
technological change upon values, Nicholas Rescher sees the following
values being upgraded: humanitarianism, internationalism, rationalism,
social welfare, social accountability, public service, social order and
aesthetic values. The following values will be downgraded: nationalistic
chauvinism, thrift and saving, economic independence, self-reliance,
self-advancement, property rights and faith in social progress.[2]

Changing values will have their greatest effect on the meaning of
work to people. In a society where work produces things of value, the
efficient worker feels good about himself, and feels *potent.* If his *work*
is not experienced as important, his free time becomes the area in
which he searches for potency. He looks for work that is independent
of his job. This work must allow him to express himself, to exert his
potency. The real opposition in his life is between *leisure* and *sloth*
rather than between *sloth* and *work,* as it was in an earlier society.
Thomas F. Green argues that in contemporary society sloth is the
refusal to enjoy the rewards of work, not the refusal to work.[3] The
rewards of work are leisure and the joy that leisure brings. Mortimer
Adler writes that the most valuable activity for men in an economy of
abundance is leisure-work[4]—that is, interesting and valued *effort* that

2. Nicholas Rescher. What Is Value Change? A Framework for Research. In
Kurt Baier and Nicholas Rescher (Eds.) *Values and the Future: The Impact of
Technological Change on American Values.* New York: Free Press, 1969, pp.
68-109.

3. Thomas F. Green. *Work, Leisure and the American Schools.* New York:
Random House, 1968, Chapter 5.

4. Mortimer Adler. *The Time of Our Lives.* New York: Holt, Rinehart and
Winston, Inc., 1970.

does not earn money—its values are service, creation of beauty, expression of emotions, and friendships.

With the pervasive change of values we have been discussing, the goals of education will be rearranged to place greater emphasis on the kinds of education that help people to achieve emerging values. This means more attention to the humanities and the arts and the social sciences.

Resource Trends

Some of the educational changes we have noted will require greater expenditures of money—notably the demand for *more* education. Other changes can be accomplished by skillful planning and creative innovation.

It seems likely that an affluent society can afford to spend more money on education. Our society now spends about six percent of the gross national product on education at all levels—public and private. This could probably be raised to eight percent, especially if the cost of military expenditures went down.

The problem of paying for education is largely one of getting the cost of public education carried by the government agencies best able to raise more money through taxes. This means state and federal government, since the local government agencies are limited generally to taxes on real property for their income. State government has assumed an increasing share of the cost of education, as has the federal government. Both will probably increase their support still further. The federal government has moved vigorously into the field of educational support since World War II, and now carries about 12 percent of the total cost. This may go up to 20 percent during the remainder of this century.

Urban Planning and Educational Development

The educational changes that we can foresee will take place largely in urban areas, and especially in metropolitan areas. These changes will consist of three elements:

1. Change in curriculum and methods of education.
2. Change in the administration structure of the educational system.
3. The location and building of new educational facilities.

Urban planning will be especially involved in the third element—the location and building of new educational facilities—but this function will be closely related to the structural changes within the educational system.

Educational Planning and Urban Planning. Educational planning is in its infancy. The relatively small amount of educational planning up to now has been confined mainly to the projection of enrollments in city school districts, the location of sites for new buildings, and the projection of costs for new buildings and renovation of old buildings ahead for five or ten years. In addition, there has been some advance planning by state boards of higher education, which have had to make plans and raise money to pay for a great expansion of state-supported colleges and universities since 1960.

With educational planning in this embryonic state, urban planning has developed at a rapid rate during the past decade. Large cities now have planning commissions staffed by competent and well-trained persons. Many metropolitan areas have planning agencies. Thus expressways are routed, airports are sited, parks are created, convention centers are located, shopping centers are laid out, and vacant railway yards and stations are allocated to new uses.

Generally speaking, these planning operations have been carried out with little or no coordination or consultation with the educational system. The reason for this is basically the lack of planning by school systems, combined with a prejudice against being "involved" with other agencies of government.

It is significant, then, that we now hear leaders in educational administration call for a partnership in planning among city government, school government, private business and cultural agencies. As long as five years ago, Professor Roald Campbell, one of the country's leaders in school administration, urged a closer collaboration among such agencies. He said:

> To cope with the problems of schools and neighborhoods in our cities, we have established many programs and agencies, including those in education, housing, welfare and employment. Each of these programs is organized as a separate service, each has its own bureaucracy, each its own policy-making machinery, and each tends to be independent of the general government of our cities. In many cases, housing patterns do more to determine the nature of the schools than any action

of the board of education. One might cite the decision to erect the Robert Taylor homes, 28 highrise public housing apartments down State Street in Chicago, as one of the most dramatic examples. Apparently city council members were pleased not to have public housing dispersed over the entire city as had been advocated by Elizabeth Wood, then director of the Chicago Housing Authority. In any case the four-mile strip of public housing on State Street did more to perpetuate *de facto* segregation in schools than any policy decision by the school board or any other body. But why was there not more collaboration among the board of education, the Housing Authority and the city council? This lack of collaboration among agencies at both program and policy levels is a notable problem in our cities. . . .

. . . board members and administrators have tended to be jealous of the independence and power of the board of education. Americans have long thought that education should be removed from politics; hence school government, particularly at the local level, has been more or less independent of city government. Some city councils can adjust the school budget; many cannot. Some mayors or city councils name the school board members; many do not. Even where city government influences school board selection and school budget allocations, seldom does city government play any role in establishing the program of the schools. The courts have often sustained the point that school boards are created by the state, that the state has delegated to such boards powers necessary for the operation of the schools, and that board members are state, not city, officials.

Thus, there is historical and legal precedent for the feeling of independence found in school board members and administrators. Unfortunately, this feeling can get in the way of cooperation with other agencies when the problems require collaboration. The matter is further compounded when representatives of each of the other agencies also exhibit similar feelings of independence, as is often the case. The situation often gets worse while the agencies that might *help* waste their energies over jurisdictional self-justification. . .[5]

5. Roald F. Campbell. *School Community Collaboration in Our Cities.* Paper presented at the White House Conference on Education, Washington, D.C., July 20-21, 1965.

The Optimal Area for Urban-Educational Planning. We have already noted that the metropolitan area is the most appropriate unit area for the financing of education and for the operation of certain educational functions, such as vocational education, education of the physically handicapped, educational television and other forms of education that can be more efficiently and economically operated over the entire metropolitan area than in the individual small school districts.

However, the metropolitan area may be too large for the most effective attack on certain socio-educational problems which require close cooperation among a variety of people and agencies that identify their interests with a relatively small area. A metropolitan area of 2 or 3 million inhabitants may be too large to serve as an effective unit for collaboration and planning over the location of such institutions as community colleges and high schools. Probably the smaller areas, those ranging in size from 100,000 to 500,000 population, are appropriate areal units for this and other kinds of urban and educational planning. But areas of a million or more population should be divided into smaller units of 200,000 to 500,000 for some planning purposes.

An example of the kind of area in need of urban and educational planning is the near south and southwest area of Chicago. This is a square area roughly four miles on a side, extending from Congress Street (in the City Center) south to 39th Street, and from the lake shore about four miles west. This area includes Chicago Circle, the site of the new University of Illinois, which will become an internationally as well as nationally famous seat of learning. It includes Illinois Institute of Technology, one of the nation's three or four greatest centers of instruction and research in technology. It includes Michael Reese Hospital, one of the great research and treatment hospitals of the city. It includes McCormick Place, the city's Convention Center on the shore of Lake Michigan. Facing Lake Michigan and McCormick Place are Prairie Shores and Lake Meadows, new high-rise integrated dwelling complexes. It also includes Chicago's Chinatown, which produces some of the brightest boys and girls in the public and parochial schools of the city.

This area contains acres of old railway yards. On many blocks, old houses have been cleared for urban renewal. Thus there is ample land for new housing and new schools.

There are thousands of people already working or soon to be

working in the scientific, educational and research institutions of this area who do not feel that they can live here because the public schools do not offer what they want for their children. However, they *will* build homes on the vacant lots, and they *will* rent apartments in new apartment blocks to be built, *once they know that their children can be sure of attending first-class integrated schools.*

By the end of the 1960's the Board of Education was cooperating with the residents of a large integrated middle-income housing project to maintain an integrated elementary school for their children.

There is no integrated high school in this area, although there are several integrated elementary schools, public and parochial. Until an integrated high school is provided, with high academic standards, and a good commercial and mechanical arts program, there is no possibility of attracting a stable multi-racial family population to take root in this area. Here the City Plan Commission, the planning office of the School District, the real estate interests in this part of the city and the Chicago Park District should get together to make a plan that would enable each agency to do its part in creating and maintaining a viable socially and economically integrated area in the inner city which could serve as a model for other cities and for other areas in Chicago.

Another unit of this kind is the upper West Side of New York City, extending from Lincoln Center to 125th Street, with Central Park and Morningside Park as the eastern boundary and the Hudson River on the west. At the southern end, the new Lincoln Center has attracted many residents who can afford to pay high rents, and there are several low-cost public housing units. The new midtown center of Fordham University is located there. At the northern end there is Columbia University, the Union and the Hebrew Theological Seminaries and several new high-rise middle-income housing projects. The population between the northern and southern ends of the area is mixed Puerto Rican, Negro, Jewish and middle-class non-ethnic white.

Here, the school system, the several institutions of higher education, the city planning agency and the city housing administration and private real estate interests have it in their power to create an economically and socially integrated area that will be a model to big cities all over the world.

Bi-State Areas. A number of metropolitan areas straddle state boundaries, and thus bring two state governments into any situation that requires the area to be treated as a unit. St. Louis is one example.

There are the state universities of Missouri and Illinois in the area, several community colleges and many school districts. This area suffers from a lack of overall planning and coordination, which leaves the small suburban governmental units helpless to plan effectively for their own future development, while the large central city government and school board see themselves losing power and significance as the suburban area grows in population and resources. It would appear that a solution might lie in a metropolitan area planning agency for governmental and educational affairs, with substantial support from the federal government.

Conclusion

The great task of urban development for the 1970's may be that of bringing the central cities and the suburbs together into effective cooperation, sharing the responsibility of governing and developing the metropolitan area. If this is so, metropolitan planning will become a recognized essential function of government.

The educational systems of a metropolitan area are themselves widely varied in their quality and in the populations they serve. When populations change, as they have done rapidly and will continue to do but with perhaps greater satisfaction of human needs, the educational systems must change. The changes in educational systems must be coordinated with broad social and civic changes in the metropolitan area.

PLANNING FOR
A MOBILE SOCIETY

Karl Otto Schmid

Contemporary urbanization holds enormous challenge for social mobility. In choosing a migrant pattern, professionally, socially and physically the contemporary urban dweller or would-be resident of an urbanized realm enjoys an unprecedented set of opportunities which would be seemingly unavailable if he stayed in his place, his position, or in any one exclusive occupation. On a world-wide basis, modern technology makes these opportunities accessible. For millions of people the ensuing lure to chase after a better life becomes increasingly irresistible. But the same mobility which serves to bring people into contact with a broader range of opportunities also helps them to move on and away. In the United States, this is no longer just a phenomenon but a nightmarish occurrence, since it has become all-pervasive. The implications of the collective urge are tremendous for urban planning. Reference to place and custom, the age-old back-bone of subconscious security, is inadvertently discarded in favor of the prospect for material security. Inter-urban and intra-urban migration, and particularly in-migration from non-urban areas, tend to disrupt cultural stability, and they bring tremendous pressures onto those societal values which have historically developed in a less turbulent social context.

Karl Otto Schmid is deputy chief planner and head of the Department for Urban Design and Research, City Planning Agency, Zurich, Switzerland.

In becoming foot-loose, are we not in danger of succumbing to an abandonment attitude toward even fully compatible elements of the environment for lack of an enduring relation to them? True, in a time of seeming abundance, built-in obsolescence and quick amortization methods permit us to discard industrial products ever faster. Yet when property is written off, or transacted as we move, has it outlived its usefulness? Many an old city suggests the contrary. Can we afford to conceptualize environmental transformation as a state of recurrent obsolescence? Is there not overwhelming evidence that we lack the resources, or the resourcefulness, for the renewal of an environment such as the "Inner City" if we just classify it as obsolete? How can we prevent environmental deterioration if steady migration erodes and disrupts concern for the physical environment? From a European perspective it seems imperative that a stronger sense of continuity be regenerated. The freedom of mobility demands concurrent constraints. This refers in particular to the retention or preservation of existing assets and resources, specifically when they constitute functional linkages, crucial to the functioning of a whole. Just as a single deteriorated commercial establishment or structure can seriously hurt a whole shopping area, so does a single neglected residential structure adversely affect the neighborhood. This calls for a more sensitive attitude toward what is left behind by a mobile society and particularly toward a strengthening of physical cohesiveness. Attention needs to be focused at the level of the micro-environment with programs for remedial action before large-scale neglect occurs. Once environmental quality can be successfully preserved or improved, a serious impediment of mobility will have been removed.

Strong new sensitivities and hostilities have erupted in the recent past, concerning the inadequacies of urban planning in dealing with social values, material and immaterial. As a typical outlet for these sensitivities, the less mobile urbanite begrudges the lack of access to decision-making about urban development. He feels alienated and victimized by a life style which is not of his own choice. He forgets that many discouraging conditions or symptoms, many of the detrimental forces, are not the result of deliberate planning or policies. He deduces, however, that urban growth exceeds the professional capacity of those entrusted with its control (by means of development policies). Through daily experience of the high price for unsatisfactory rewards and services, the disillusioned urbanite builds up resentment against some myths of democracy or against the benefits of a "consumer society" where there is supposedly a high regard for the individual to protect him from abuses. Such protection must originate from local initiatives, assisted through budgetary allocations of the local government to self-help mechanisms.

At a time when every large U.S. city relies on outside assistance and competes with others for federal funds to resolve large-scale renewal, it seems imperative to generate more tax resources at the local level. The necessity for large-scale renewal is far more attributable to unchecked mobility than to obsolescence. We slowly comprehend that urbanization both generates and destroys resources; it challenges the intellect, but it also breeds ignorance. The next decade is likely to make us more apprehensive of both the challenges and the built-in frustrations. Participatory democratic planning processes conceivably supply the best precedents for the attitude necessary to preserve environmental balance and to reduce alienation through social and spatial integration. Combined with new local tax resources they can also alleviate sensitivities due to lack of community participation in urban planning decisions.

Urban planning professionals now register the suffering of the groups which are least favored by material progress. They record the loss in environmental quality. They watch the growing list of demands on their profession. They ascertain an interdisciplinary assault on the two most fundamental of their targets: the understanding and the guidance of urban development phenomena. But the urban planner is caught in a set of dilemmas. He cannot project well-tested institutionalized value judgments into people's expectations any longer; yet he is expected, and frequently forced, to work through institutional channels established long ago. Moreover, on an unprecedented scale, urban planning becomes entangled with the neglected residue of past development, rather than being in command of models for the future. In a deprived environment, which previous occupants have left for lack of satisfactory stimuli and services, it is difficult to address the pride of the newcomer to the scene, as he in turn will likely move on soon. As a consequence, aside from a concern for tangible resources of environmental quality in durable physical terms, the urban planner will have to include less tangible and less amenable factors of security, safety and health. As he shifts the emphasis in any new direction, however, he is subjected to the criticism that the innovative aspects of his approach have not been submitted to testing. Or maybe they have been—in a different cultural context! Are they subject to transferral? Urban planning depends urgently on the testing of comparative methodology.

The following discussion outlines some new avenues toward a better understanding of the forces at work, through educational processes both for professionals and for the public at large. It is (somewhat naively) assumed that information gaps are at the source of public ignorance, misunderstanding and lack of interest. For professional urban planners, the lack of knowledge about comparative situations and the need for shifts in emphasis are taken as a point of departure for an experiment in structured exposure to different cultural environments, and hopefully, the eventual transferral of environmental control-mechanisms.

A New Model for Professional Reorientation

Through the application of the best ingredients of mobility, a unique exchange-experiment has been launched to lift urban planning professionals out of their routine environment. The new program invites urbanists from all across Europe to spend an *extended period of time* (from three to nine months) in the urban laboratory of Detroit, hosted by Wayne State University. In its Division of International Urban Studies, through the Foreign Fellowship Program, 26 urban planning professionals have been committed so far to direct their widely differing experiences towards the unresolved problems of Detroit's development. For all of them, the established scholar or practitioner as well as the younger planning specialist, Detroit provides the scene for a certain shock therapy. Its diversity of societal values and the magnitude of its development vectors, constructive and destructive, make Detroit an excellent testing ground for new planning philosophy for a mobile society.

The program deliberately draws upon vastly diversified intellectual resources from all across Europe to exploit the latent potentials of exposure to one of the gravest problem areas of urbanization in the United States. It also draws upon the wealth of social and political heritage in the home-countries of the fellows. A fruitful generation of ideas stems from the confrontation of the various fellows with their American colleagues as well as from their exposure to one another. A research format which focuses on the Inner City and its people has been developed, with the expectation that European precedents might shed light on the possible re-emergence of an urbane culture despite sub-urbanization. It is felt that a great source of information and inspiration is available, if the components of compactness and of continuity in metropolitan centers are comparatively analyzed and evaluated. It is further assumed as a premise for focusing on this theme that the resources generated by an urbane life style, economically and technologically, are epitomized by high density development. Needless to say, this is a hypothesis, and there is strong evidence to the contrary in the factual development of many cities. But indispensable is the understanding of the increasing social fragmentation within urban societies, and the ability to discern whether the ensuing decline of cohesive forces is indeed irreversible. While the centrifugal forces are seemingly overwhelming, a European perspective might be a catalyst for uncovering the hidden values of a strong metropolitan center, symbolically, culturally and, last but not least, economically.

To test the validity of this hypothesis, the exchange program includes specialists from a great variety of professional backgrounds: economics, political science, urban design, etc., out of governmental and private institutions as well as from universities. While their expertise may not be directly applicable, their contributing to the formation of new beliefs about what is feasible can be instrumental in redirecting the gloomy outlook about the future of the Inner City. Each fellow will also portray the planning philosophy and the institutional mechanism for planning implementation in his home-country, in the light of their potential transferability to U.S. urbanization.

Attempts at guiding urban development show the extremes of success along with the extremes of failure. While success tends to become publicized, all too many failures remain unknown and are therefore lost as valuable learning experiences. Detachment from the constraints of their home-operations makes it possible for the foreign fellows to evaluate both success and failure. If it were assumed that the urban planner often invites failures, despite his forebodings or even better knowledge, because of inertia or resistance in a part of the system, how could he be helped in his efforts? Are there constructive ways to overcome resistance, to break down inertia and to interfere with the comfort of routine-dominated processes of development? Or, conversely, when a drastic change is advocated, is it possible to avoid disastrous effects of disruption?

It is assumed that this exchange program also provides answers to these problems, since it effectively disrupts occupational patterns of the professionals engaged in it. Through change in place and immersion into a completely different cultural context, strong impositions on one's ability to understand, adjust or even assimilate ensue. This generates vast resources for reflection about the "normal" familiar background of past experiences. There is a significant time-lag involved, before it is possible to calmly subject both the familiar and the new environment to the scrutiny of comparison. Some differences must be recorded immediately before an assimilation process takes place. The web of conditions in an alien environment, however—the rationalities between innumerable conflicting forces or claims—can only be discovered gradually. It is for this reason that the exchange program is based on stays of a significant length of time. Eventually the new environment would be taken for granted and routine responses start to predominate. At such a time comparative research can be better performed by local specialists again; the foreign fellows return. But it may be expected that their expertise will have had an impact on some conceptual approaches of local agencies and institutions.

The exchange program also specifically evaluates the institutional framework within which urban planning takes place. If, for example, good public relations programs produce a flow of information to both the public at large and from the people back into institutional and governmental operations, if a broader understanding were made available to a large base of interested parties and individuals, and finally, if as a consequence urban development could occur in more direct response to a well-informed citizenry, maybe even the inertia of the public at large in relation to development programs could be successfully overcome.

As just one example, Switzerland might provide some valuable insights into the impact on planning decisions by an above average quality of information submitted to its people. Much of the information on development programs is presumably digested, since the hurdle of the public vote is consistently built into Swiss governmental processes. This has brought an elaborate and effective procedure of public review into existence: public hearings and other semi-public mechanisms for amendment eventually produce a solid "middle-ground" base for policies as well as implementation measures. The public thus has the opportunity, but also the obligation, to consume a large enough dose of information to take an intelligent stand on the issues presented for a vote. It will typically insist on being well informed, and it will equally insist on the government's assuming the burden of proof that the measures brought before a public vote are objectively and comprehensibly presented. Subtle and pervasive forces are built into the network of information. Of course, the news media play an important role in challenging various controversial opinions prior to policy-formulation. As a rule these challenges tend to be constructive, since professional expertise is invited into public debate. It would be essential to evaluate this public participation mechanism in comparison with procedures in different cultural, political and social contexts. Such comparisons should elicit the ability of various decision-making procedures to cope with necessary changes for a mobile society, without disruption of environmental integrity. Significantly, the Swiss equivalent of decision-making is commonly referred to as opinion-making. The process of opinion-making connotes appropriate consideration of minority-interests and subcultures and their assimilation as a result of mutual learning processes.

The increasing mobility of the Swiss society has not engendered extremes of social or cultural disruption, and environmental quality has been sustained with a governmental structure similar to the one in the United States. This constitutes just one of the innumerable European development phenomena which warrant very careful comparative evaluation.

As mobile societies generate an endless flux of people, the physical environment may well become a dominant stabilizing factor in an otherwise turbulent development context. The urban planner on the operational front, and to a lesser degree the theoretician, will be in a position to comprehend the undercurrents of change only through participation and immersion in them. The Foreign Fellowship Program initiated by Wayne State University will undoubtedly expand; there are already several other institutions both in Europe and in the United States which will partake in this pooling-operation based on professional mobility and exchange. As mobility becomes a preoccupation of his society, the urban planner will profit greatly if he personally experiences the benefits and constraints of this emerging life style. To regenerate and constantly renew urban cores with new meaning may be society's greatest challenge, as people on the move depend on strong stable points of reference. While urban cores often symbolize motivations of the past, their steady regeneration may also constitute a strong cause for the present, and they do not inherently contradict the concept of social mobility.

TRADITION AND CHANGE
IN CITY PLANNING

Giorgio Piccinato

While the tradition of modern city planning goes back to the first decades of the 19th century, institutionalized teaching of the discipline is surprisingly rare. A degree in planning cannot be obtained in Italy, as well as in most European countries and in Latin America. British and American experience in the field is unique and is now being eagerly weighed abroad.

In continental Europe, if you want to deal professionally with urban problems, you must be an architect or a civil engineer.

The first hypothesis reflects the concept of city planning as an extension of architecture and the city itself as a complex of architectural objects. The aristocratic tradition—established in ancient times and revived in the Renaissance and Baroque eras—of designing cities like palaces, in the image and to the major glory of the prince, is reflected in the popular concept of the buildings, not the inhabitants, being most relevant to the idea of city.

Schools of civil engineering have placed greater emphasis on *technical* aspects of building in their curricula.

In this way, the two souls of official city planning were set; furthermore, the technocratic tradition has supported the establishment of the daily planning practice as it is carried out in the town planning

Giorgio Piccinato is professor of urban planning at the Instituto Universitario di Architettura, Venice, Italy.

offices of most great cities. Here the emphasis is usually on so-called technical matters and only very seldom on problems of design. While this does not prove that great city offices have not carried on a design policy, it shows that popular thrust has been more attached to technique than to design as a problem solving tool.

There is, of course, another stream in the history of modern city planning: the one which is known as the line of the Utopian socialists, where the garden city movement has its roots. Here "new town" means new social organization in the first place, and the emphasis is more on the size of the settlement and on the amount and quality of services as a way to evaluate the kind of life which becomes available. Not surprisingly, this group counts the largest number of non-designers, from Fourier to Owen and Ebenezer Howard, from Patrick Geddes to Lewis Mumford; under their impact city planning developed an ample sector of social interests, in which community life and social interchange are given priority in spatial relationships among buildings.[1] To admit that these people were not always correct in discerning causes and effects in the dynamics of urban growth must not detract from their essential contribution toward the definition of city planning as a specific field of interest.

Traditions of City Planning

Origins of modern city planning have to be recognized in the complaints, studies and provisions aroused by the formative process of the large urban concentrations of the industrial age. Social injustice and exploitation, particularly harsh in the "paleotechnic"[2] age, were often attributed to spatial rather than social structures. In this way the city became the source of ills and evils: delinquency, prostitution, overcrowding, epidemics and social "unrest."

City planning had the form, at its beginning, of a curative approach to the ills of the city. Our culture, traditionally city-oriented, led us to see only the ultimate effects of transformations which were taking place on a much larger scale and often at levels other than that of spatial organization. If cities were growing bigger than ever before (and poor housing was the obvious by-product) and the overall urbanization rate was rapidly increasing, the causes were to be found (and faced) in the changes occurring in the land uses of entire regions, in the location factors of new productive activities, and even in the demographic explosion that marks this stage of development in Western countries.

Yet urban planning, in practice as well as in theory, was for a long time constricted within the city limits. All the great infrastructural works—railways, roads, waterways, land reclamation—occurred outside any coordination and, most of the time, also outside any consideration by the official planners.[3]

The emphasis was, and in many cases still is, on master plans and in the attempt to control urban growth through zoning and building ordinances, thus avoiding a confrontation with the forces and the structures actually shaping the environment. The inevitable result was, in the greatest majority of cases, a sad failure; there is practically no large city in the world which is not suffering from planning problems of some kind (whatever was the official attitude toward town planning policies), be it a housing shortage, traffic jams, commuting distances, etc.

Planning Today

Responsibilities for this situation largely outgrew the possible impact of town planning operations alone; however, together with mixed feelings of impotence and guilt for the city planners, this gave way to serious efforts in order to include in the discipline a broader range of non-spatial components, primarily dealing with implementation policies in terms of legal institutionalization, economic and financial programming and management, and social participation and control.

Nowadays, the old image of the city planner as the man who designs the city seems, at least in the proclaimed theories, obsolete. Or, what is the same, design becomes only a part of the discipline, where it used to be practically the whole.

The term "design" itself, as used in this context, is necessarily ambiguous; it happens that even its connotations have changed, and the old and the new ones overlap each other. Many people today believe that design at the urban scale is something like "formal programming" rather than definite spatial design. The awareness of planning as work in progress, or process planning, is therefore brought to the extreme consequences; urban form is also a process-form and new tools must be devised in order to control the process.[4]

This has little to do with the approach which was feasible in the past, when Baroque principles of organization were shaping urban growth; but, as always happens, modern theories meet all sorts of difficulties on the practical field. Habits, interests and institutions are obviously constraining any effort for change.

The resulting situation is such that (when everybody admits the net decay of the urban environment, even in its visual and, more generally, formal aspects) we appear to be still trying to grasp some new result using old approaches. There is an incredible amount of money being wasted everywhere in the world for "improvements," that is, for building absurd pieces of "urban design" which are only bigger architectural objects sharply detached from the urban context.[5]

The gap existing between the levels of design research and actual practice is also to be ascribed to the increasing distance between major studies on architectural typologies and the development of most city planning branches. Not only has the social or even psychological impact of one kind or another of architecture *not* been satisfactorily explored, but city planning itself has largely ignored, in recent times, the problems of spatial environment.

More and more the environment is man-made, and more and more it assumes urban characteristics; yet, we still refuse to take into account interactions among different kinds of spatial decisions, and we are extremely suspicious of the role of design as an institutionalized form-shaping tool within an urban context.

After an era when it was simply an extension of architectural design, and through a period where it seemed to cover only the spatial arrangement of the subject considered of public interest (health, transportation, housing, open spaces, etc.), official city planning seems now detached from spatial design. The practice of zoning, as a bi-dimensional translation of all urban-elements-to-be-considered, together with its legal ties and connotations, has done much to erase physical space from the mind of the urban "expertis." However, once again, it remains to be analyzed why, in a world where human manufacts are so overwhelmingly present, the place of the form-giver is being constantly reduced.

The suspicion arises that the environment of a consumer society comes out of a simple process of addition of goods, therefore refusing any process of synthesis (which implies a value judgment) like that of environmental design, so common in other cultures.

Here is exactly where the progressive thinkers' support for form applies: the lack of form (or its heavily diminished role) in our present society is taken as a sign of its inhumanity, and many left-wing scholars, rejecting an old tradition, see a high formal emphasis as the only radical alternative to current planning practices.[6]

A more articulated approach to planning is also required by the situations created by fast economic development. In Italy, for instance, huge internal migrations, from the countryside to the city and from the South to the North, have been definitely changing the pattern of population distribution. Growth of large metropolitan systems, industrial development, and escape from non-productive lands and from urban centers left aside by economic growth determined enormous uncontrolled transformations in land uses and increased the demands for infrastructures.[7]

Waste of existing resources grows together with unsatisfied needs of services; despite many efforts, the economic distance between developed and underdeveloped areas continues to increase. The rise of individual income and the development of international tourism place a strong pressure on open spaces, particularly mountains and seashores. Water and air pollution, consequences of poor control and strong economic interests, are part of any urban area and often overflow to the remaining countryside.

The last factor to take into account is the situation of the university. Students are today, more than ever before, the most positive and progressive force available. Beyond all troubles and misunderstandings, they reestablished the idea of a "critical" university. Thus, a school pretending to give all the needed answers through the use of technique alone seems finally unthinkable.

No more a docile instrument of the existing power structure, the university can be the place where scientific research is freely directed and conducted and where all social groups can find technical advice and propose their own problems. This might be especially true (and more at hand) for the schools more socially oriented, as is city planning, and offer an alternative to the present lack of commitment in general scientific policies by the universities.

Analyzing the present and designing the future is not necessarily a futile exercise, but it depends on who is involved in what more than on the state of the art.

Notes

1. Raymond Unwin's *Town Planning in Practice* (London, 1909) appears emblematic of this kind of approach, if compared to contemporary continental literature, though the professional milieu was small and compact enough to allow frequent and thorough exchanges of ideas and experiences, and Unwin himself had many contacts with foreign planners.

2. The term was created by Patrick Geddes to define the first (that is, his contemporary) industrial age: paleotechnic age is characterized by spirit of competition, "diffused and habitual fear," "dissipation of energies," alcoholism ("the quickest way of getting out of Manchester"), corruption and sexual perversion. See for this his *Cities in Evolution* (London, 1915 and New York, 1968, Chapters IV, V). Morton and Lucia White's *The Intellectual Versus the City* (Cambridge, Mass., 1962) is an accurate and vivid description of American anti-city tradition, but the literature on the subject is enormous in all industrial countries.

3. Limiting city planning to consideration of the building aspects of human settlement in an era of unprecedented social, economic and cultural changes coincides with the increased impact of land speculation: 19th century cities' extensions and improvements reinforced the power of private land ownership, which has become since then one of the most conditioning forces of urban development.

4. Here is where current artistic theories may find, in the context of urban design and planning, a direct contact with scientific research on programming, evaluating and decision-making processes. However, this also could be the place where advanced management techniques could be weighed in the light of one or another set of social goals, thereby feeding deeper and more substantial characterization of the different policies involved.

5. This could be said of 80 percent of the public enterprises in the field, be it the civic centers of American urban renewal projects, the restructuring of the historic districts in the European cities or the "prestige" architecture in so many developing countries. There is probably also a lack of public interest in the matter (with the obvious exclusion of the people more or less professionally involved).

6. This explains also the renewed interest in a little known chapter of the modern tradition: architecture and planning in Soviet Russia before the Stalinist era. The fantastic qualities of those projects and schemes, their multilevel symbolic significance and their strict relationship with a revolutionary image of the society, seem to indicate a way towards a restoration of design as an instrumental goal into a general social perspective.

7. In 1961, 28 percent of the population was living in 8 metropolitan areas. The figure is expected to be 37 percent in 1981 and 44 percent in 2001. Internal freight traffic is expected to double by 1980, passenger traffic to quadruple and international traffic to double; and the needed investments in transportation will be around $3 billion in the same decade. Public expenditure should be multiplied 4 times for education, 3 times for health, twice for social security, 3 times for soil protection and 4.5 times in urban infrastructures.

URBAN DESIGN
RELATED TO SOCIAL NEEDS

Isadore Candeub

In the earlier decades of this century the problems of the city were considered to be primarily physical and financial. A listing of these problems would include such items as traffic congestion, slums, inadequate parks, obsolete schools and inadequate sewers. Unfortunately, these conditions and others of a similar nature still continue. But we seem to be moving into a period in which the priority order of a listing of city problems will be headed by those of a social nature, with the physical ones being delegated to positions far down the list.

It has been argued that physical design has little relevance to the social problems of our cities. These are said to be primarily influenced by such factors as social and economic inequality, the availability of economic opportunities, the quality of social services and the political cohesiveness of ethnic and economic groups. It has been further argued that man, next to the roach, is the most adaptable creature in the animal world and can readily adjust to *any* physical setting.

These arguments probably have considerable validity when urban design is viewed as an isolated element. They are not valid when we recognize that the physical environment is very much part of the set of urban forces to which man reacts and with which he is involved as part of daily life. A few recent events may be indicative of this.

Isadore Candeub is president of Candeub, Fleissig and Associates, planning consultants, headquartered at Newark, New Jersey.

In Berkeley, California, the desire to use a vacant lot as a "people's park" was apparently of sufficient social relevance to generate a riot by students of the University of California.

In Harlem, the use of a site on 125th Street for a state office building was so strongly objected to by some groups that it nearly generated riots until work on the plan was stopped and a review made of the use of the site.

In New York, and in some of our other large cities, thousands of buildings a year are being abandoned in the face of a critical housing shortage. While this process of abandonment is the result of several factors, it is noteworthy that abandonment has not occurred indiscriminately but generally in selected areas of poor environment.

Despite the current housing shortage, sizable vacancies exist in a number of public housing projects in various cities throughout the country. People, Black as well as white, have left subsidized housing projects rather than accept an environment they consider undesirable.

My first encounter with the effect of the interaction of people with their environment occurred in 1950. At that time, I was directing a study of housing conditions in Paterson, New Jersey, leading to the selection of redevelopment projects. As a first step, we made a review of U.S. Census data by rentals, availability of private bathrooms and density of population for each block in the older portions of the city. We supplemented this with information on land use, lot sizes and age of buildings. We completed our inventory of existing data prior to field surveys and then anticipated that the field review would support our initial office determinations on the location and extent of probable slum conditions in the city.

To our considerable surprise, there were major discrepancies between our expectations and what we encountered in our field examinations. Some of the areas in which we expected severely blighted conditions evidenced considerable vitality and neighborhood cohesion and were in the process of being upgraded through the individual efforts of property owners and tenants. Other areas where the census findings had not indicated major problems were in a very poor state of repair, seemed to have no neighborhood cohesion and were undergoing rapid and continuing change of occupancy.

Our observations indicated that there were significant differences in street layout, mixture of heavy commercial uses and the extent of commercial traffic between the areas that were retaining vitality and those that were declining rapidly.

But the most important difference was the reaction of families—individually—in how they rated the varying areas for living. Their collective judgment, applied to the whole range of variations in the characteristics of the different blocks under study, made the critical difference between the areas that would decline and the areas that would be improved. Without any observable organized group efforts, group reaction and group judgment were decisive.

One of my most vivid impressions of a group reaction and judgment of their environment is the memory of a visit that I made to a large public housing project in New York in 1952. It was a cold and blustery Sunday morning in mid-January under fairly clear skies and bright sunshine. Starting at the nothern end of the site, I observed a black-topped playground in the deep shadow of one of the buildings, with not one child in sight. Buffeted by the wind, I walked down the central mall of the project and, looking on all sides, I couldn't see a single person. At the southern end there was a wall with a drop in elevation to a parking area and to the location of the project's heating plant, around which there were a number of ash cans and some maintenance trucks. Here there were boys at play in the sunshine and protected from the northwest wind by the wall.

As I continued my tour I found a large number of people crowding the sidewalks in front of the stores of the old tenements across the street on the west side of the project, sidewalks bathed in sunshine and protected from the wind.

The project had been "attractively designed" with high rise buildings well set back from the street, with ample space between buildings to provide light and air and a large open mall in the middle. As a design for people, it was a disaster. The site was intolerably cold in the winter and intolerably hot in the summer. The open quality provided no sense of privacy to either individuals or small groups. The open space existed in fact but had no real function.

One of the most discouraging aspects of some of our large public housing projects to a planner is the sense of broken promises; of defeat where there should have been victory. Consider that our sociology textbooks, with their pictures of grim slums, have traditionally taught that these were the result of the greed of private enterprise, the overcrowding of land, development by small parcels, the lack of a comprehensive plan, and building that was carried out without public-oriented control and supervision. None, I repeat, *none,* of these conditions prevailed in the design of the environment of one public housing project.

At a later date, I found that the project I had examined in 1952 could be rated as well-designed by comparison to some others. In Newark, New Jersey, I observed a project of bleak, overpowering height and length of buildings lined up in parallel rows of red brick walls which needed only watch towers to complete the illusion of being prisons. The entries to these buildings have small asphalt areas and a few benches, with no trees facing on a long sidewalk that is completely fenced by five foot high chain link wire fencing to protect a grass strip.

How shall we explain situations of this type? We could begin by advancing the possibility that the architects and planners of such projects are incompetent. This raises a second question: what of their clients, the housing authorities? We can forgive them, since they are presumably laymen, not competent to judge the implications of a design. But then, what about the architects, planners and other technical review specialists at the federal level? Are we to assume incompetency throughout?

This explanation is not logical and is not in accordance with the facts. A review procedure functions to provide determinations on items the procedure is designed to review. Site coverage, access, adequacy of utilities, building set backs and other items are reviewed. These and similar items are identifiable, they can be measured, and there are standard criteria that can be applied to determine whether requirements have been met. Because the review process is explicit, the design of a project relates to the review requirements, and projects are designed so that they will be approved.

There is no review with reference to living *quality,* because the attributes involved are not itemized, and there are no criteria or standards of adequacy. This applies not only to housing projects but to neighborhood design, town design and regional design.

Having made the statement, I can already hear cries of anguished protest from the design professions. The first such cry is the one dealing with creativity, so let's hear it out.

If we are to believe the purists, all good design is a creative act. It is derived from the talents, experience and imagination of the designer dealing with the variables of space, form and function. Truly creative design rises above mundane solutions in achieving patterns that are exciting and stimulating and that enrich human experience. Therefore, let it be unshackled; do not encumber it with an increasingly onerous set of requirements that will impinge on the creative scope of the designer.

The proper response to comments such as this should be "bunk." Our automobile designers have been untrammeled for over fifty years. So now we have cars that are uncomfortable, too bulky, too expensive, and that pollute the atmosphere.

An artist painting for his own account in the privacy of his studio is free to do as he pleases. The design of land and buildings for the use of the public should be guided by public regulation. Far from diminishing creativity, expanding the range of requirements will make greater demands upon the imagination and talents of the designer.

Now, for the second argument of the purists—that design will be regimented by the fixed requirements to meet a uniform concept of social need. This comment can be forgiven, because it is based on ignorance of the facts. The look-alike patterns of subdivision developments, garden apartments and high rise projects that we now have are the result of inadequate investigation into the social needs of the users of such housing. With requirements set for the identification of user groups, of desirable relations with adjoining community patterns and with thorough study of the diverse needs of user groups, we may make some significant breakthroughs in the uniformity that is now overpowering our landscape.

A third and final argument against change is that we already know enough about the requirements of the people served by urban design and have a wide enough range of design concepts to adequately serve society. This argument bears some investigation and a brief review of some design elements may be helpful in our evaluation.

Streets

Streets were traditionally designed in grid-iron fashion for easy platting and land sale and the orderly development of our cities and towns. As we have learned in our textbooks, this pattern, applied rigidly and without discrimination, resulted in some streets running up grades of twenty percent or more and street and block patterns of deadly uniformity and boredom. Hence, we have been taught that streets are to run along the contours that nature has given us and should be designed with fewer intersections and more graceful curves.

The general application of these principles has resulted in elaborately contrived subdivision layouts from coast to coast. In the flatlands of Illinois there are street layouts that are so convoluted they might well have been designed for the steepest grades in Pittsburgh. If, for unforeseen reasons, a design student should inadvertently design a grid-iron pattern as the most appropriate for the subdivision on which he is working, he would have to camouflage it to avoid severe criticism. In the process, much of the simple order and clarity and ability to locate oneself within a community has been lost.

Cul-de-sacs were originally stressed as a device to separate automobiles from pedestrian walks and the play areas of children, which presumably could be set in the rear of housing clusters. Since the children seemed to prefer the paved area of the cul-de-sacs for play purposes, these are now being designed with larger turn around areas to give children more surface area in which to play—among the cars.

Land Use—Commercial

Stores were considered anathema in residential areas by early reformers. "Undesirables" congregated around saloons and barber shops, tradesmen were coming and going, and service vehicles cluttered up streets. So we have zoned them out of residential neighborhoods and with them much of the points of social intercourse and personal contact that were invaluable in the strengthening of community ties.

Land Use—Industrial

Industry was ugliness, dirt and refuse in the eyes of early urban reformers and was to be banished as far from homes as possible. So we now have the long commute to work and highly distorted regional patterns unnecessarily separating residential dormitories from the primary economic resources of the region and creating one way patterns of road utilization which require traffic capabilities for limited peak periods at tremendous costs.

Land Use—Residential
Somewhere in the history of planning and zoning in this
country the conclusion was reached that apartment dwellers
and single-family home owners are not compatible and
should not be mixed.

"Neighborhoods" are designed for home owners. Apartment dwellers are assigned living area along major roads, in
left-over space adjacent to shopping centers and on the
fringes of industrial areas.

The designation of these sites for apartments is con-
doned in our town master plans on the grounds that these
areas are not well suited for single-family homes. Thus we are
assigning our higher density dwelling areas beyond the
boundaries of our community areas and speeding them on
their way to becoming the slums of tomorrow.

Building Placement
At the turn of the century, our city slums suffered from
overcrowding, narrow streets, buildings that lacked light and
air, and a pathetic lack of open space. These were the
conditions on which the city design goals for the second half
of the century were set. And we have paid for our mistakes in
vacuous projects, useless open space and faceless streets.

The cul-de-sac being used for play purposes and the project open
space that is a nuisance rather than a blessing may be symbolic of much
of the urban design efforts of the last few decades. Many of our design
features stem from early reactions to negative conditions. Their
applications to current needs are frequently counter-productive.

We should not delude ourselves about the ease of changing the
environmental design forces that are now entrenched in government
regulations; in the training being given to a new generation of architects
and planners; that have been incorporated into our marketing and land
development financing procedures; and in our value systems and status
symbols. We should further recognize that systematic research into
social needs and systematic evaluation of the impact of design upon
people and groups is still to come.

These deficiencies notwithstanding, there are some beginning points that may serve to orient us until they are replaced by more definitive directives.

At the top of our list we must place the concept of "community." Please note that we do not mean that banal word which is used to describe every new subdivision and every new housing project. We mean "community" as describing the society of man occupying a given area within fairly definable boundaries, interacting within that area, with many interests in common despite differences and even antagonisms. If man is a social being, let's treat him as one and provide him with an environment in which he can function as a social being.

The cultivation of a sense of community through urban design involves the development of strong connecting links between sub-elements, providing diverse activities to focus interests and to secure interaction, and the provision of definable boundaries and functional centers.

Related to the concept of "community" is the concept of "place." Man's sense of security is dependent upon a set of stable relationships with family, society at large and his direct environment. In designing our urban environment, we can establish a sense of order and specific spatial relationships. However, we can also create a sense of confusion similar to that of a rat's maze, or a sense of indefinite space in which there are no firm points of orientation and in which spatial relationships are constantly changing.

The patterns we create can be repetitive to the point of completely lacking interest, or they can engage attention, stimulate, and excite interest. The environment can be dreary and dull, or can offer a continuing challenge and sense of discovery. If we consider the full range of variables presumably at our disposal—topography, views, lot size, block size, building placement and open space treatment—there are endless opportunities for the generation of interest and excitement in our urban areas.

This range of treatment can be even greater if we recognize our responsibility to plan for a pluralistic society—one of poor and rich, young and old, homeowner and renter, adult and teenager, manual worker and professional. Does this sound too utopian? No!

It can be done and has been done. A visit to the twenty block area of the West Side Urban Renewal Area in upper Manhattan will show the results, a truly stimulating and dramatically interesting environment.

This is only the beginning of a list of directives that can and should be drawn to guide urban design for the future. The list should certainly include provision for privacy, safety, ease of travel, public gatherings and the proper placement and design of public parks.

In drawing this list we have not once mentioned the word "beauty," the original function of urban design. This was not an oversight. The civic beauty that we should strive for is not the civic beauty of the building facade but the beauty that is inherent in the total urban environment that we will achieve. This will come about not in the deliberate striving for "beauty" but as a by-product of our total concern with the creation of a livable human environment.

Thoughts on Urban Schools

Turning our attention to schools within the urban scene, we find we have one of two alternatives.

Alternative 1

We may decide that we now know the proper size of a school site and the optimum number of children per school facility—and this shall apply in every instance. Under this dictate the only area of discretion to be decided upon within any given community or segment of it is the location for that facility.

In doing this we will, of course, have a priority decided that:

a.   There is a definitively "proper" size for a school facility;

b.   That the size is truly relevant to the educational function;

c.   That this function is clearly separate from other aspects of community life and shall supersede them in level of importance when a school facility decision must be made.

Alternative 2

Under Alternative 2 we might want to list a series of assumptions as follows:

a.   We are not sure what the "optimum" size of a school facility should be;

b.   We are not even sure there is an "optimum" size;

c.   However, there are diverse communities with diverse needs and problems; and

d.   Rather than relate to "optimum" size or other features, we might better serve community needs and possibly the educational needs of our children if we related the school facilities to the community rather than trying to force an inflexible school format on the community.

Unfortunately, most local school authorities are thoroughly committed to Alternative 1. Educational facilities have become so standardized in form and function that it has become almost impossible to utilize them with any freedom in the community building process.

There are tremendous potentialities that would be available, if the entire function could be unfrozen. Some of these are as follows:

a.   Combine day care centers and schooling for kindergarten and lower grade classes in centrally located community centers.

b.   Combine schooling, art centers and theatrical workshops in community creativity centers.

c.   Clearly separate athletic activities from the school facility. Why must every "temple of learning" be attached to a ball field?

d.   Integrate school facilities directly into an office-business complex, not merely at the university level, but also at the high school level where it can be done to good advantage.

We should be reaching out for the diversity that we need for a pluralistic society of multiple interests, instead of standardizing and homogenizing our facilities and services as if such diversity does not exist.

We should be building a more differentiated pattern with relations to community needs and interests, rather than striving for greater uniformity.

We should be reaching out to the local community to relate to it, to respond to it and to utilize what it has to offer to the maximum degree. This cannot be done if we start with the presumption that all schools should have one prescribed form and format.

AMERICAN AND EUROPEAN
URBAN PLANNING

Jack C. Fisher

There is a growing conviction on the part of European professionals that European cities are beginning to face many of the same social problems that we do here in the States (e.g., social tensions, housing problems, police attitudes, and economic competition, as reflected in the Catholic-Protestant clash in Belfast, the Algerian minority in Paris, the "coloured" immigrant problem in London, and South European worker-immigrants in the Common Market). There is the expressed conviction that there is much to learn from the American experience on these problems; if nothing else, Europeans feel that there is much to learn from American mistakes.

It is equally clear that both European and American urbanists share the common problem of finding new and better answers to the basic problem of humanizing the urban environment. Urban planning in Europe, particularly in Great Britain and Scandinavia, appears to have made great progress in terms of implementation programs that reflect competence of physical design and progress toward the development of comprehensive national urban growth policies. However, the Europeans emphasize their inability to come to grips successfully with the human factor in city planning.

Jack C. Fisher is associate director, Center for Urban Studies, Wayne State University, Detroit, and director of the American-Yugoslav Project in Regional and Urban Planning Studies, Ljubljana, Yugoslavia.

The strands linking economic and physical planning have been analytically weak in both planned and unplanned economies. The so-called requirements of physical planning methods are a mixture of average past practice, social aspiration and currently fashionable technical solutions.

The two major decision areas for urban and regional planners are land use and capital investment in infrastructure. Land use decisions involve amount, location and other elements of demand by type of use. The prescriptions of the land use planners are based upon projection of demand (to meet the test of reasonableness) and upon norms which are independently validated (the standards of the profession). Capital budget decisions of the physical planners are concerned chiefly with priorities, since the levels of the budgets are matters of economic determination. Priorities are set in accordance with judgments of need (based on obsolescence of existing facilities or deficiencies in meeting standard conditions). Physical planners, however, have contributed little to the development of criteria of choice among competing projects, leaving this issue to welfare economists or public administration experts.

The style and content of city planning practice in the United States has moved far from the European practices upon which it once drew so heavily. This difference is particularly marked in the matters of specialization and professional division of labor. The European planner remains the humanist-generalist, particularly in the South-Central European milieu. Though urban economic theory owes a great deal to the southern Alpine area, where Bavarians, Swabians and Czechs developed location theory in various forms, contemporary regional economists are, with a few exceptions, remote from city planning practice. Even more than his counterpart in the United States, the urbanist is an expansive architect, and the regionalist is a rural-oriented geographer or economist.

Urban planning institutes throughout Central Europe rely, for reasons of scale and financing as well as staffing, upon the individual artist method of planning. In Europe generally, the division of labor in planning teamwork is not so far developed as in the United States, nor are European urban planners as likely to be specialists. The Europeans have as yet made much less use of planning-related social science work; and policy-directed social sciences and the management sciences are still relatively rare.

American city planning places much greater demand on substantiating data than does European practice. Elaborate defenses of the planners' judgments, such as cost-benefit analyses, are not often found in European practice outside of Great Britan and (recently) France. When he utilizes social science, the European planner does so primarily in a descriptive, rather than normative, fashion. The techniques of evaluation are subjective in both cultures of planning, but American planners have developed more elaborate aids to buttress their decisions in the form of the trappings of science and "objective" findings. In addition, American planners are more prone to believe in a "best" solution that can be discovered by mathematical optimization or other techniques.

While in many American universities professional schools are moving toward more "theoretical" or general formulations, there is substantial demand in Central and Eastern Europe for the application of relatively well-known American techniques. That is, the professional "know-how" based on experience is more in demand than contributions to new knowledge on the frontier of a subject. For many of these countries, contact with American professional work is much more limited than in England, Scandinavia, Holland or France. Accordingly, work of planners using established techniques in housing and transportation studies, project analysis and programming is welcome and useful even when not noteworthy from a professional perspective in the U.S.

Funds allocated for planning education, for planning research, for studies of specific problems, and for planning itself are rather meager in many parts of Central and Eastern Europe. When funds are made available for planning studies, there is great political pressure to realize these studies in direct program actions. When Americans cooperate in these studies, they must expect to fall under this political accountability. Accordingly, pressures are placed on such work which exceed those to which many American planners are accustomed.

European governments enjoy a wider sphere of legitimate action in planning and public works than is afforded the typical U.S. local government. Secure in this position, European decision-makers will eschew the elaborate calculus built up for American planning decisions, for there is less need to defend decisions with such justification. Accordingly, American planners may find some of their techniques unwelcome, and may be in turn intolerant of the style of the Europeans.

Though the typical European does not need social analysis for the defense of his planning decision-making, there is a lively interest in the application of social science work for planning, and in part it is symptomatic of the growing concern about the social consequences of physical planning. But social science training in the socialist bloc is largely ideological and doctrinaire. American social science, with its engagement in practical problems of urbanism and the social issues of planning, appears to be more useful to the practitioner of city planning in Europe as well as in the United States. As a general rule the American "planner," far from being an architect-civic designer, may well be a generalist in command of a number of specialties, or more probably, is himself a specialist in a very large team of other specialists. Such information resources and networks of expertise are badly needed in continental planning.

Americans, in turn, can benefit from comparative planning studies. Further, the academic planners in the United States have developed techniques that are in sore need of being tested, but which have had limited testing in the States. European planners frequently have possibilities for the direct implementation of planning concepts. This possibility influences the conceptualization in turn. Americans learned a good deal about the behavior of pet ideas under such direct testing. And they learned how to modify their models to suit the limitations of local data and resources. Finally, the cooperative enterprise may well be instructive in an informal as well as formal manner, showing Americans something of the European working methods, with their strengths as well as weaknesses, and showing them the advantages and disadvantages of our university training system.

"NEW CITIES" AND EDUCATIONAL PLANNING

Charles S. Benson

Perhaps my chief qualification to write on this topic is that I lived for two years in a "new city." Admittedly, that new city was far away—in Pakistan—but it incorporated a number of the concepts pronounced in 1898 by Sir Ebenezer Howard. Islamabad has limitations of numbers and area, as exemplified in a master plan of housing, commerce, education, public offices, recreational areas and green belts—a master plan that was drawn up by Doxiadis. Most of the residents—those who are in the labor force, that is—find their employment in the city of Islamabad, though a minority commute to the old parent city of Rawalpindi. The growth of Islamabad has definitely been carried out by a process of colonization; indeed, the government had been quite ruthless in expropriation of land of the villagers.

At one point, however, Islamabad departs from Howard's principles: the increase of value in land is seldom retained by the public authorities. Islamabad has come to be known as an expensive city to build and to operate and as a place where persons who stand in favor of the government can make fortunes in real estate speculation. The antagonism that this knowledge has created is partly to blame for the continuing strife between East and West Pakistan.

What can be said in favor of Islamabad as a social experiment? In

Charles S. Benson is professor of education at the University of California, Berkeley.

terms of a kind of physical and intellectual demonstration effect, a great deal. Islamabad provides the most advanced university facilities in the country, the best laid-out and equipped colleges, schools of all kinds, parks, playgrounds, tree-lined streets, underground utilities as well as an underground garage, large air-conditioned office buildings, a country club, a bit of a freeway, a traffic circle that did not quite come together, and the most elegant Islamic firehouse in all the world. Much of this had not been seen in Pakistan before. Islamabad showed what can be done in the rest of the country when resources become available.

Does Islamabad hold promise of producing a better way of life? The initial impression of a Westerner might be to the contrary, in that the city appears to idolize what many Westerners deplore most in South Asia. Life in Islamabad is hierarchical in the extreme. One's house, garden, water ration, access to given grades of school and health facilities, as well as one's social companions, are all determined by the "job." The job is found primarily in the bureaucracy. Young people have little in the way of work models to observe except that of the white-collar administrator. The opportunities for recreation are fairly well utilized, but the Westerner does not sense much richness of cultural life.

On the other hand, longer-term changes are clearly in evidence. A major characteristic which distinguishes Islamic nations from the rest of the world is isolation of women from work (outside their own households). It is only in Islamabad that school and college enrollments of females approach that of males. These newly educated women will surely be a force for change in the country. Further, it is only in Islamabad that one sees much evidence of fathers and sons playing games together—games such as field hockey, cricket, tennis and badminton. This will make a difference. One might think that the pleasant rural surroundings of Islamabad would give detachment from the horrifying problems of poverty and disease that abound in most of the country. It is true that Islamabad lacks the color, the smells and the gay tongas of the city bazaars, but as compared with Karachi, a person in government in Islamabad senses with even greater reality the enormous gulf that separates him from the animal-like existence of the nomads and tent dwellers, who, along with their animals, have managed to settle themselves down in vacant fields and green belts alike. This reality shock will stand to benefit the country in the long run. Hence, the message I start with is that at the greatest distance one can move in the mind's eye, there is a new city. It is thriving and it is yielding benefits in the near-term and in the future alike—not all of which might have been easily predicted at its building.

Turning to matters closer to home and thinking now about regionalism in education, I would like to suggest that there are two practices developing strongly. Neither is new in principle, though neither has yet been well developed. The first is the regional delivery of certain important, specialized services to schools and similar institutions. Let us call this "functional regionalization." The second is the use of large governmental units to finance and administer long-term experimental programs, free of those conventional bureaucratic constraints that are commonly imposed by state and local bodies. This might be described as "experimental regionalism."

Let us first consider functional regionalization. The direction of development can be seen in New York State. The most visible regional unit is the Boards of Cooperative Educational Services (BOCES). These Boards stand ready to provide occupational educational services on contract to local school districts, as well as to provide services in special education. Some BOCES are beginning to operate programs in in-service education. Some are doing important work in data processing, educational research and educational technology.

No one claims that regionalism in New York State is working perfectly. There are actually two main kinds of regional units, the BOCES and the Title III centers; and the boundaries, generally speaking, are not coterminous. In parts of Long Island, the whole structure of local government has a complexity that passes human understanding. The linkage between the regional units and the school districts of the larger cities are weak, where they are not non-existent. Private educational agencies have been largely excluded from the mainstream of regional planning and development. Relations with county and municipal planning agencies are poorly developed as yet.

Nevertheless, BOCES are regarded as one of the brightest and most hopeful developments in education in New York State. The reason is fundamental and it is related to the continuing drive, as Wilbur Thompson[1] has put it, to obtain economies of scale in the provision of

1. Wilbur R. Thompson. *A Preface to Urban Economics.* Baltimore: Johns Hopkins Press, 1965, p. 259 ff.

public services while at the same time expanding the range of household choice. If small school districts tried to provide themselves with occupational education, in-service training of teachers, educational research, etc., they would face the choice of paying heavily (per capita) for their services or of limiting the choices open to the clients of the district. One can easily extend this kind of argument to urge regional provision of a number of services that fall outside the field of instruction: student transport, food services, health services, building construction and maintenance are examples.

The movement toward functional regionalism has now acquired a new driving force behind it. Our state governments are being urged, rightly I think, to move toward "full-state financing" of educational services. Simultaneously, pressures are mounting to place decisions about operations of schools in the hands of the parents, teachers and students who are involved with a given school. These two proposals—thanks to an unfortunate, though understandable, shortcoming in social science research—place state governments in a quandary. If money for education is to come wholly from state coffers and if it is to be distributed to educational authorities in small (e.g., single school) attendance areas, how is one to decide which schools receive how much money? Social science has advanced far enough to tell us that equal dollars do not mean equal education in different schools of the state, but it has not advanced far enough to tell us how unequal the dollars should be. Regionalism offers the only way out of this dilemma (pending such time that we can become truly scientific about resource allocations in education): the idea is that the state would distribute more or less equal dollars to all the schools, making perhaps some adjustments for easily documented differences in necessary costs, while at the same time establishing regional units to offer local schools on their order a wide range of specialized services. These would be available on the basis of diagnosed needs of students. Needs could refer to medical treatment, requirements for remedial work, requirements for specialized instruction to assist a student in developing an unusually great musical talent, etc.

This process is one of distributing educational resources from the state to the schools as "aid-in-kind," rather than as cash. The Miller-Unruh Basic Reading Act in California (1965) is an example, though that program operates in the unfortunate lack of regional centers to aid in its administration.

Regionalism of a kind to serve diversity in tastes, while at the same time serving criteria of fiscal good sense, requires better planning than we have so far been engaged in. I recently commented that we tend to settle for *ex post* evaluations of highly fragmented educational projects as a substitute for a fully developed set of planning activities.[2] A more complete set will have at least the following features: that educational planning occur in a governmental body which is powerful and which provides means for coordinating educational planning with other public sector planning programs; that educational plans provide definite time horizons for the meeting of targets; that those targets be related to the uses of education, whether in occupational assignments or non-market situations; that planning provide a continuous process of control and monitoring of educational activities; that the planning processes employ computerized planning models; and, finally, that these processes be conducted by teams of specialists in demography, finance, curriculum, survey research, measurement and architecture. If we are to have an education structure which is more rational, and at the same time more openly complex, we must allow the body politic of education to exist complete with a system of nerves, e.g., the planning apparatus.

Now let me turn to the topic of experimental regionalism. In 1970, the California Assembly passed Assembly Bill No. 1035 to establish a set of innovative schools to be administered by a public commission. It was stated that the California Legislature sought improvement of educational programs through an organized and concerted effort in experimentation and research. The goals were to: (a) identify both the exemplary school programs which lead to pupil success in school and the programs that fail to produce success; (b) examine the effectiveness of various instructional programs; (c) conduct research and experimentation on a clinical basis to seek improved methods of instruction; and (d) discover ways to improve instruction in reading and mathematics. These schools were to be administered by an Education Research Commission of nine members selected for their familiarity, standing, competence and attainment in research methods applicable to the physical, behavioral and management sciences. The Commission had the power to employ a staff for its own use and for

2. Charles S. Benson. How the American Education System Looks from the Standpoint of Systematic Planning. Paper presented at the Annual Meeting of American Educational Research Association, New York, 1971.

the innovative schools, to establish and operate the schools, to receive and expend funds in support of its programs and to contract with other governmental agencies and private organizations for services and equipment. Generally speaking, the Commission was free of the requirements of the state education code and it is free of the natural constraints of client pressure, unions and political factions that may serve to limit bolder kinds of experimentation in the local setting. It was not anticipated that all of the experimental practices tested in the innovative schools would be immediately transferable to the conventional school setting. The idea was to explore effectiveness first and cost-effectiveness later. The first innovative programs began late in 1971. The ideas were somewhat similar to the proposal that schools in the pattern of the "teaching hospitals" of the medical service be established by the state governments in inner city areas, schools which would serve simultaneously the functions of research, experimentation, teacher training and high-grade instruction of students.[3]

Having sketched two kinds of developing practices in regionalization, what can be said about the role of the cities? It was Henri Pirenne who pointed out that formal, non-religious education is a child of the city.[4] This was true in Europe, and it could clearly be seen in England at the turn of the century. On its own initiative, London began to explore secondary education for those youth who did not intend to enter the university (though this was quickly squashed by the central government). It was repeated as recently as when Philadelphia produced the open high school—Parkway.

Education does not lack for critics. Insofar as the new generation of critics are hitting true targets, one may say that our schools are sick in the first instance, because life in our cities has gone sour. The *new cities* may be seminal in a process of educational renewal.

What is the place of new cities in the rejuvenation of American education, and how is their role affected by the two kinds of regionalism we have discussed? Plainly, the new cities are well designed to be seminal institutions of reform. They have the advantages of freedom from the constraints of older forms of physical plants and they

3. Charles S. Benson. The Economics of Education in Urban Society. *Phi Delta Kappan,* March, 1967.

4. Henri Pirenne. *Economic and Social History of Medieval Europe.* New York: Harcourt Brace Jovanovich, p. 124, undated.

have the freedom—if they choose to exercise it—of hiring staff who are amenable to experimentation.

Functional regionalism can add a third freedom to the educational life of the new cities, namely, minimizing the need to build and operate specialized facilities in the early stages of a new city's development. Resources can be husbanded for what are, one hopes, more interesting kinds of experiments. Hence the new cities might become the primary locus of work performed under the program of experimental regionalism, with the state's interest in that program offering the link between what is learned in the new cities and the broader educational community.

Along with these freedoms goes a peculiar kind of stability, specifically, the maintenance of a given cohort of students in the schools of the new city over an extended period of time. One of the difficulties of our California experimental program is that if we want to include students from poor households in the experimental programs in reading and mathematics—and we very much do want to include them—we have to face the hard facts that we will be dealing with a rotating body of students, given (a) the propensity of poor households to change their residence frequently and (b) the difficulties of maintaining a transport network for the special benefit of a small number of mobile pupils. In the new city it will be possible to conduct longitudinal studies for this class of student. It is probably our first opportunity to do so.[5]

The freedom to experiment and the stability of the student population argue strongly for the establishment of research wings attached to elementary schools. These units would provide special services in diagnosis, in reduction of data, and in carrying on various kinds of clinical activities. Obviously, one is saying that the schools need to be staffed not only with superior teachers, but also with a body

5. Section 712 (a) (7) of the Housing and Urban Development Act of 1970 (Public Law 91-609) lays down the following as a condition for a new city to receive federal assistance: that the community development program "makes substantial provision for housing within the means of persons of low and moderate income and that such housing will constitute an appropriate proportion of the community's housing supply." We are assuming, of course, that the advantages of life in a new city, as compared with conditions in the ghetto, will lead low income households to change their residence less frequently.

of research teachers. Please recall that earlier I took the position that applied research in education needs to be free of the requirement that practices be immediately transferable into the conventional classroom. The initial objective is to explore effectiveness; cost-effectiveness considerations must enter later.

What are some other possibilities open to education in new cities? One is to establish the high school as a community center open seven days a week and "around the clock"—not literally, of course, but from early in the morning until late in the evening. There are two clear objectives. First, to bridge the generation gap in learning; that is, to have the school as a place where adults as well as young people enter happily in pursuit of new learning. Second, to allow young people to pursue their specialized interests in subjects including literature, mathematics and science; in the arts—painting, music, etc.; and in the crafts. I feel our country is remiss in delaying too long the opportunity for young people to work intensively with experts in their special interests during the years of their late teens when their mental and physical energies run so strongly. It is unrealistic to expect that these special interests can be served within high school programs that—let's face it—must continue to place their primary emphasis on preparation for college entrance. So the way out is to extend the availability of educational facilities in the time dimension.

Another task is to explore diversification of school staffs. The possibilities are greater at the secondary level, but they exist to some extent at the elementary level as well. Presently, much of what is done in the schools is boring to students and teachers alike. What we need is diversification within staff to allow diversification of activities within the school day. Not every school day needs to be the same dreary progression of a given pattern of one subject after another. Many persons in the community have special skills which they would gladly teach to young people, if they could do this free of certification requirements and free of the obligation to be full-time employees. These might be musicians, artists, scientists, persons with high-grade office skills, and the like. Many would be housewives—though some might be college and university students. The new surplus of Ph.D.s might well be channelled into careers that allow a work life split between teaching in a college and university and teaching in a secondary school. Strong effort should be made to involve housewives and students from low income families.

Finally, it should be possible to explore changes around what I call the "productive margin" of education. For the student who does not intend to go to college, one possibility is to establish for him adult high schools, on the one hand, and to offer him vouchers to attend proprietary training schools, on the other. Centers in the style of Russia's pioneer palaces might be established to allow students to see what their capabilities are in scientific and artistic fields. These would be complements to the use of the high school as an all-day community facility, and they would allow the accumulation of a critical mass of instructional materials in one place. Voluntary programs in early education of many types would also be useful.

Experimental regionalism would allow a dissemination of results from educational experimentation in the new cities to the remainder of the state. It is easier to see the general form of such statewide networks than it is to see the locus of long-term, concentrated and well-planned experimentation. This is the particular contribution that new cities can make. Whatever they discover will not be lost on the larger community.

SYSTEMS ANALYSIS AND MANAGEMENT INFORMATION SYSTEMS IN EDUCATION

Harold Weitz

Exploring Alternatives in Education

The urban educator of the early 1970's is being challenged by the complex problems of a changing urban environment. Metropolitan areas have been expanding, the population of the cities has been increasing rapidly and the socio-economic and ethnic composition of the population in the central cities has been changing. Furthermore, the urban school system is under increasing pressures to find the funds necessary to meet the rapidly rising costs of education, to satisfy the demands created by new and changing labor markets and to overcome the relative ineffectiveness of the school in compensating for the deficiencies of the culturally disadvantaged. These new problems and pressures have, in turn, increased the demand for innovation in education, which is being promoted and facilitated by the use of federal funds. New theories from the field of child psychology, new technology and new curricula are being increasingly applied by educators as they seek means for improving the educational process.[1] [2]

Such innovations present mixed blessings to the administrator. Although each may represent a possible means for improving the schools, the administrator is forced, because of financial limitations, to make choices between alternatives for which he often has limited

Harold Weitz is with the Advanced Systems Development Division, IBM Corporation, Yorktown Heights, New York.

information concerning effectiveness and actual cost. Thus, the administrator approaches his decision-making with much uncertainty. Furthermore, because he often has to base his planning upon the marginal resources available, the administrator often chooses to continue the traditional patterns of education and administration. This occurs in spite of the fact that changes in the student body and the services needed may require a totally innovative approach to the use of the school resources. Current planning is a reflection of: the limited amount of funds available for new programs; contractual obligations; legal constraints; prior commitment of funds; the force of tradition; and, finally—but not least—a lack of resources to formulate a number of alternative plans and policies and to evaluate their consequences.

What we need are tools for planning that would permit the administrator to:

1.   Explore a wider range of alternatives in the deployment of the school's resources;
2.   Generate the resource requirements and consequences dictated by several strategies; and
3.   Evaluate the consequences of each alternative strategy.

An attempt at the attainment of these objectives is the subject matter of this chapter.

Computers, Models and MIS

Within recent years several developments have taken place which offer some promise that the needs of the educators, as briefly enumerated above, might be coming closer to fulfillment. These developments include those of sophisticated communication and information-processing technology (in which the principal component is the computer) and systems analysis.

Although the computer has gained an accepted position in industry, its role in education is still in the early innovative stage, despite its rapid introduction during the past decade. Beginning with such mundane administrative applications as payroll, the computer is now being employed for a wide variety of student services (e.g., attendance reporting, grade reporting, test scoring and scheduling) and business services (e.g., accounting, inventory, purchasing and bus routing).[3] Many of the student service applications stem from a desire to make more effective use of the teaching staff by reducing its ever-increasing clerical and administrative duties, whereas the business service applications are intended to reduce the administrative and business staff burdens and generally to make more efficient use of the education plant. More recently, the use of the computer in providing instructional services, such as computer assisted instruction and student problem solving aids, has gained in importance. And, finally, there is the advent of the modern management information system (MIS), which seeks to more systematically and efficiently provide information needed by the school administration. But the computer, together with systems analysis, may also make significant contributions in the area of policy making. Certainly the need exists to increase the "staff support" available to the education administrator as he attempts to resolve the numerous policy making problems confronting him.

The application of systems analysis to education also is still in its infancy, although its use in the military and industry has been widespread. It offers much promise of making choices more rational and systematic; however, it offers no panacea. It cannot completely substitute for factual data and tested quantitative relationships upon which real knowledge is based and which are so lacking in the field of education (and, for that matter, in all fields touching on human behavior).* Modeling, which is the essence of systems analysis, provides a method and rational structure that, together with progress in experimentation, holds the promise of providing additional staff support for the education administrator. The merit of modeling and computers lies in the fact that they force a discipline upon the user; in addition, the computer can store large volumes of data, process many variables, represent complex relationships and assist in investigating numerous alternatives.

The position of models in the modern MIS can be seen in Figure 1, which portrays some of the information flows in an educational MIS for a large school system that is divided into four regions. Routine data on schools, pupils, teachers and expenditures periodically flow into the computer center and are used to update the appropriate files. Results of any special tests or questionnaires also are entered into the data base. In response to queries, the computer will generate reports pertaining to

*This is not to imply that systems analysis can be employed only where tested quantitative relationships are known; on the contrary, individual judgments, values and estimates are almost invariably embedded to varying degrees in any systems analysis study.

Figure 1

Computerized Information Flows for a Centralized Education System

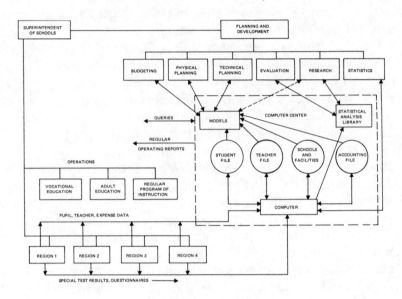

Figure 2

Methods for Deriving Solutions from Models

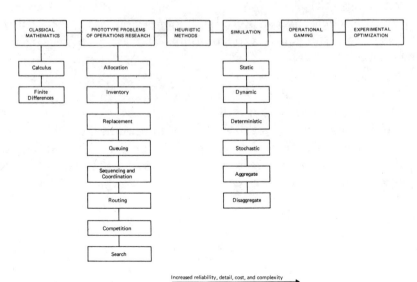

current or past operations as reflected by the data files. The use of the models will permit responses to questions of a policy-planning nature: for projecting requirements, for selecting and allocating resources and for the evaluation of alternative strategies.

The Structure of the Decision Process and the Role of Systems Analysis

The Structure of the Decision Process

The making of a decision regarding the best solution to a problem can be viewed as having a certain structure with the following elements:

1. Establishing objectives.
2. Enumerating the possible alternative strategies within the control of the decision maker (e.g., the administrator).
3. Delimiting the possible states of nature (i.e., the conditions outside the control of the decision maker) that may occur and affect the achievement of the objective.
4. Selecting a payoff measure by which the achievement of the objective under each alternative strategy may be determined.
5. Predicting the payoff for each combination of strategy and state of nature.
6. Choosing a decision criterion (i.e., a principle for selecting a strategy given the predicted payoffs).

The Role of Systems Analysis

Within this structure of a decision process, the systems analyst can assist the administrator by: suggesting quantitative measures of payoff; constructing mathematical models (whenever feasible) that predict the payoff for each alternative strategy; and forcing the administrator to be explicit. He may, in fact, contribute significantly to all elements (levels) of decision making, but it is the administrator who has the ultimate responsibility for accepting a statement: defining the objectives; identifying the relevant strategies and states of nature; selecting the measure of payoff or performance; and choosing the decision criterion.

A striking example of the importance of carefully defining objectives (and an illustration of how a system analyst may contribute to the solution of a problem) arose in World War II, as reported by Morse and Kimball.[4] At the beginning of the war a large number of British merchant vessels were being heavily damaged or sunk by aircraft attacks in the Mediterranean. One answer to this was the installation of anti-aircraft guns on the vessels. This, however, was quite expensive; and little training could be given the merchant vessel crew in the use of the gun, so the accuracy of fire was very low. Some guns were installed, and data on their effectiveness were obtained. It developed that in only about four percent of the attacks were the enemy planes shot down. This strongly suggested that the guns were not worth the price of installation. However, this conclusion would follow only if the objective in installing the guns had been to shoot down enemy planes. Was this the real objective? Second thoughts by the systems analysis staff showed that it was not. The objective in installing the guns had been to protect merchant vessels, and it was in terms of this objective that they should have been evaluated. Data were collected in terms of this objective; and it was found that for the vessels that fired anti-aircraft guns when under attack, 8 percent of the bombs dropped hit and 10 percent of the ships attacked were sunk. For ships that did not fire anti-aircraft guns, 13 percent of the bombs dropped hit and 25 percent of the ships attacked were sunk. Therefore, on the basis of this latter objective, the installation of the guns was worth its cost. The original objective would have resulted in an incorrect decision.

The Methodology of Systems Analysis

Systems analysis had its origin in World War II in Great Britain when the military, faced with immense operational problems concerning the tactics and strategies of a new technology of warfare, called upon the scientific community for assistance.* The techniques and methodology have since grown rapidly, and the range of their application is ever increasing.

Characteristics of Systems Analysis

The essential characteristics of early systems analysis were: (1) a systems orientation; (2) the use of interdisciplinary teams; and (3) the application and adaptation of the scientific method. *Systems orientation* regards every part of an organization as having some effect on the activity of every other part; in order to examine any problem, it is

---

*In Great Britain the work of the group of scientists was termed operational research; in the United States and Canada a variety of names were used: operational analysis, operations evaluation, operations research, systems analysis, management sciences, and others.

necessary to identify all the significant interactions and to evaluate their combined impact on the performance of the organization as a whole. This approach also reflects the notion of Gestalt psychology, where the whole is regarded as being greater than the sum of its parts. It is dramatically opposed to the approach of "cutting a problem down to size" to make it more tractable.

The *interdisciplinary team* was composed of members representing several fields of specialization. It was composed of engineers, physicists, mathematicians, biologists, educators, social scientists and even lawyers. What is particularly striking about these groups is not so much their passion for scientific methods nor even the particular knowledge they possess about a problem, but rather the unique way in which each discipline tends to view a problem. Leavitt drives home the point with an anecdote in which an executive with a single problem calls in three consultants, who recommend (because of their different views) a mathematical program for inventory control, a people-oriented cycle of sensitivity training and a change in the formal organization and procedures.[5] While the use of interdisciplinary teams has increased over the years, it is no longer regarded as essential; rather, teams are composed based upon the nature of the problem and could consist of only a single individual.

The use and adaptation* of *the scientific method* are the remaining essential characteristics of systems analysis. It is due to the nature of the kinds of problems that confront a systems analyst that he cannot readily manipulate a large system to perform controlled experimentation, except in limited ways. Rather, he must behave like an astronomer who constructs a representation of the heavenly bodies based upon observations from a ground position. This representation of the heavenly bodies and their motions or behavior constitutes a model. It is this model that the astronomer then uses to simulate the behavior of the heavenly bodies, which is to say, he conducts experiments upon this model. Symbolically, a mathematical model can be described by the following equation:

---

*The scientific method is commonly regarded as one that involves controlled laboratory experimentation. This is often not feasible in problems confronting a systems analyst. Mathematical models hence are constructed through empirical observation rather than under laboratory conditions.

$$P = F(C,U) \qquad\qquad (1)$$

where   P = the payoff or measure of performance,
            C = the variables that can be controlled,
            U = the uncontrollable variables that affect P, and
            F = the relationship between P and C and U.

In a typical problem, payoff might be measured in profits, costs, delivery time, travel time or achievement. A controllable variable might be the teacher's age or experience, the kind of audio-visual equipment being used or the size of the class. An uncontrollable variable might be the type of student assigned to a classroom, i.e., his social-economic background, his attitudes and race.

In some problems, a single measure of payoff would be sufficient; often, however, it is necessary to consider several measures of performance. In certain instances it is possible to combine into one single measure two different measures of performance: cost-benefit and cost-effectiveness are examples of such single-multiple measures. The use of these single-multiple payoff measures permits the examination of alternatives in which the economic costs of a particular strategy or program are compared with their utilities or benefits. In cost-benefit studies, both benefits and cost are expressed in dollars; and, when their ratio is found, one can obtain a measure of the extent to which benefit exceeds the cost of a program. Such a measure is frequently applied to evaluating job training and school drop-out programs (where benefits are taken as the change in income over the person's working life), although it is not the only measure.[6] Cost-effectiveness measures, on the other hand, compare the costs of a program with some nonmonetary measure of benefit, such as, for example, the incremental cost of teachers' having a particular characteristic (e.g., verbal ability, experience or degree) with the associated change in students' verbal ability.[7]

Often a second set of relationships is necessary to adequately define a mathematical model: namely, an equation or inequation describing constraints on the values of the controllable variables. For example:

$$N \leq C$$

$$0.70 \leq \frac{W}{N} \leq 0.90 \qquad\qquad (2)$$

where   N = the number of students assigned to a class,
          C = the maximum class size permitted, and
          W = the number of the students that are white.

These inequations state that the number of students assigned to a class must be equal to or less than C and that the percentage of white students in each class must be between 70 percent and 90 percent. The two equations [Equations (1) and (2)] constitute a mathematical model of the system and the problem we are trying to solve.

In assigning students to schools to minimize travel time subject to certain constraints, such equations are appropriate. Equation (1) could represent the total student travel time or cost as a function primarily of distance from the school, school assigned and number of students. Equation (2) would represent the various constraints imposed by the administration: class size, integration levels and so on. The object would be to use these relationships to find assignments of students to schools which minimized the total travel time but which also satisfied the constraints. The view of a mathematical model as consisting of only two equations, however, should not be taken too literally; quite frequently many equations are required to represent complex problems. Furthermore, mathematical models are not the only ones of relevance to a systems analyst. In some situations, physical, analog or even conceptual models of a problem can be resorted to with profit. However, where mathematical models are feasible to construct, they are preferable over the others.

The Nature and Uses of Models

In simple terms, a system is a set of objects united by some form of interdependence or interrelationship. A model is a representation of that system, its elements, their attributes and the relationship among these elements. The performance equation (1) above is one example of a mathematical model of the relationship between some measure of performance and the elements that make up the system.

With a mathematical model one can experiment on paper when experimentation in the real world would be infeasible or too costly. In particular, one can: (1) make *predictions* as to the outcome of specified changes in the controllable variables or strategies, (2) *compare* alternative strategies, (3) *evaluate* a proposed system (e.g., an instructional system) in terms of specified measures of performance, (4) perform *sensitivity analyses* to determine the critical factors among a complex of variables (e.g., to predict the change in student verbal ability that results from an increase of one year in the average level of teacher experience), and (5) search for *optimal* solutions (i.e., find what values of the controllable variables result in performance that comes closest to satisfying the stated objectives. Thus, models permit one to investigate more rigorously the use of alternative plans, resources and operating rules.

Techniques of Analysis

Once a model has been constructed and tested for validity, it can be used to derive a solution, i.e., to find the optimal or near optimal values of the controllable variables. Over the years since the inception of systems analysis, a large body of techniques for deriving solutions has evolved. An excellent, readable discussion of some of these techniques is given by Ackoff and Rivett.[8] For purposes of discussion these techniques may be grouped as follows: classical mathematics, techniques for the prototype problems of operations research, heuristic methods, simulation, operational gaming and experimental optimization (see Figure 2).

When the model consists of elementary algebraic equations with relatively few constraints, *classical mathematical techniques* such as differential calculus and finite differences can be used to find the best, or optimal, values of the controllable variables. Where such is not the case, one of the several *techniques of operations research* may be applicable. These techniques have been applied to a wide variety of tactical problems (i.e., where the emphasis is on how rather than what to do) such as: allocation, inventory, replacement, queuing, sequencing and coordination, routing, competition and search.

Allocation problems encompass the general problem of assigning resources to a set of tasks to be performed. In one case the resources may be inadequate for the tasks to be performed; in another the resources may be adequate in total, but the particular matching of resource to task makes a significant difference in overall performance. In both cases the question is how to make allocations to maximize overall benefits. A third case arises where resources may be added or changed; hence, the question: What resources should be added and where, and what resources should be disposed of? Most of the techniques for solving allocation problems involve mathematical programming, where allocations are made to maximize an objective function consistent with specified constraints. The assignment of students to schools to minimize overall travel time subject to the constraints of classroom capacity and desired integration levels is typical of problems amenable to mathematical programming.[9] The scheduling of students into courses is really a form of allocation problem, for which numerous computer programs are available and in use today.

Inventory problems involve generally the holding or storing of resources and the determination of how much to acquire or when to acquire it. Such decisions entail balancing the costs of increasing inventory (storage, spoilage, insurance) against the cost of decreasing inventory (shortage, setup, lower purchase price). Such problems appear to relate primarily to production or retail operations; however, the problem of how many teachers to hire for next year's school enrollment can be formulated as an inventory problem. An excess of teachers results in a costly inventory; an inadequate number may result in critical shortages.

Replacement problems pertain to decisions about the replacement and maintenance of equipment. Almost all equipment deteriorates with age or usage unless action is taken to maintain it. Sometimes it is more economical to replace equipment rather than maintain it. This category of problems encompasses: (1) major capital equipment that can be used indefinitely but at a cost that increases with age; (2) equipment that is replaced in anticipation of failure, the probability of which increases with age; and (3) the selection of a preventive maintenance scheme that is designed to reduce the probability of failure.

Queuing occurs whenever lines of people form waiting for service, whether at the supermarket or barber shop, or when students await guidance from a teacher in an individualized instructional school system. Such systems nearly always involve waiting clients and idle service, facilities and/or personnel, with their associated costs. Queuing theory relates to the problem of how to minimize these costs, including the use of different priority rules for servicing clients.

Sequence problems involve the selection of an appropriate order in which to service waiting customers or to perform tasks. In some cases the order in which these tasks are carried out has a significant effect on the total time required to do all of them or on the distribution of completion times about the dates on which they are due. Analysis is required to find the sequence in which. the jobs should be done to achieve some objective in terms of total time or completion times. Coordination problems entail projects or jobs that consist of tasks that must be performed in a specified sequence. These problems involve determining how much effort should be put into the performance of each task and when to schedule the task so as to optimize some measure of overall performance. The techniques used are commonly called PERT and Critical Path.

Routing problems also deal with the order in which certain jobs or tasks are to be performed. What is unique about this class of problems, however, is that the equipment or mean must be prepared for doing each job and the amount of preparation depends on the order in which the jobs are done. Here, setup costs and time must be considered. In a paint factory the cost of change-over from one color to another is significant and varies with each color; the cost of going from red to white differs from that of white to red.

Competitive problems are among the more complex, since they entail consideration of the behavior of outside parties that affect the organization's performance, such as parents, school board or competitors. The techniques of the theory of games are most often applied to these problems.

Search problems involve the determination of how much and what information to acquire, how to acquire it and how to treat it once it has been acquired. This class of problems had its origin in the determination of the best methods to "search" an area to locate enemy submarines or a pilot whose aircraft was lost at sea.

Such prototype techniques have the general characteristic of directly yielding optimal solutions satisfying the objectives and constraints.

Heuristic methods are the third category of general techniques for deriving solutions to problems. These techniques are employed where the optimal values for the controllable variables cannot be found directly, as, for example, in finding the best layout for a manufacturing plant or the proper locations for a set of warehouses. Characteristically, these problems entail the evaluation of a large number of possible arrangements. In such situations a procedure (called an algorithm) is specified for selecting successive trial values for the controllable variables, so that they tend to converge on the optimum solution. In the case of the plant layout problem, a heuristic algorithm successively exchanges each department in location with every other department, evaluating the incremental transportation cost resulting from each exchange and retaining only those layouts that incur a lower incremental cost. A solution (not necessarily optimal) is reached when further exchanges of departments do not result in any reduction in cost.

In many complex situations analytical tools for finding solutions directly are inadequate. In these cases, *simulation* can be used profitably. By simulation we mean conducting experiments on the model itself, in which we specify values for the controllable and uncontrollable variables and observe the performance of the system or its model under these conditions. Each experiment results in a particular set of outcomes. By conducting a series of planned experiments, one may find the values for the controllable variables that best satisfy the objectives. More than any other technique, simulation shows considerable promise for the problems of education. It has the advantage of permitting solutions of complex problems that defy analytical techniques, and yet its method can be more readily understood by an administrator.

Simulation models may differ in the structural characteristics of their design. A static model is designed to describe or predict the total response of the system as if it occurred at a single instant of time; a dynamic model is designed to explore the changes occurring within the system over some period of time. A deterministic model contains no probabilistic elements; a stochastic model contains one or more elements or mechanisms involving random or probabilistic characteristics. An aggregate model is so structured that it can answer questions only of an aggregate nature: for example, the average level of achievement in a particular course or test; a disaggregate model (there are various levels of aggregation or disaggregation) is so structured as to yield information of a more detailed nature, such as the number of students having IQ's between x and y who score between r and s on an achievement test.

To be successful, simulation requires that the processes and relationships be made explicit. Where such cannot be the case, particularly when the behavior of a decision-maker cannot be specified, then *operational gaming* may be employed. With this technique humans are placed in a role-playing capacity and their behavior is observed. War games are typical of such applications, since the behavior of the commander cannot be adequately described and represented in a model.

Finally, in some situations in which we are able to construct the model but unable to solve it even by simulation, *experimental optimization* may be used. In these cases, one can conduct experiments on the real system in such a way as to locate an optimal solution to the problem.

Stages of a Systems Analysis Project
In brief, a systems analysis project consists of the five following stages:

1. Formulating the problem*
   a. Establishing the objectives
   b. Defining the variables (controllable and uncontrollable) and the constraints
   c. Defining the measures of effectiveness
   d. Enumerating the alternative strategies
2. Constructing the model
3. Deriving a solution
4. Testing the model and evaluating the solution
5. Implementing and adjusting the solution.

The first three stages of a project have already been discussed. By *testing a model* we mean ensuring the validity of its representation of the system and problem being studied. By *evaluating the solution* we mean comparing the solution with the policy or procedure that it is meant to replace. If it is not a significant improvement, why bother changing? Because the objective of a study is not simply the production of reports but is, rather, the improvement of systems, the results of the study must be *implemented.* Once the results of the study have been implemented, any significant change in the system and its environment must be detected and the solution and/or model adjusted.**

Operations Research and Systems Analysis
As stated previously, during the early years of World War II groups bearing a variety of names were formed to attack quite similar problems

---

*Often, it is this stage of a project that is most troublesome and time-consuming.

**A model or procedure developed, for example, for the early detection of drop-outs may no longer be valid five years hence, if one or more of its underlying assumptions or relationships have changed.

of an operational nature using similar approaches. This confusion in terminology has continued without resolution, although some writers have attempted to delineate the distinctions between operations research and systems analysis. Operations research is sometimes considered as emphasizing quantitative techniques and optimization in the solution of problems that are characterized as low-level—well-defined, tactical problems.[10] Systems analysis is often less quantitative and less concerned with seeking optimal solutions. The problems are generally strategic, complex and ill-defined; and, consequently, one is often limited to tracing out the consequences of a particular strategy. The techniques of operations research are inadequate for these problems.

Other views abound in the literature. Some contend that systems analysis is simply the study of systems by simulation. Others regard systems analysis as the study of *the flow of information through an organization, the decisions that are made and where they are made and the information required to make these decisions;* this is generally the point of view of the computer systems specialist who desires to establish an information system. The latter is also the viewpoint of some operations researchers who regard systems analysis as a technique simply for defining and understanding a problem.

This confusion over terminology should not discourage the use of rigorous, systematic approaches to the solution of administrative problems. One uses quantitative models only where feasible and economic. Since 1964 numerous educational planning models have been developed. The nature of these models will be described briefly in the following section.

Educational Planning Models

Common Elements of Educational Planning Models
A planning model may be defined as a formal procedure, usually mathematical or computerized, for projecting requirements, for selecting and scheduling resources and for evaluating alternative programs or strategies. Educational planning models tend to have one or more common elements: (1) demand populations (i.e., students), (2) service units (i.e., teacher, classrooms and other resources), (3) rules for the allocation and assignment of the various service units to the student

populations and (4) mechanisms for measuring and evaluating system performance. Accordingly, it is convenient to classify planning models according to the following scheme:

Enrollment population models—which project the number and kinds of students to be enrolled at the various levels of a school system, including the dynamics of the flow of students through the system over time.

Resource requirement models—which determine the need for classrooms, facilities, equipment, personnel and budget based upon projected enrollments, historical relationships and/or specified policies on: curriculum, staff and facility utilization, integration, transportation and other factors.

Resource allocation and scheduling models—which assign students to schools and classrooms; allocate and schedule instructional resources; explore organizational strategies for instruction (e.g., continuous progress plans) and methods for sequencing curricula to maximize mastery levels.

Evaluation models—which evaluate a specific educational program, strategy or system configuration; they include achievement and related cost-benefit and cost-effectiveness measures.

The above classification is primarily one of convenience, since a particular planning model may in fact include one or more or all of the above categories.

Survey of Educational Planning Model Applications

The applications of models to educational planning are numerous. Any attempt to exhaustively catalogue these applications would prove futile, for progress is continuous. The listing below is intended only to summarize the diversity of current applications and to indicate references for their study:

Enrollment Population Models
    Predicting student enrollment
        National[11]
        State[12]
        Local[13][16]

Higher education[1][7][5][3]
Evaluating subsidy policies
National[1][8][1][9]
Higher education[2][0]
Predicting school drop-outs
State[2][1]
Local[2][2]
Higher education[2][3]

Resource Requirement Models
National
Teacher supply[1][1]
State
Teacher supply and demand[2][4]
Local
Location and size of the schools[2][5]
Instructional staff budgeting[2][6]
Long-range planning[2][7][2][8][2][9]
Planning, programming, budgeting system (PPBS)[5][4][5][5]
Higher education
Planning and budgeting[2][9][3][4]

Resource Allocation and Scheduling Models
Attendance area assignment[3][5]
School bus routing and transportation[5][7][5][8]
Course scheduling[3][6][3][7]
Instructional organization evaluation[3][8][4][0][5][2]
Instructional resource allocation[4][1]
Optimum curriculum sequence[4][2]
Policies for hiring substitute teachers[4][3]
State financial aid allocation[5][9]

Evaluation Models
Input-output achievement models
International[4][4]
National[4][5]
State[4][6][4][7]
Local[4][8][6][0]
Cost-benefit models[4][9][5][0]
Cost-effectiveness models[7][5][1]

Concluding Remarks

Models for use in educational planning may take many shapes and forms. An input-output model used to determine cost-effectiveness is an example of a descriptive model; i.e., one that expresses statistical relationships between inputs and outputs but does not describe the causal relationships (which, for example, might explain how verbal ability or teacher experience affects student achievement). A dynamic simulation model is an explanatory model, for the causal relationships accounting for the various changes over time are made explicit. Clearly, the latter model is the more desirable, for it permits exploration of alternatives not entirely feasible with a descriptive model. It is also obvious that, in many situations, to go beyond a descriptive model is infeasible, considering the current state of knowledge. A goal of educational research is to establish hypotheses based upon the descriptive models and conduct further research in order to permit the development of the more powerful, explanatory models.

With regard to the relationship between models and an MIS, it should be apparent that models require data for their implementation, without which they are almost valueless. What kind of data depends upon the model, and, until the model or models have been adequately defined, their data requirements cannot be specified. This is not to suggest that data files for an education MIS must await definition of the various models to be created, but it does suggest that some consideration be given to the kinds of models likely to be constructed.* More important is the need to create an information-processing system that is open-ended in its ability to permit additional attributes to be added to the elements within the existing data files (e.g., attributes such as personality measures or IQ scores which could be added to the teacher files at a later date). A second need is the ability to relate elements within one file to elements in another file, such as, for example, particular teachers to particular students. Research needs can never be fully anticipated and for this reason the information system must be designed for flexibility and growth.

---

*The definition of data for administration and research is never complete, for new insights continually cause changes to occur.

References

1. Notes and working papers concerning the administration of programs authorized under Title III of Public Law 89-10 as amended by Public Law 89-750, prepared for the Subcommittee on Education of the Committee on Labor and Public Welfare, U.S. Senate, April 1967.

2. Caweth, Gordon. Innovations in High Schools: Who Does What and Why and How. *Nation's Schools*, Vol. 79, No. 4, April 1967.

3. Bushnell, Don D. and Allen, Dwight D. *The Computer in American Education.* John Wiley & Sons, Inc., New York, 1967.

4. Morse, Philip and Kimball, George E. *Methods of Operations Research.* MIT Press and John Wiley, Cambridge and New York, 1951.

5. Leavitt, Harold J. *Managerial Psychology.* Second edition, University of Chicago Press, 1964.

6. Ribich, Thomas I. *Education and Poverty.* The Brookings Institution, Washington, D.C., 1968.

7. Levin, Henry. *Cost-Effectiveness Analysis and Education—Profusion, Confusion, Promise.* Stanford University, September 1968.

8. Ackoff, Russell L. and Rivett, Patrick. *Manager's Guide to Operations Research.* John Wiley & Sons, Inc., New York, 1964.

9. Koenigsberg, Ernest. *Mathematical Analysis Applied to School Attendance Areas.* Matson Research Corp., San Francisco, 1967.

10. Quade, E.S. and Boucher, W.I. *Systems Analysis and Policy Planning Applications in Defense.* American Elsevier Publishing Company, New York, 1968.

11. Zabrowski, Edward K. *Student-Teacher Population Growth Model.* Department of Health, Education, and Welfare, U.S. Office of Education, OE-10055, Washington, D.C., 1967.

12. Nordell, Lawrence P. *A Dynamic Input-Output Model of the California Educational System.* Technical Report No. 25, Center for Research in Management Science, University of California, Berkeley, August 1967.

13. Brown, R.C. *Predicting School Enrollment.* New York University Center for School Services, New York, 1961.

14. Loughary, John W. Administrative Applications. *Man-Machine Systems in Education.* Harper & Row, New York, 1966.

15. Cross, R. and Sederberg, C.H. Computer Assisted Enrollment Projection Procedures. *Journal of Educational Data Processing,* Fall 1968.

16. Schmitt, John and Griffin, Mary. *A Monte Carlo Model for Prediction of Public School Enrollment.* Boston College, November 1966.

17. Baisuck, Allan, Koza, Russell C. and Neuhauser, John J. *A Projection Model for Higher Educational Systems Planning.* Rensselaer Research Corp., Troy, New York, May 1968.

18. Froomkin, Joseph. *Cost-Effectiveness and Cost-Benefit Analysis of Educational Programs.* U.S. Office of Education, Symposium on Operational Analysis of Education, Washington, D.C., November 1967.

19. *Students and Buildings: An Analysis of Selected Federal Programs for Higher Education.* Office of Program Planning and Evaluation, U.S. Office of Education, OE-50054, Washington, D.C., May 1968.

20. Hoenack, Stephen A. *Efficient Allocation of Subsidies for College Students.* Institute for Defense Analysis, presented at Symposium on Operations Analysis of Education, Washington, D.C., November 1967.

21. *Reducing the School Dropout Rate—Report on Holding Power.* State University of New York, State Education Department, Albany, 1965.

22. Fitzsimmons, Stephen J. *et al. A Study of Longitudinal Patterns of Failure Among High School Dropouts and Poorly Performing Graduates.* Abt Associates, Cambridge, Massachusetts.

23. Panos, Robert and Astin, Alexander W. *Attrition Among College Students.* Annual Meeting of American Educational Research Association, New York, February 1967.

24. Morton, Anton S. *Supply and Demand of Teachers in California.* Paper presented to Symposium on Operations Analysis in Education, Washington, D.C., November 1967.

25. O'Brien, Richard. *A Model for Planning the Location and Size of Urban Schools.* U.S. Office of Education, paper presented to Symposium on Operations Analysis in Education, Washington, D.C., November 1967.

26. *Computer-Based Instructional Staff Budgeting for Public Schools.* IBM Advanced Systems Development Division, Yorktown Heights, New York, 1968.

27. Sisson, Roger. *Some Results of a Simulation of an Urban School District.* University of Pennsylvania, March 1967.

28. Weitz, Harold. *A Model for Planning and Budgeting for Elementary and Secondary Schools.* IBM Advanced Systems Development Division, Yorktown Heights, New York, April 1968.

29. Keller, John W. *The Use of Models in University Decision Making.* University of California, Office of the President, Berkeley, California, November 1967.

30. Judy, R.W. and Levine, J.B. *A New Tool for Educational Administrators.* University of Toronto Press, 1965.

31. Koenig, H.E. *et al. A Systems Model for Management, Planning, and Resource Allocation in Institutions of Higher Education.* Division of Engineering Research, Michigan State University, East Lansing, Michigan, September 1968.

32. Firman, Peter A. *University Cost Structure and Behavior.* School of Business, Tulane University, New Orleans, Louisiana, 1969 (available from Regional Educational Laboratories, Mutual Plaza, Durham, North Carolina).

33. Little, Edward F. *A Computer Program for Budget Forecasting.* Harvey Mudd College, Claremont, California, March 1964 (available from Regional Educational Laboratories, Mutual Plaza, Durham, North Carolina).

34. Scott, R. and Willard, H.H. *Computer-Aided Campus Planning for Colleges and Universities.* Duke University, sponsored by Educational Facilities Laboratories, Interim Report, August 1967.

35. Koenigsberg, Ernest. *Mathematical Analysis Applied to School Attendance Areas.* Matson Research Corp., San Francisco, 1967.

36. Holz, Robert E. Computer Assisted Scheduling. *Journal of Educational Data Processing,* Spring 1964.

37. Oakford, Robert V., Allen, Dwight D. and Chatterton, Lynne A. School Scheduling—Practice and Theory. *Journal of Educational Data Processing,* Winter 1966-67.

38. *The Use of the Computer in Planning Buildings, Flying a College on the Computer.* St. Louis Junior College District, Missouri, July 1964 (available from Educational Resources Information Center, ED 024240).

39. Glasserman, J. *Organizational Strategies in Schools: A Computer Model for Their Analysis.* IBM Advanced Systems Development Division, Yorktown Heights, New York, 1968.

40. *Analysis of Instructional Systems.* TM-1493/201/00, System Development Corp., April 1966.

41. Taft, Martin I. *et al. Evaluation of Educational Programs: A Systems Approach.* California State College at Los Angeles, Los Angeles, 1968.

42. Taft, Martin and Reisman, Arnold. Toward Better Curricula Through Computer-Selected Sequence of Subject Matter. *Management Science,* July 1967.

43. Haussmann, R.D. and Rath, G.J. Automated Teacher Assignment—A GPSS Simulation. *Journal of Educational Data Processing,* Summer 1965.

44. Husen, Torsten. *International Study of Achievement in Mathematics.* John Wiley & Sons, 1967.

45. Coleman, James E. *Equality of Educational Opportunity.* FS5-238:38001, U.S. Department of Health, Education, and Welfare, U.S. Office of Education, Washington, D.C., 1966.

46. Firman, William D. *The Quality Measurement Project in N.Y. State.* Presented to the American Association for the Advancement of Science, Berkeley, California, December 29, 1965.

47. Scovell, William, Haller, Archibald and Portes, Alex. The Educational and Early Occupational Attainment Process. *American Sociological Review,* February 1968.

48. Burkhead, Jessie *et al. Input and Output in Large City High Schools.* Syracuse University Press, New York, 1967.

49. Ribich, Thomas I. *Poverty and Education.* Brookings Institution, Washington, D.C., 1968.

50. Spiegelman, Robert G. *A Benefit-Cost Model to Evaluate Educational Programs.* Stanford Research Institute, Menlo Park, California, January 1968.

51. Abt, Clark. *Design for an Educational System Cost-Effectiveness Model.* Abt Associates, Cambridge, Massachusetts, January 1967.

52. Bratten, Jack E. *The Organization of Interrelated Individual Progress and Ability Level Courses in Math at Garber High School: System Analysis and Simulation.* TM-1493/162/00, System Development Corp., February 1966.

53. Reisman, Arnold and Taft, Martin I. *On the Generation of Doctorates and Their Feedback into Higher Education.* Reprint No. 5, Department of Operations Research, Western Reserve University, Cleveland, Ohio.

54. *Planning, Programming, Budgeting System Manual for California School Districts.* California Department of Education, Sacramento, California, 1970.

55. Haggart, Sue A. *et al. Program Budgeting for School District Planning: Concepts and Applications.* RM-6116-RC, RAND Corporation, Santa Monica, California, November 1968.

56. *Project Yardstick.* The Yardstick Project (Brochure) The Alcazar Hotel, Cleveland, Ohio, November 1969.

57. Tracz, George C. *A Quantitative Approach to the Design of School Bus Routes.* Ontario Institute for Studies in Education, Ontario, Canada, March 1970.

58. Elwood, Bryan. *Student Transportation: A Comparison of Alternative Methods for Providing Service.* Report No. 2, Ontario Institute for Studies in Education, November, 1969.

59. Bruno, James E. *Minimizing the Spread in Per Pupil Expenditures in School Finance Programs.* RAND Corporation, Santa Monica, California, March 1969.

60. Pinsky, Paul D. *A Mathematical Model for Measurement and Control of Classroom Achievement.* Stanford University, presented at meeting of Operations Research Society, Washington, D.C., April 1970.

SYSTEMS ANALYSIS FOR
SCHOOL DECISION-MAKING

Francis Tannian and Jon Magoon

Effective educational planning in urban environments demands the recognition of many forces at work within a community, and interpretation of these processes requires expertise in many separate areas. Particularly apparent is the fact that urban schools are only one part of a large scene for hotly contested social change; and demands on these schools go far beyond the traditional 3R's into basic social, political and economic issues. When communities decide that schools should attempt to meet these wider and nonconventional demands, much of the independence school systems have strived to achieve simultaneously comes under attack. When schools move to take up functions traditionally performed by other institutions (notably the family), demands to be involved in school policy can be expected to grow rapidly. Moreover, when the schools request added funding to allow them to do more, they then are forced into deeper political competition in the sweepstakes for city budget shares against requests for added police protection, advancing requirements for pollution control and cost erosions due to inflation.

The work described herein is being carried on at the Division of Urban Affairs, University of Delaware. Francis Tannian, an economist, is school project director. James Cox, a political scientist at Urban Affairs; James Elsbery, a sociologist at the Center for Urban Education, New York; Jon Magoon of the College of Education, University of Delaware; and Shigeo Nohara of the Department of Sociology, University of Delaware, combined with Francis Tannian to develop the model. This paper has been written by **Jon Magoon** and **Francis Tannian**.

In a systems analysis sense, city school demands are but one element of local public demands competing for shares of public revenues. Optimum social policy would lead a city to provide the most valuable mix of schools, fire protection, snow removal and many other community goods by using up the least valuable amounts of city resources. Similarly, within the complex subsystem which is the city school program, the hope must be to make decisions which generate the most valuable services at lowest burdens to the community.

One purpose of this paper is to outline a comprehensive school system model which, when put into operation, could aid school program decision-makers. A second purpose is to briefly point out the utility along with some of the difficulties of this systems approach. An important research precedent for our work is the limited input/output model described by Jesse Burkhead for city school systems. The purpose of Burkhead's model was to (1) examine resource allocation within school systems and tie this to educational outcomes, and (2) give operational definition to input/output variables.

The effect of several kinds of constraints left Burkhead with approximately four output and ten input variables that were measurable. Nevertheless, the model enjoyed limited success, for outputs could be predicted utilizing a linear prediction scheme. The most predictable outputs were test scores, being highly dependent on the socioeconomic status of pupils.

The model outlined here describes sociological, political, economic and educational interactions in an urban school system in order to describe how the system is performing and might be amenable to change and reform. To do this, it is necessary to take into account both how the system operates and how changes can be brought about. Unlike most previous educational systems models, this one is aimed at having direct practical utility to educational administrators and local educational interest groups in a specific small-city situation.

A School Decisions Model

The school system model described here can be generally characterized as a multistage input/output scheme. The model structure has borrowed heavily from work of various people in many disciplines. Among the major works, including Burkhead's, from which ideas have been adopted are Coleman's model for describing policymaking, and Gamson's sociological notion of trust as it relates to community policy.

The debt owed to the work of these and others will be seen in the model which is outlined in Figure 1.

Figure 1

School System Interaction Processes Model Framework

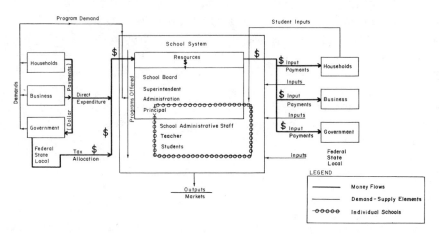

Households provide student inputs (right side of Figure 1) which are processed over a series of years in the school system by a series of programs. Ultimately, these boys and girls graduate out or drop out of the school program after passing a series of grades where achievement goals are met. Simultaneously, governmental, business and household groups maintain various program demands (left side of Figure 1) on the school system. Households and businesses back up these demands with money payments. Legal steps are taken allowing federal, state and local governments to collect money (heavy lines in Figure 1) through a variety of taxes and then allocate the funds back to the school system for use. Private support in terms of corporation grants or personal bequests provide some supplementary funds.

These financial resources are then spent back into the community in terms of payments to business for books, paper and electricity, as salaries to teachers, and less often in terms of user charges to governments for services such as water or police protection. Top echelons of the school system guide this spending and buy a mix of various resources which are allocated down to individual schools. At this stage, money flows become cost functions.

The central block of Figure 1, labeled "School System," can be viewed as the decision-making structure which guides the funds it receives, listens to various demands for programs, accepts the student inputs and actually manages programs offered. Operating responsibility for the present and planning responsibility for the future rests with this formal organization or bureaucracy.

Principals of individual schools behave as middlemen to some extent between schools and the bureaucracy. The dotted lines within the larger school system block of Figure 1 represent individual schools where the central business of education is carried out through teacher to student interactions.

Implementing the Model

Generally the model described here suggests that systematic school policy decisions involve at least: student inputs, teacher-student interactions, bureaucratic processes, funding arrangements, expenditure patterns, varieties of different program demands, physical input mixes and output performance evaluation, including the relationship of student skills to job market characteristics of the local economy. To operationalize the model in a school district, measurement is required for each of these multidimensional factors.

First, in many senses, are the students. Clearly, numbers of students are important, school by school, as are age, race and sex of the students. Such information is normally available in school records. Characteristics of the student's family as perceived by the student, student self-concept, perceptions of school, career aspirations, reading achievement and arithmetic achievement can be measured by survey instruments. The general goal is to be able to describe the student body in a quantitative and qualitative fashion.

The community environment from which students come to the schools can be quantified through survey of neighborhood character-istics and student family factors. Attitudes of parents toward the schools, including appraisal of school goals and descriptions of program demands, can be measured through a community survey instrument. The role of families in the political life of the city and the social life of immediate neighborhoods can also be described.

Moving away still further from the direct environment of the classroom, school policy effectiveness and community satisfaction relate to the complex general policymaking environment of the community. Attempts are being made to identify the nature of political decision-making networks in the city.

Participation of various party officials, union leaders, bankers and spokesmen for various racial groups in school decision-making is being measured by a political survey instrument. Levels of demands and supports for various school policies by these leader groups will be identified.

Within the school system itself (see Figure 1, central block), the key persons directly able to affect student performance are the teachers. Age, sex, race, education and teaching experience are some standard qualitative characteristics of teachers being quantified from school records. Attitudes of teachers toward students, salaries, communications and program content can also be surveyed.

But just as students enter and pass through the educational process under the influence of family and neighborhood characteristics, all of which must be taken into account by school policymakers, teacher performance is also affected by a complex set of backup factors. These backup factors can be called the school organization or bureaucracy. Program policy changes, information about salaries, day-to-day communications and rumors circulate between classes, within schools, between schools, to the administrative staff "downtown," through to members on the school board in a series of formal and informal ways. The nature of these channels structures the nature of how decisions get processed. Through observation and interview techniques in the administration the structure of these channels can be identified.

A rich mix of program analysis options becomes available once this information is gathered. Flexibility of use and dependability as to level of alternative revenue sources can be estimated. Such information, known only informally before, can become a more explicit aid to program planning.

Since student reading, math and self-concept can be measured school by school, individual schools in the school system can be ranked by performance on these variables. Relationships of school program inputs to pupil achievement gains are of special interest. Explanations for variations can be sought statistically through relationships of student performance to family structure, income levels, teacher attitudes and school cost functions. Changes in self-concept or in student attitudes toward authority can be interpreted. Do student attitudes toward authority seem to change between the fourth, sixth and seventh grades? How might school reward and punishment systems be modified to take into account actual student-by-grade level perceptions of authority? In those schools where student self-concept or reading levels are relatively below the city average, explanations can be sought and policy changes worked out perhaps to modify spending patterns, teacher qualities, or levels of community participation in school policy if these factors appear to explain this lower performance.

Teacher satisfaction is hypothesized to depend in part upon teacher perceptions of student quality, malleability, educational facilities and community support as well as teacher wages and status. Evaluations of the relative importance or relative weakness of these factors are made possible from data provided by the operationalized model. Moreover, demands and supports for a wide range of school programs can be estimated. Differences in demands and priorities for programs among school teachers, parents, school administrators, business leaders and political leaders and between blacks and whites can be evaluated. Estimates can also be made as to whose demands and priorities are actually being met. Community trust in the schools is hypothesized to depend on relative levels of socioeconomic status, openness of communication with respect to the system and the existence of formal group membership patterns. Where trust is low, explanations can be sought and policy steps taken.

Concluding Comments

The conceptual difficulties of operationalizing each of the steps described above are formidable. Many measures must be exploratory. For example, to our knowledge, relationships described in the theory of bureaucracy have not been empirically tested. Critics with an eye to statistical fine tuning who review the instruments developed and data collected may find little praise for many of the adaptations we are being forced to make. Difficult indeed are the major steps of (1) building the model, (2) constructing ways to operationalize the model, (3) actually measuring the variables and (4) the matter of releasing results once they have been gathered. Here we face many problems, such as the time of information release and the sequence of releases. Who in the community should get the findings, and what form should these releases take? Clearly, the standard professionalized report is not enough. Probably what is necessary is a lengthy interaction and dialogue between all recipients and the producers of this technical information.

The goal of our case application of this model is to provide a description of processes at work in a real-world school system. Particular types of processes (e.g., bureaucratic perceptions) are thought to be related to other inputs or processes (e.g., community demands) and to school performance (e.g., reading level gains). It is important to describe these relationships as fully as data allow. While one can characterize this approach as a complex multistage input/output mechanism, the information gathered can have practical utility to all concerned with an evolving school system, without full understanding of the model. One vehicle for increasing involvement may be the opening up of information to all sectors of the community before issuing a final report. By providing data, analysis and information to a community and school administration, prescriptions for reforms may be easier to reach and carry out; moreover, many costly confrontations and policy changes made under crisis conditions without adequate and systematic information may be avoided.

REGIONAL EDUCATIONAL PLANNING:
A SYSTEMS VIEW

David I. Cleland and William R. King

School administrators are caught in a dilemma of social unrest, inadequate funding and the need for maintaining educational excellence. In an era of rapid change, they find themselves in a poor position to cope with change.

Any organization which exists in a world of dynamic change—particularly one with such complex and significant responsibilities as a school district or county education office—needs to *plan for change and to structure its organization to effectively respond to changing environments.* In the sense used here, planning is not simply ensuring that facilities, personnel and other resources are available to meet projected enrollments, but rather it is " . . . the process of preparing for the commitment of resources in the most economical fashion, and, by preparing, of allowing the commitment to be made less disruptively."* This modern view of planning requires that specific objectives be established and that policies, programs and procedures for achieving them be selected and implemented.

To accomplish effective planning requires that a systems view be

---

*Warren, E. Kirby. *Long-Range Planning: The Executive Viewpoint.* Englewood Cliffs, N.J.: Prentice-Hall, 1966, p. 21.

David I. Cleland is associate professor of systems management, School of Engineering, University of Pittsburgh. **William R. King** is professor of business administration, Graduate School of Business, University of Pittsburgh.

149

adopted. In its simplest interpretation, the systems view means that logical boundaries must be drawn around segments of the overall educational system which are more alike than they are unlike, and that planning must be done on this level. In many instances, this means that various school districts will find it essential to cooperate in conducting *regional* educational planning. Planning at the regional level then provides the context within which local planning can be done.

Coping with Change

A radically changing environment creates great problems *and great opportunities* for the educational system. If the system is to be able to take advantage of these opportunities, it must be able to rise above day-to-day crises, look into the future and develop ways of coping with change. If it is able to do this, *it can take advantage of the changes which are occurring, rather than simply reacting to them.*

The only way in which a complex organization system can effectively cope with change is through a *planning system.* A planning system permits the establishment of goals and objectives and the implementation of programs to accomplish these objectives. Without such a system, the school administrator has little basis for operating effectively. For instance, few organizations find it as difficult as do school administrators to define the basic "clientele" which they serve and to whom they owe allegiance. School administrators must interact effectively with many "claimants"—faculty, students, citizenry, local, state and national government, school boards, other educational institutions, business and industry and other organizations (both legal and extra-legal)—each with their own objectives and value systems. When these goals and values come into conflict, the school administrator must be able to allocate his severely limited resources in a fashion which best accomplishes overall educational objectives. He has little hope of being able to do this if he is not guided by explicitly stated objectives and does not possess a capability for evaluating and comparing the degree to which alternative programs and actions achieve those objectives and satisfy the various clientele.

The Planning Process

The process of planning and developing organizational strategy in the educational system environment may be cast in terms of the following three-stage cycle:

(1) Analysis and establishment of a school system's objectives and goals.
(2) The implementation of a contrived dynamic planning system which is focused toward the achievement of the objectives and goals.
(3) Procedures for re-assessing and re-establishing objectives and goals.

Analysis of Objectives and Goals

Organizations which are not oriented toward profit making activities often operate without the establishment of explicit goals and measurable objectives. The objectives of a school system emanate from a set of "consumer" needs. However, one of the initial problems is a precise definition of the relative roles of the community, students, faculty, etc., as consumers of the system's services. Another major problem is the assessment of the degree to which the school system is currently satisfying a basic set of consumer needs.

The planning process involves a formalized procedure for determining the goals and objectives of the various clientele groups. In this way, mutually inconsistent goals can be recognized and evaluated.

Even though no planning system can magically provide everyone with everything he desires, such a process provides a forum for the articulation of everyone's views, so that each clientele group is at least assured that their needs are being *considered.*

A Dynamic Planning System

On the basis of a prescribed set of goals and objectives, a continuous procedure can be evolved for achieving these objectives by foreseeing opportunities and making decisions regarding the allocation of resources among various programs.

The planning process is a continual one which takes the following form:

1. The development and promulgation of objectives, planning guidelines, goals, strategies, key assumptions and forecasts.
2. Preparation of tentative plans for major school organizational elements.

3. Review at the overall system level.
4. Final review by top school administrative management.

The overall *strategy* for the achievement of the school system's objectives which evolves from the planning process must be *dynamic* and *adaptive* rather than fixed and static in nature, for the school system must be able to adapt to changing conditions in the same fashion as do living organisms. Thus, the organizational instruments of adaptation—the plans—must not only involve forecasts and predictions of the future, but also they should entail the specification of appropriate responses to contingencies which may occur.

For example, the school organization may have available a prediction of future demand for student services. Around this prediction, it establishes a set of planning premises, develops its goals and establishes its strategy. However, it should clearly not "place all of its eggs in a single basket" and assume the very considerable risk that the predictions are not precisely correct. Rather, it should establish programs which are based on the predictions but which are also capable of being adapted to a range of demands which may ensue. Such an adaptive planning process is described in Figure 1.

Such an adaptive planning process illustrates how planning differs from simple forecasting. A non-adaptive plan might be so tied to a particular forecast of the environment that the failure of the forecast would imply the non-achievement of the plan's goals. However, an adaptive mechanism will permit the forecast to be changed and actions taken which take advantage of the change. Thus, forecasts and the actions based on them are not rigidly "believed" in adaptive planning. Rather, they are thought of as dynamic quantities which are subject to re-evaluation and revision.

Re-Assessment of Goals and Objectives

Just as the programs and actions which make up a plan are not fixed, neither are the objectives and goals on which it is based. Just as the goals of the various clientele groups change over time, so too will the goals expressed in a system of plans. Therefore, the planning system must itself entail explicit provisions for re-evaluation of goals—for, rigid adherence to outworn goals causes no less difficulty than does protracted commitment to inaccurate forecasts.

Figure 1

The Adaptive Planning Process

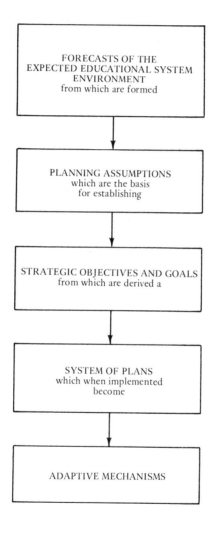

FORECASTS OF THE
EXPECTED EDUCATIONAL SYSTEM
ENVIRONMENT
from which are formed

PLANNING ASSUMPTIONS
which are the basis
for establishing

STRATEGIC OBJECTIVES AND GOALS
from which are derived a

SYSTEM OF PLANS
which when implemented
become

ADAPTIVE MECHANISMS

The Systems Approach to Planning
    The development of the dynamic planning system will involve the use of systems techniques to develop a clear understanding of the future impact of present decisions, to provide means for anticipating areas requiring future decisions, to permit the relative evaluation of programs and to provide for faster and less disruptive implementation of decisions.

    The basic idea of the systems approach revolves about the view of a region, a country or a school district as *a complex of interrelated and interdependent parts.* Thus, any action taken on or by one part of the system has reverberations throughout many parts of the system.

    Implicit in this approach is the notion of "wholeness" which makes the whole something different from and more than the sum of the individual parts considered separately. While it might be indeed easier to say, "Let's look at the school district as if it existed all by itself," such is highly impracticable in terms of today's social and educational environment.

    A basic premise of the planning effort—developed through the experience of school administrators, their problems and their discussions with school officials—is that school administration has not adequately applied *systems* ideas to its day-to-day operations or to its long-range thinking and planning. Certainly, little of the planning in school administration thus far has been directed toward gaining an understanding of the total relationships among the many organizations and forces involved in effectively managing a school district or county office, and in developing a sense of direction for the school system *in terms of its future generation of products or services.*

    A System of Plans
    The output of a planning process is a system of plans which are documentary manifestations of planning activities. In a real sense, the organizational and program changes which the plans bring about are the real output of the planning process, but the system of plans provides the organized base for these changes.

    An illustrative system of plans for an educational system is shown in Figure 2. The elements of the system of plans are regional strategic plans, county/district development plans, operational plans and project plans.

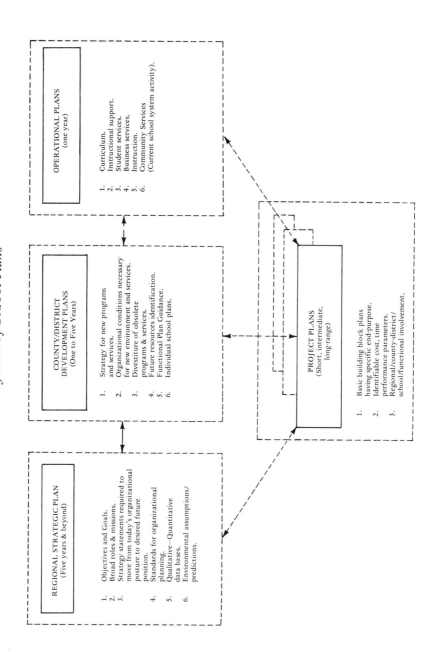

Figure 2
The System of School Plans

REGIONAL STRATEGIC PLAN
(Five years & beyond)

1. Objectives and Goals.
2. Broad roles & missions.
3. Strategy statements required to move from today's organizational posture to desired future position.
4. Standards for organizational planning.
5. Qualitative—Quantitative data bases.
6. Environmental assumptions/ predictions.

COUNTY/DISTRICT DEVELOPMENT PLANS
(One to Five Years)

1. Strategy for new programs and services.
2. Organizational conditions necessary for new environment and services.
3. Divestiture of obsolete programs & services.
4. Future resources identification.
5. Functional Plan Guidance.
6. Individual school plans.

OPERATIONAL PLANS
(one year)

1. Curriculum.
2. Instructional support.
3. Student services.
4. Business services.
5. Instruction.
6. Community Services (Current school system activity).

PROJECT PLANS
(Short, intermediate, long-range)

1. Basic building block plans having specific end-purpose.
2. Identifiable cost, time performance parameters.
3. Regional/county-district/ school/functional involvement.

Regional Strategic Plan

This plan outlines the broad educational goals and objectives for the region and outlines the broad mission and role of education in the region. It establishes:

(1) the general strategy for moving from current organizational postures to desired future positions;
(2) the ground rules and standards for organizational planning;
(3) the establishment of a qualitative-quantitative data base;
(4) the environmental assumptions and forecasts which are to be used by planners.

The concept of wholeness which is inherent in the systems approach to planning indicates that individual school districts or counties, particularly small ones, cannot themselves do comprehensive systems planning. Although every district and county must obviously have its unique set of plans which reflect its own goals and resources, all districts and counties should not and *cannot* perform each of the activities necessary to adequate planning.

They cannot do so because it is unlikely that any could afford to finance the myriad activities which are essential to good planning *and* because the development of effective plans by districts and counties must be done in the context of broad goals and planning outlines for a relatively homogeneous region.

To perform planning on a regional basis will offer the establishment of a regional agency to facilitate planning. Such an agency would not necessarily do planning and it could never substitute for planning activities and organizations at the county and district levels. Rather, it would provide the regional guidance and integration which is essential to effective comprehensive regional educational planning.

Moreover, since all districts and counties do not equally recognize the need for formal planning, there is a clear need for an organization which can act as an agent of change in demonstrating the values of planning, the need for planning, and in developing an awareness of effective planning practices. Such an agency could serve both as a focal point for regional planning activities and as a motivator of these activities.

County/District Development Plans
These plans develop the activities which are necessary for the creation and implementation of current new generation of educational programs for the counties and school districts. Such plans offer further guidance to the achievement of the organizational posture which has been suggested in the strategic plan and which is essential to the offering of new programs and disciplines. They specify the techniques for evaluating alternative programs, delineate the resource requirements of each proposed program and provide guidance for the development of operational plans.

Operational Plans
The operational plan is the blueprint for action in the current year. Operational plans exist for each functional area of effort in the school organization and for each major educational program. Each specifies the objective to be achieved, the jurisdictions, the work flow, allocations of resources, authority and responsibility patterns, schedules and budgets.

Project Plans
The basic building blocks of the planning system are *project plans.* Currently, many school districts have taken on the responsibility of administering federal projects as a means of enhancing the learning environment for the student. Instructional content and objectives are being examined by school districts. The management of these projects requires the formation of a new and smaller "organization" within a parent organization such as a county or district office. An example of this in a school district is a Title I Project in which an individual appointed as a project manager has authority to involve the project staff, other school district personnel and outside consultants. The resulting pattern of organizational relationships creates a management system whereby there is a mix or web of horizontal and vertical authority between the project staff and other school district person-nel.* Thus, the need for developing a philosophy of project planning is clear.

*The emerging concept of project management is aptly described as a revolutionary management technique in the Apollo program: " . . . projectization has evolved in Apollo to the point of being a management revolution. It carries to its most elaborate development the task force concept now becoming the fashion in

Projects are identifiable *ad hoc* efforts in the organization having specific time, cost and performance parameters. Typically these projects go through a distinct life cycle, i.e., a natural order of thought and action which is pervasive in terms of all time periods and all organizational involvement. Projects emerge as *ideas* from the mainstream of organizational activity and constitute the building blocks of the overall strategic planning system. As such they go through a distinct life cycle in which specific thought and action are required within the organization to measure the efficacy of the project in developing and implementing overall organizational strategy. The "phases" of this cycle serve to illustrate the life cycle concept and its importance.

The Conceptual Phase. The germ of the idea for a project may evolve from other research, from current organizational problems or from the observation of organizational interfaces. The conceptual phase is one in which the idea is conceived and given preliminary evaluation.

During the conceptual phase, the environment is examined, forecasts are prepared, objectives and alternatives are evaluated, and the first examination of the performance, cost and time aspects of project development are performed. It is also during this phase that basic strategy, organization and resource requirements are conceived. The fundamental purpose of the conceptual phase is to conduct a "white paper" study of the project requirement in order to provide a basis for further detailed evaluation.

There will be a high mortality rate of potential projects during the conceptual phase of the life cycle. Rightly so, since the study processes conducted during this phase should identify projects that have high risk and are technically, environmentally, or economically infeasible or impractical.

The Definition Phase. The fundamental purpose of the definition phase is to determine as soon as possible, and as accurately as possible, cost, schedule, performance and resource requirements and if all elements, projects and sub-systems will fit together economically and technically.

---

management doctrine." See: The Unexpected Payoff of Project Apollo, *Fortune*, July, 1969. Also see: *Systems Analysis and Project Management* by David I. Cleland and William R. King, McGraw-Hill Book Company, 1968.

The definition phase simply tells in more detail what it is we want to do, when we want to do it, how we will accomplish it and what it will cost us to do it. The definition phase allows us to fully conceive and define the project before we start to physically put the project into the total system. *Simply stated, the definition phase dictates that you stop and take time to look around to see if this is what you really want* before the resources are committed to put the project into operation and production. If the project has survived the end of the conceptual phase, a conditional approval for further study and development is given.

Decisions that are made during and at the end of the definition phase might very well be decisions to cancel further work on the project and redirect organizational resources elsewhere.

Production or Acquisition Phase. The purpose of the production or acquisition phase is to acquire and test the project elements and the total system itself using the standards developed during the preceding phases. The acquisition process involves such things as the actual setting up of the project, the fabrication of hardware, the allocation of authority and responsibility, the construction of facilities and the finalization of supporting documentation.

The Operational Phase. The fundamental role of the manager of a system during the operational phase is to provide the resource support required to accomplish the project objectives. This phase indicates the project has been proven economical, feasible and practicable and will be used to accomplish the desired ends of the system. In this phase the manager's functions change somewhat. He is less concerned with planning and organizing and more concerned with controlling the project's operation along the predetermined lines of performance. His responsibilities for planning and organization are not entirely neglected—there are always elements of these functions remaining—but he places more emphasis on motivating the human element of the project. It is during this phase that the project is placed in its proper place in the ongoing total system. Eventually the project will lose its identity and be assimilated in the "institutional" framework of the organization. The project organization and the management of the project as such will thus cease during this cycle.*

*A detailed outline of the project life cycle and the elements of the various phases is available from the authors on request.

The Role of Forecasting in Planning

The role of forecasting is to project future school system conditions and expected demands for the school system's performance as related to a future environment. The function of forecasting by a school planner is clear—given the present position of the school system, forecasting seeks to determine the effect that future economic, legislative, social and technological factors will have on the environment of the school system. Such a task demands that the planner develop, by collection of existing intelligence and by the forecasting process, a quantitative and qualitative data base concerning such things as:

(1) Demographic changes.
(2) Government statistics affecting education.
(3) Changing social mores and conditions.
(4) State and national legislative actions.
(5) Political environment.
(6) Technological progress in educational hardware.
(7) Government fiscal and monetary policy—changing tax bases.
(8) Technological progress in teaching, research and communication techniques.
(9) Expected educational products and services to be offered at future periods of time.
(10) Advanced forecasting and planning techniques having application to school systems.

Forecasting is not planning *per se*. Rather it is the projection of the future organizational environment and organization environment related to the future environment. Forecasting does not have the innate function of acting to affect the course of organization progress. The system of plans prescribes the organizational objectives and the means for attaining these objectives.

Summary

Many of the needs of a school system are regional in nature, e.g., the needs of specific minority groups who may populate an entire region. Since such needs are inherently regional, they can best be assessed on a regional basis. So too can much of the forecasting which is necessary for effective planning be more economically performed at a regional level.

The concept of an educational planning system for a region does not mean that individual school districts should not develop their own development and operational plans. They must have overall strategic objectives, guidance, forecasts and assumptions which provide a basis for their planning and which assure consistency across districts and counties. Without such guidance, individual districts and counties are likely to be seeking inconsistent goals and expending resources in mutually contradictory ways.

The authors are indebted to Blaine Wishart, executive director of the Educational Resources Agency of Sacramento, California, for his helpful suggestions in the development of this paper.

REFORMING URBAN EDUCATION WITH COST-EFFECTIVENESS ANALYSIS

Clark C. Abt

Cost-effectiveness analysis is a well-known technique of management science for increasing the efficiency of complex systems, but it has not yet been applied to the improvement of urban education on any significant scale. Yet there is growing public clamor for more and better education for more people, within tax cost constraints that demand vastly increased efficiency if much more is to be done with only a little more in resources. The application is urgent and the technique exists, yet inaction persists. Why?

Organizations of all types are basically homeostatic mechanisms that mobilize their internal forces in the direction of stability. If this were not so, they could not survive as organizations. The equilibrium conditions reached are always a balance of the external forces for change and the internal forces minimizing the impact of those external forces on the inner organization by adaptation. These considerations suggest that urban education systems are unlikely to change unless external forces require such changes as conditions for organizational survival.

Governments at all levels are forced to change by external political forces expressed as public opinion that anticipates elections—elections creating peaceful changes of leadership that, if long denied, result in

Clark C. Abt is president of Abt Associates, Cambridge, Massachusetts.

violent changes. Governments operate in a political market, and consumer preferences force the changes. In democracies the market mechanism is that of elections, in totalitarian nations it may be that of revolutions. Either way, political competitors force the changes.

Businesses are forced to change by external economic forces expressed as consumer demands that anticipate sales and revenues and profits. Businesses operate in an economic market in which consumer preferences, often mobilized by economic competition, force the changes. Again, it is the consumers' access to alternatives that creates the market mechanism that forces changes responsive to the preferences of consumers—at least when there is no monopolistic concentration of industrial power.

Public education systems, in contrast to governments and businesses, are much more insulated from the forces that can be exerted by their consumers. Public schools have both a political and an economic monopoly with respect to all those consumers of their services who cannot afford to place their children in private schools or obtain the information necessary to migrate to areas of better schools. The administration of public schools is usually insulated from political markets by several protective layers of administrative vertical supervision and lateral coordination, and from the economic markets by the same means.

What can cost-effectiveness analysis do to introduce the market mechanism to public school systems so that they will respond positively to consumer needs for reform? What conditions must be created for cost-effectiveness analysis to do its job of increasing educational efficiency?

To apply cost-effectiveness analysis to the reforming of urban public education, we must apply what we know of urban economics and urban politics to the education system itself. This "system" is not only the formal public school system, but also encompasses the consumers of the public schools' services: the students, parents, teachers and administrators (who are provided employment and some educational or at least training services also). Less directly, the education system is also linked to its inputs: teacher training colleges, preschool, formal and family education, municipal budgets and facilities, and whatever part of the urban infrastructure is vital to the delivery of educational services; and to its outputs: job and college placements, citizen socialization, professional development of the staff, etc.

Given this more comprehensive view of the urban education system, of which the formal public school system is really only a subsystem, what can be said of the economics and politics of this larger system that would permit and encourage cost-effectiveness techniques to be applied? In economic terms, the elimination of the public school subsystem's monopoly with the introduction of competitive alternatives would offer incentives for educational institutions to become more responsive to consumer demands. In political terms, the politicization of school administrations, or alternative and possibly competing educational institutions, would force them to operate in a political market much like other governments, and to be more responsive to voter demands. The combination of an economic and a political market mechanism for educational services would be a most powerful one for achieving educational reform in consonance with consumer demand.

Three Basic Conditions

For either economic or political market mechanisms to operate on the formal public school system to force internal reforms, three basic conditions must be satisfied: First, economic and political *alternatives* must exist, and have sound economic and political reasons for existing. Second, the consumers of educational services—the students, parents, teachers, administrators, employers and operators of advanced educational institutions—must have *information* on the alternatives and their relative cost-effectiveness in terms of criteria based on their own priorities. Third, the consumers must be able to exercise *control* over their own choices of alternatives, because information on alternatives that one cannot exercise is of no use at all.

A Market Mechanism

Given that the reform of urban education requires an economic and political *market* mechanism for educational services, and that this market mechanism is achieved by *alternative sources, information* on alternatives, and *control* over the choice of alternatives by the consumers, we can now be specific about the contribution of cost-effectiveness analysis to the reform of urban education. Alternative sources to the formal public school system can be identified and stimulated by cost-effectiveness analysis and comparison of the components of the current educational process in the home, in the school and on the streets. (In order of decreasing influence, they are parents, peers and teachers.) Widely disseminated results of cost-effectiveness comparisons among schools can provide the information for consumers to exercise intelligent choices among the alternatives. And cost-effectiveness analysis of alternative mixes of public, institutional and private control over the choice of educational alternatives can approach a socially optimal policy.

Cost-effectiveness analysis of specific educational and educational-supporting programs will suggest better alternative methods and programs, provided there is an audience for the results of such analysis and that the audience has entrepreneurial and technical capacity. At present such cost-effectiveness analysis as is done rarely reaches those most likely to respond to it: the educational entrepreneur, innovator or investor. Rather, the results of the few usually government-funded cost-effectiveness analyses are usually disseminated to the sponsoring government agency and its staff. Here it rests, to be used as one more input to policy deliberations at best, or at worst—and all too often—simply to be perused and filed. Thus one of the conditions necessary for the application of the results of cost-effectiveness analysis of education systems to the generation of educational alternatives is the wide dissemination of such findings to those most capable of responding—entrepreneurs, innovators, community leaders, and of course the operating managements of existing educational institutions.

Voucher Payments

The dissemination of the very modest amount of cost-effectiveness analysis conducted on educational processes thus far is not likely to be sufficient to satisfy the market research needs of a careful entrepreneur or educational investor. For alternative forms of educational institutions to be developed and offered to the general public, clear financial rewards must be offered, and such analysis as has been done fails to promise this, given no changes in the currently operating public school system. One interesting proposal for creating financial incentives for the development of alternative educational institutions is the *voucher payments* approach, in which each school-age child (or his parent) receives a voucher worth the average annual per-pupil expenditure in that community, to spend on the public school system or as they wish. Obviously, such a program would immediately offer the possibility of new schools being started and funded by tax money previously committed exclusively to the public schools. Whether or not this approach will actually result in such alternative schools being started by community or private groups is about to be tested experimentally by Christopher Jencks in a test program for the U.S. Government Office of Economic Opportunity.

For alternative educational institutions to be developed that offer improvements over the public school system at the same cost, effectiveness obviously must be increased. And the way to identify how to increase effectiveness in a complex process is to make cost-effectiveness analyses and comparisons of the components of that process. For example, if a community group decides that anything would be better than the educational services it now receives from the local public school system, and decides to set up its own school with funding from student vouchers, it must immediately face the school system. If the design of the new community school is to proceed rationally, the question of what to do differently should be answered on the basis of comparisons of the relative cost-effectiveness of different component programs and mixes of programs in terms of the community's objectives and local conditions.

The annual school audit would consist of a sample survey of the quantitative and qualitative outputs of a school as viewed by the student, parent and teacher consumers, and the money and other resource inputs. The outputs could be expressed in the form of a measure of educational effectiveness on the basis of community priorities, and the inputs as a cost, to form a cost-effectiveness rating for that particular school. The same procedure could then be applied to other local schools to provide a basis for comparison of their relative cost-effectiveness or efficiency. At the same time, different individual components or programs within a school could be evaluated for their relative cost-effectiveness in terms of the objectives of the community.

Few communities attempting to set up their own competing education system will be able to afford a complete cost-effectiveness analysis of educational processes, or even a partial one to any great extent. Some means must be found to simplify the method so as to make it widely accessible, implementable, understandable and affordable. One approach to developing such a simplified and widely available cost-effectiveness tool would be an *annual school audit.* Community groups could be trained to execute such audits at a cost of probably under $1000 per school (or less if unpaid volunteers are used).

A Typical Audit

A typical annual school audit of a typical high school having 1000 students and 50 teachers might be accomplished as follows. First a group of interviewers is recruited. For economy and for the sake of community involvement, these might be high school students from nearby schools, off-duty teachers from other nearby schools, and housewives who are parents of children in other schools. (It would be wise to avoid data-gathering by persons directly involved in the school being evaluated, so as to avoid the obvious biases and recriminations.) A stratified random sample of students, parents of students, and teachers would then be selected for interview. For the size school given, perhaps interviews with 100 students, 70 parents and 30 teachers might be adequate for fairly representative results.

The standardized survey instrument that would be administered to the stratified random sample of students, parents and teachers by other (out-of-district) students, parents and teachers must be brief, clear, and yet comprehensive of major evaluative factors. Ideally it would have both quantitative and qualitative, both objective and subjective data. Typical data to be collected would be respondents' answers to such questions as: How many teachers have turned you on, or off, in the last two years? How many of your courses do you find worthwhile? How many are a waste of time? Are the clubs and sports interesting? What is the greatest deficiency of the school? The best thing about it? Do you expect to go to college? Parents might be asked: What do you think of the instruction at the school? Is your child interested in his school work? Has he shown improvement as a result of school work in his grades, behavior, general knowledge? Teachers might be asked: How does this school compare to others in which you have taught, in terms of quality of leadership, curriculum, equipment, facilities and students? Do you find most of your fellow teachers above average, average or below average?

In addition to these open-ended responses from school consumers, the school audit would also obtain archival data on graduation rates, college and job placement rates, dropout rates, average achievement scores on standardized achievement tests, teacher qualifications, teacher turnover rates, the annual school budget by major cost categories (including per pupil annual costs) and the positive and negative changes and rates of change in these characteristics from year to year (showing improvement, decline or no change). Some of this archival data requires the cooperation of the school authorities, unlike the randomly sampled opinion data. In those cases in which schools refused to cooperate in supplying the archival data, much of it could be estimated on an interview sampling basis at some added cost in both accuracy and interviewer salaries.

The annual school audits, published inexpensively and disseminated widely (or sold) in communities, would also serve the function of providing *information on educational alternatives* currently available, even if the community did not decide to create its own competing school. Parents, students and teachers could exercise a much more selective choice of school placements through their choice of residence, application or employment, respectively. This greater exercise of public choice of the available public schools would itself go some of the way toward creating an educational market mechanism, and might foster productive competition among the schools of a district compared in the school audit publication.

Unfortunately, those individuals who have most to gain from improvements in public education through its facilitation of upward socioeconomic mobility are also the least able to execute *control of the alternatives*. Parents are unlikely to be able to control their home location in order to place their children in the best schools identified by the school audits, if they are poor and dependent on a particular low-rent home location. Students who need the greatest amount of help as a result of various environmental and other handicaps are precisely those least likely to be able to exercise control over placement in different schools by selective application or competitive examination. And teachers who are teaching in the least cost-effective schools may feel duty-bound to stick to their burdens lest replacements do worse. For all these reasons, the information on currently available educational alternatives offered by an annual school audit is likely to be effective chiefly with middle-class populations and of little direct help to the poor, unless more alternative educational institutions actually are developed.

COST-EFFECTIVENESS ANALYSIS FOR EDUCATIONAL PLANNING

Margaret B. Carpenter and Sue A. Haggart

Cost-effectiveness is both a powerful and an often misused technique of analysis. Its misuse stems from its very power, for it gives superficially simple, quantitative "answers" to highly complex problems whose sources and repercussions are very poorly understood. So that the results of cost-effectiveness analysis may be used most wisely in educational planning, it is necessary to know how to structure, conduct and interpret the analysis.

Educational planning is ultimately concerned with achieving a more effective use of educational resources in improving pupil performance. There are several intermediate steps in the realization of this goal. The educational planner must first determine what resources are being used directly to produce specific educational performance or outcomes. From this base of knowledge, he may then estimate the resources required to make changes in various aspects of the educational process. These changes may range all the way from changes in the objectives of education, *per se*, to changes in instructional methods. This means he must be armed with an informational framework about his current system that is as complete as possible and with a methodology for estimating the future consequences of proposed changes.

Margaret B. Carpenter and Sue A. Haggart are with The Rand Corporation, Santa Monica, California.

Cost-effectiveness analysis is a tool that can assist the planner in relating the resources required by an educational program to its effectiveness, often measured by pupil achievement. For the purpose of analysis, we look at schools as "systems." From this analytical viewpoint, an educational system is perceived as being an arrangement of elements (such as teachers, classrooms and the like) and processes (such as instruction and counseling) that combine to produce student learning. There are factors within the system that influence the relationships between the resources used by the system and the student learning that results; there are also factors external to the system that have impacts on these relationships. Just what these factors are is being widely discussed now and will be for some time to come. We will not directly explore the many facets of this question here. (Their consideration is, of course, an integral part of analyzing the educational process.) Our purpose is to look at the problems involved with the use of the technique of cost-effectiveness analysis in educational planning.

We mentioned that cost-effectiveness analysis is concerned with *educational programs*. The term *educational program* can have many meanings, such as *the inservice teacher training program*. From this point on, we shall restrict the term to apply to *a set of activities and resources that, taken together, bring about a specific kind of student learning*. A program must be described in terms of certain basic characteristics—its effectiveness, its cost, its resource requirements, and the way it is carried out.

Cost-effectiveness analysis is, quite frankly, a technique for comparing programs, and may be used

- to help assess the relative worth of several innovative programs with the same educational outcome (such as improvement in reading achievement),
- to determine whether a single program is becoming more or less effective as time passes so that steps may be taken to improve it, if necessary,
- to help assess the relative worth of the same program for different student populations (such as those with differing socioeconomic backgrounds) or in different school settings.

The goal of the analysis is not to provide the planner with the alternative that "maximizes" or "minimizes" specific characteristics;

the goal is to provide information which together with the judgment of the planner permits a compromise among the characteristics of the alternatives within the various environmental constraints, such as budget level or political atmosphere.

The term *cost-effectiveness* should be broadened to *resource-effectiveness* for reasons which will be made clear shortly. *Resource* will be used in the common way to mean *a source of supply*. The way in which the resource requirements of a program are analyzed is inseparable from the purpose of the analysis—to relate the resources used by the program to program effectiveness. Ideally, program cost should include only those resources that can be directly related to program effectiveness.

Problems concerning resource-effectiveness analysis can be broken into two largely parallel sets, one focusing on resource analysis and the other on the analysis of effectiveness. Common problems are those of definition, of the misleading nature of single measures and of the lack of well-developed methodologies for analysis. We shall discuss these two sets of problems in turn and then conclude by addressing problems concerning resource-effectiveness analysis itself.

Resource-Oriented Problems

In order to be able to choose among alternative programs as applied to different educational situations, the planner must have techniques for comparing and evaluating estimates of the resources required by the programs throughout the time span of interest.

Determining the Resources Required by a Program

In the past, educational institutions have accounted for the cost of doing business primarily for the purpose of financial control. Funds for different purposes have come from different sources and may not be traded from one account to another. Keeping track of these accounts in terms of end-items of expenditure was the major task of the budgeting and accounting activity.

When cost is used for choosing among alternative programs, however, the source of funds is of secondary significance. Rather, it is necessary to know what each alternative will require in terms of personnel, facilities, equipment, training activities, dollars, and the like, not only at present but throughout the foreseeable life of the program. Few school systems can describe the resources that go into existing programs, let alone estimate what existing programs or alternative programs will require in the future.

This is not, however, an insurmountable problem. It is possible to draw up a set of variables describing the resource requirements of alternative programs that is sufficiently broad to encompass the major variables in each program and, at the same time, sufficiently compact to be manageable. This must be undertaken at the outset if cost-effectiveness analysis is to be carried out.

There is a more subtle problem, however, whose solution may not be so easily reached. This is the problem of definition of the "real" resources in education, that is, the resources that actually are the *source of supply* of learning. Many attempts are now being made to identify such resources, and some small progress has been made, viz., teacher verbal ability appears to have a positive effect on student learning. The amount of time a student participates actively in some learning process may well be another resource, but there seems to be no easy way to measure this at present. The amount of time that a teacher devotes to the subject in the classroom is only a proxy measure. Much work in this area will be necessary before it is possible to identify the real resources in education.

The Misleading Nature of a Single Measure

Resource analysis has a seductive quality engendered by the availability of a single measure, the dollar, by which most resources can be measured. Given this, it is a natural step to add all of the dollars to obtain a single indicator of resource requirements—the "cost of the program." Although in some cases such a number might be quite sufficient for resource-effectiveness analysis, in most instances the single measure buries many characteristics of the program of which the planner should be aware in making his choice.

One significant aspect concerns the timing of the expenditures; are they required in a lump sum, can they be spread over several years or will they recur as long as the program is in existence? Thus, projections of expenditures over the expected life of the program are required to provide a true picture of dollar needs. A display of the expenditures required over several years contrasts with the usual practice of assessing the cost of a program solely in terms of the initial research, development and implementation costs.

Another significant aspect is that in general the resources required are of very different kinds, and dollar measures do not reflect these differences adequately for decision making. For example, a program may require that a certain percentage of the teachers belong to a particular minority group, but these teachers will receive the same salary as any teacher with similar background and experience.

Thus, the cost-effectiveness analysis should always display the major resources required for each year of program life, along with their associated dollar costs, and should particularly note items which may be difficult to obtain (but whose scarcity may not be reflected adequately in their dollar costs). The problem is to identify and estimate the major, crucial, or scarce resources that will be required for full implementation of the programs.

The Lack of a Fully Developed Methodology for Resource and Cost Analysis

Some of the methodology required for the analysis of cost within cost-effectiveness analysis has already been developed, although it is not in general use in educational institutions. Much of the methodology can be developed in a rather straightforward fashion simply by using techniques that have been developed elsewhere to identify and cost those resources that contribute directly to a given program. Several pitfalls exist, however, of which the analyst should be wary.

The objective of cost-effectiveness analysis is to facilitate choice among alternative programs. Therefore, costs which actually will remain fixed regardless of which programs are implemented (within limits) should not be "allocated" to particular programs. For example, a school district with enrollment in a particular size range will require a relatively fixed administrative function. If all of the cost of central administration were to be allocated to instructional programs, it would have to be done by largely arbitrary rules (except in some special cases where curriculum experts work in specific subject areas); worse, if such allocations are made, changes in the direct cost of a program will appear to generate corresponding changes in the indirect, or allocated, cost, when in fact such changes would not actually follow. The key to realistic cost analysis in these instances is to identify those resources that will not change in response to program changes and to set them aside under *unallocated* functional categories such as *administration* or *student services.* The question of which costs to allocate to which programs is of very real importance and will have to be resolved.

Special problems of resource allocation are also posed by "core" programs, programs that teach two or more subjects within a single session. If student achievement on each subject is measured separately, some decision must be made on how resources and activities within the program are apportioned among the subjects. If, however, a single measure of student achievement that encompasses the several subjects has been devised, there is no need to allocate resources within the program.

These problems of resource allocation are most easily, and consistently, handled if a resource/cost model of the district has been developed. The development of a resource/cost model is also an essential step in achieving a workable methodology of analysis for educational planning. This model would comprise a set of mathematical expressions that relate variables describing the district and the programs to estimates of resource requirements and cost. With such a model, the analyst can formulate a description of the district at each future date and simulate the results of conducting each alternative program within the district.

The model must be broad enough that each of the alternative programs can be fully described by the basic variables and relationships that make up the model. For example, requirements for teachers are usually directly related to projected enrollment, but if a program is largely self-paced, the number of teachers required may be more sensitive to the number of points in the learning sequence at which a teacher's assistance is needed than it is to enrollment.

Often analysis will suggest that alternative programs be combined or that parts of programs be used in ways in which they were not used before. The model should be able to accommodate such variations as these, also. At the same time, care should be exercised to keep the model to a manageable size. There are so many aspects of school districts and educational programs that it is very easy for the number of variables included in the model to reach astronomical values. The only way to avoid this is for a skilled model builder who is well informed on the workings of educational institutions to tailor the model to the questions being addressed.

Effectiveness-Oriented Problems

The effectiveness of a program is a set of measures or indicators that describes the learning that the program has brought about. The impact of the program on such groups as parents, teachers or the community at large may suggest peripheral benefits and can be used to choose among programs of apparently equal teaching effectiveness, but these benefits are not central to the problems surrounding effectiveness.

Measuring Effectiveness

The problems of defining and measuring the effectiveness of educational programs must be dealt with before the cost-effectiveness of alternatives can be analyzed. A central problem is the selection of instruments that measure attainment of program goals validly and reliably. In many academic areas, there are tests of student achievement that may be used with some confidence. But if program goals include such objectives as changes in a child's conception of his own self-worth or improvements in the child's relationships with his peers, it may be more difficult to obtain or devise instruments that are valid and reliable; sometimes very expensive techniques such as individual observation or interview by trained psychologists must be used.

Even if acceptable measuring instruments are at hand, care must be taken to assure that they are administered in a consistent fashion; otherwise, the comparability of scores may be in question. This may require, for example, that a single team of testers administer all pre- and post-tests that are to be used as measures of effectiveness.

Finally, in interpreting measurements, the evaluator must decide which scoring mode is appropriate for the program goals. Grade-equivalent scores show the grade level at which the students are performing, but are not appropriate for inferences about the effect of the program on the rates of growth of children who started at different grade levels. For this purpose, percentile scores, which allow comparison of the relative position of students at different time points, are preferable. But the comparison of percentile scores is misleading as a measure of the *amount* of change, although it is useful as a measure of the *direction* of change in relative standing. A more accurate representation of the amount of change would be given by standard scores.

The Inadequacy of a Single Measure

Because of the complexity of the learning process, a full analysis of effectiveness should produce a *set* of measures and indicators, rather than a single measure. These measures and indicators should be kept track of for several years in order to determine the effects of specific programs, because temporary spurts in growth may be of little value in the long run.

It is also important to determine the effects of specific programs on student performance in other educational programs, for example, the effect of a reading or mathematics program on those programs that make use of reading and computational skills such as history, science, and the like. Although it seems logical to assume that improved performance in reading would carry over into improved performance in most other areas, some programs may encourage more of such carry-overs than others and some could even have negative effects. These considerations are important. In spite of the fact that they add a considerable burden to the task of analysis, parallel longitudinal testing programs in several subjects should be conducted. This is a potentially more valuable approach than just measuring achievement in a single dimension such as reading or mathematics. This means that setting up a research program specifically designed to test hypotheses about the interdependence of student achievement among academic subjects may be required to obtain a full description of the effectiveness of a single program.

As suggested earlier, educational programs may be directed specifically to goals other than improvement of student achievement in such subjects as reading and mathematics. For example, the program may seek to change the attitudes of the parents toward their children's schooling. Objectives such as these are usually thought of as fostering the attainment of the primary objective of student achievement, but the causal relationship may go in both directions. In any event, if the program devotes resources specifically to attain such ends, some means for determining to what extent the ends have been gained should be set up; and experimental design should include similar programs that do not devote resources to attaining such goals. This is particularly important when questions arise concerning whether to apply a successful program as a "package" or to use only those portions of it that seem to have been most conducive to its success.

If it is accepted that a single number for the dollar cost of a program conceals most of the information needed for decision making, it should be even clearer that no single measure of program effectiveness will tell the whole story about the worth of the program because any program promotes several different kinds of change in the student. Because these changes are different in kind, no unit exists by means of which the changes attributable to a particular program can be made commensurate. Thus, the effectiveness of a program can only be presented as a *set* of measures and indicators. In order to choose among alternative programs, the planner must then judge the relative importance of the various aspects of program effectiveness *as they apply to particular schools*. For example, the teaching of reading may be of primary importance in inner-city schools but may carry much less weight in schools in upper middle class neighborhoods. One of the major tasks is to decide how to rank measures and indicators of effectiveness vis-à-vis schools in various socioeconomic areas.

The Lack of a Methodology for Estimating the Effectiveness of Future Programs

Many aspects of the effectiveness of past and ongoing programs can be measured by pre- and post-tests of student achievement. The relationships among test results and educational resources of various kinds can also be inferred by using standard techniques of regression analysis. Unfortunately, such analyses can only describe what has happened in the past and cannot be relied upon to predict future program effectiveness if major changes in factors influencing learning (such as the social environment) are likely to take place. In addition, because the "real" resources in education may not yet have been identified, regression analyses may fail to treat the resource-effectiveness relationships that are crucial to the success of the program. Longitudinal studies address just such matters as these. Hopefully, such studies will contribute to the future development of models of program effectiveness that can be used in educational planning in the same way that resource and cost models could be used today.

The Need for Criteria of Effectiveness

Lacking reliable models that relate educational resources to program effectiveness, it is necessary not only to weight the relative importance of measures and indicators of different aspects of effectiveness but to judge what levels of effectiveness are acceptable. If, for example, growth in reading achievement of one month-per-month of schooling is acceptable, is a growth rate of .95 month-per-month unacceptable? What if the latter growth rate is provided by a program that has more evident peripheral benefits than the former? Or what if the latter program reaches more students for the same cost?

A rationale for the resolution of issues such as these is an integral part of the analysis; setting criteria, or standards for judging effectiveness, can help to supply this rationale. An important problem is whether different criteria are to be chosen for students with different characteristics, such as socioeconomic background, or whether the same criteria are to be applied to all students. An obvious need is to know what is the average achievement of students with different characteristics under current educational programs. Whatever criteria are chosen, they should only provide general guidelines to the planner, rather than draw fine lines between the acceptable and the unacceptable. This is because the measures available are subject to error and, at the same time, are only proxies for what we would really like to assess—student learning. And this is why peripheral considerations can often tip the balance of decision between one program and another.

Analysis for Educational Planning

From the foregoing it should be clear that a single number purporting to be a cost-effectiveness ratio must hide more than it reveals about the overall value of an educational program. This is because the requirements of a program for resources are multidimensional and time-variant; the same may be said for indicators of program effectiveness. The educational planner, whether the analysis is aimed at a modest change in the current way of doing business or whether the analysis addresses the question of incorporating a major innovation, must have adequate information—information about the change and about its impact on the resource requirements of other programs and on the effectiveness of other programs. When the planner is considering the implementation of promising innovations in his district, he will need to know, for example, to what extent the success of the innovations depends on the *characteristics of the schools in which they have been used,* particularly the socioeconomic status of the school population. Because of the great variability among school districts and among schools within a given district, it seems unlikely that any innovation can be replicated in a new school without some modification. For example, the new school may already have some of the equipment needed for the program or may have to add more or fewer specialized personnel. Therefore, the resources required to implement the alternative innovations will have to be estimated for the new school.

Ideally, this work should be done by collaboration between people familiar with the original programs and the school district personnel. If each district has information readily available about the resource requirements of its programs, it should then be able to estimate the resource requirements of the innovations as alternatives.

In addition, there are characteristics of a school that are related to the effectiveness of an innovation. It is very unlikely that the characteristics of the new school will exactly match those of the school successfully using the innovation. The characteristics of the student populations will differ in some respects; the relationships among the teachers, students, administrators, parents and community will not be the same; and other educational programs in the schools will also be different. The impacts of these differences on program effectiveness will need to be estimated, through collaboration between people familiar with the original programs and the school district personnel. During the course of this work, a rationale for ranking criteria of effectiveness will be developed that will be tailored to each school in the district.

Because of these problems in comparing programs, the best way to use cost-effectiveness analysis is to construct *equal-cost alternatives*, that is, to adjust the dimensions of each program (such as the number of students enrolled) so that each program will incur approximately the same total cost over some appropriate period of time. In this way, the educational planners will be freed from having to consider cost when choosing among alternatives and can concentrate on the more difficult aspects of effectiveness, the phasing of dollar requirements, and the requirements for scarce resources. Because the use of a single measure of effectiveness (since any program brings about student change of several kinds that are not commensurable) is less defensible than is the use of dollar cost, the reverse of this procedure—to construct *equal-effectiveness alternatives*—is a dubious approach. Moreover, the projection of the estimated cost of a program can be done with a great deal more confidence than can its effectiveness.

In educational planning, one alternative, simply to continue current practice, should be included for baseline data. Although this alternative will usually not incur the same cost as will the innovative programs being compared, it is important to know its projected future cost and effectiveness so that the added resource and cost requirements incurred by the innovative programs may be estimated. Then the

incremental requirements that are associated with improved effectiveness will be known. (It often turns out that these incremental
requirements are small compared with the requirements simply to
maintain current practice, even though they might seem large when
considered in isolation.) Thus the first step toward cost-effectiveness
analysis must be to estimate the future resource requirements and
effectiveness of current programs.

There are many instances in which the future resource requirements of an innovative program are quite uncertain. This may arise
because of uncertainties in projected enrollments, for example. In such
a situation, it is important to know whether the choice among
alternative programs would change if the future were different from
some "most likely" case. If one program appears desirable under a wide
range of future possibilities, it is obviously a good choice. If not, it is
possible that the educational planner will want to choose a program
that hedges against future change rather than the one that seems best in
the most likely case.

The results of all this work will be estimated measures or
indicators of resource requirements, cost and ranked aspects of
effectiveness projected over the time period of interest for each
program and for alternative futures. The display of these items, along
with supporting explanatory text, will provide planners with the
information on the resource requirements and effectiveness of alternative innovative programs that they will need for making informed
choices. Thus, a carefully designed display and textual presentation is a
significant part of the resource-effectiveness analysis. Only in this way
can the educational planner guard against the indiscriminate use of a
single cost-effectiveness "number" so far removed from its limitations
that it is not only useless but dangerous.

Any views expressed in this paper are those of the authors. They should not be
interpreted as reflecting the views of The Rand Corporation or the official opinion
or policy of any of its governmental or private research sponsors.

References

Carpenter, M.B. *Program Budgeting as a Way to Focus on Objectives in Education,*
    The Rand Corporation, P-4162, September 1969.

Carpenter, M.B. & S.A. Haggart. *Analysis of Educational Programs within a Program Budgeting System,* The Rand Corporation, P-4195, September 1969.

Haggart, S.A., S.M. Barro, M.B. Carpenter, J.A. Dei Rossi & M.L. Rapp. *Program Budgeting for School District Planning: Concepts and Applications,* The Rand Corporation, RM–6116-RC, November 1969.

Rapp, M.L. *Evaluation as Feedback in the Program Development Cycle,* The Rand Corporation, P-4066, April 1969.

WAYS FOR SCHOOL DISTRICTS
TO USE EFFECTIVENESS AND COST
INFORMATION IN PLANNING

Sanford Temkin and Margaret J. Jones

Introduction
It is increasingly evident that urban school administrators have problems of an economic nature. These problems arise because in schools the supply of resources is insufficient to meet educational needs, given the level of technology. If these pleas for more resources are sincere, then it is safe to assume that administrators are unable to conduct some programs and activities which they feel are necessary. Further, it implies that planning is important in order to obtain the best possible educational outcomes from a level of resources inadequate to meet all the needs of children.

This chapter describes a way of thinking which can be applied to many school planning and decision-making problems. It also offers ways to plan for and gather the kinds of information which are needed to support planning decisions.

Permission for use of this original paper has been granted by Research for Better Schools, Inc., Philadelphia, Pa., a private nonprofit corporation. The opinions expressed herein do not necessarily reflect the position or policy of the Office of Education, and no official endorsement by the Office of Education should be inferred. Funded in part by the Cooperative Research Act (P.L. 83-531 as amended) in cooperation with the USOE.

Sanford Temkin is director of comprehensive planning, and Margaret Jones is program coordinator, Research for Better Schools, Inc., Philadelphia.

Questions an Administrator Asks

Currently, many "prescribers" attempt to tell administrators *how* they should plan and make school decisions. These prescribers, however, make little effort to communicate supportive information to the school administrator so that he can become comfortable with the *planning prescriptions* which are offered to him. It is not surprising that administrators think and behave differently from prescribers. The kinds of questions which are raised by school administrators in their planning often appear to be different from those which prescribers suggest. Is this really the case?

At the risk of oversimplification, two school situations that administrators frequently face will be described. The questions which administrators generally raise in these situations will be presented and compared with the language which prescribers might use in the same situations.

In *School Situation I*, the administrator is considering whether or not to *modify* a program. Usually the administrator is aware of the need for change but is caught up in his day-to-day operations. When the *need* for change is brought to his attention by others he is likely to raise two initial questions:

> How well is Program X working now?
> What is wrong with Program X?

Notice that these inquiries appear in the present tense. In the words of the planner-prescriber, such questions are labeled *evaluation and relevance questions*. Rephrased with planning precision they could appear as follows:

> Is Program X effectively meeting pupil needs?
> To what extent is Program X accomplishing what
> it is trying to do?

If the administrator receives information which leads him to appreciate that Program X should be contributing more to his learners, he usually adds other concerns such as:

> What else may we do?
> What will this contribute?
> What will this cost?

These questions signify importance for the future, as opposed to the present, and in planner-prescriber terms are cost-effectiveness or *efficiency questions.* Observe that the administrator is asking for alternatives or options to consider. In order to weigh various options, he is also requesting information on comparative contributions of options and comparative costs. Contributions which are expected if a given option is selected are referred to as effectiveness. *Effectiveness* is doing what you planned to do. *Efficiency* is being effective at a reasonable cost. Efficient organizations are those which command effective educational results from the level of dollars committed to their programs.

When the administrator has selected those alternatives to Program X which promise meaningful contributions at a reasonable cost, then he raises a final group of questions:

> What support and what opposition to this
> change would emerge?
> Who could manage the effort?
> How long would it take to get it operational?

Notice that these questions are framed in the conditional mood. *They are questions of feasibility.* Questions of feasibility come in many sizes, shapes and forms. Despite this, they have a basic characteristic which allows them to be placed in the feasibility category. When the question's intent can be reduced to three words—*Will it work?*—then it is a question of *feasibility.* Typical questions related to feasibility are: 1) Could this be done under the present state law? 2) Is the board likely to support this? 3) Will the publisher make the curriculum available to any school district that wants it? 4) Will we be able to hire the required personnel by September?

Once the feasibility or practicability of each option is judged, the number of options usually is reduced. When the number of viable options is reduced to zero, the administrator must continue with Program X until a superior alternative can be developed. Hopefully, more energy can be directed toward engineering* of educational alternatives.

---

*An "educational engineer" devises alternative ways for achieving outcomes preferred by administrators. He tries to arrive at the "best" program, project or

In *School Situation II,* the administrator is considering whether or not to *substitute* a new program for the existing program. In this instance, by way of contrast to situations for which modifications are sought, the administrator initiates his inquiry with questions of feasibility.

Questions of feasibility probably will eliminate some options from further consideration. The administrator now examines questions which deal with the contribution of each option to the total effort of the district. Basically, there are two pieces of information for each option under consideration. He needs to know about the *estimated effectiveness of the options* and he is tied inextricably to *costs.* Since he has few dollars available for new programs—that is, programs which do not replace an existing program but rather are supplements to present district effort—he must be especially careful about the effectiveness of proposed changes. Results and outcomes of modifications of existing programs are easier to explain and justify than results of new efforts. But new options, which are carefully designed and implemented, offer the real promise of being effective for learners.

The administrator may or may not raise a last group of questions (evaluation and relevance). These questions are required to assess progress after the change has been successfully implemented. Hopefully, the administrator will *not* evaluate the new program too soon. He may, however, want to use certain kinds of information to determine how well the new program is being implemented. This form of evaluation provides information (feedback) to help those responsible for implementation. Evaluation of the new program by means of standardized tests and the like should be reserved until it is reasonable to assume that the effort is *fully operational.*

This section has been concerned with questions raised by school administrators and prescribers. Four categories of concern have been discussed. These are:

1.   Evaluation and relevance—to what extent does the program meet the needs of children?

method for taking dollar resources and converting them into school outcomes. He also tries to assure that alternatives are practical and can be implemented within the framework of time and resources. He is not only skilled in planning but is expert in his knowledge of recent developments and approaches in education.

2. Effectiveness—to what extent can the program accomplish what it is trying to do?
3. Efficiency—can it be effective, yet not too restrictive on the budget?
4. Feasibility— will it work?

The order of questions and concerns is related to the specific change being considered, the context—time of the school year, size of the budget and previous commitments—and the way individuals think and approach problems. These four categories can be used to subsume most planning and decision-making questions. To develop skills in recognizing the category in which a question belongs requires careful listening as well as application of basic criteria which sort questions into the four categories. When, for example, several people are planning and have mutually agreed that questions of feasibility have been answered, it is helpful to recognize a new feasibility question as it "sneaks" into a discussion about effectiveness.

Balancing Effectiveness and Costs:
Efficiency Considerations
The previous discussion has identified four general question areas in the planning process. A precise sequencing of these question areas is not necessary. When, however, questions about needs of pupils (relevance) and questions about conditions in the district which would or would not allow a change to be implemented (feasibility) are not answered, it is often impractical to proceed. Once these questions have been satisfactorily answered, questions about effectiveness and cost of various options are in order.

When children benefit greatly from school programs their needs are being met (although it is possible that some needs may be neglected for some groups of children). It is impractical and virtually impossible to measure all the benefits that children receive from schools. Crude measures, such as standardized tests, are used and often confused with productivity of schools.

The fact remains, however, that an administrator has a need to assess how well district programs are performing (effectiveness). Not only must he assess overall effectiveness of existing programs, but he must also consider the effectiveness of each change or option. If an administrator had an unlimited amount of dollars, he would select that option which promises to most effectively meet the needs of children. Realism, however, dictated by a scant supply of dollars, compels him to select from among those options he can afford the one which promises to be most effective. Ideally these decisions are made with regard to the entire school district program—that is, each option selected is the best available. This is not practicable. It is possible, however, to suggest some ideas which could permit an administrator to balance effectiveness of various options and their costs. Certainly the need to do this is substantial.

Developing Educational Performance Indicators

It was pointed out in the preceding pages that it is important for the administrator to weigh the effectiveness of the various alternatives with their costs. Implied in the planning process is a need for methods which allow an administrator to evaluate how effective his programs are as well as how effective various alternatives will be. Performance indicators are standards against which comparisons can be made. These comparisons may be used to evaluate the effectiveness of school programs.

Performance indicators are not universal. One district may choose to use scores on the Iowa Test of Basic Skills to assess the extent to which the present arithmetic curriculum is meeting the needs of children. Another district may elect to use results of a "city test" to measure effectiveness of its arithmetic curriculum. A teacher in this school district may decide to use the city test results coupled with comments made by her pupils about their arithmetic class. Yet another teacher may want to assess how well she has met the needs of high school pupils by determining their ability to complete a 1040 income tax form. The point is that performance indicators may be used to evaluate program effectiveness in many ways. A strict determination of how good a particular performance indicator may be is meaningless, since performance indicators that are developed by a district are unique to the district. This means that they do not readily lend themselves to application in other districts. To this extent planning and decision-making processes are as individualized as people are.

Basically, a performance indicator can do two things. It can indicate how effective a particular program is, if an existing program is being evaluated; it can *also reveal how effective a program can be,* if a proposed option is being evaluated. Three steps are required to develop a performance indicator. These steps are listed below and then discussed.

Step   *Outcome*
1.   A *written statement* of what is to be observed, under what circumstances, when, and by whom.
2.   A *listing* of the *possible outcomes* that may result from observing the specifications prepared in Step 1.
3.   An assignment of preferences to each possible outcome listed in Step 2.

Step 1: Specification of a Performance Indicator

When a planner and an administrator* want to evaluate a group of options, they need a common frame of reference or standard which can be used to assess the merits of the various options. Sometimes a single standard does not adequately reflect the merits of the options, in which case several performance indicators are defined.

A clear specification of the performance indicator is usually difficult. Difficulties arise from two sources. A first source of difficulty stems from the very essence of specification. People tend to avoid specificity because it bares their problems to *themselves* and to others. To plan effectively, the planner and the administrator must be willing to be specific. A second source of difficulty emerges from the administrator's realization that others should be consulted before the performance indicator is specified. He sees that many people within the school district are affected by his decisions and, as such, he feels the responsibility for these decisions. Consequently, he may choose to involve those who will be directly affected by his decision in a definition of the basis upon which the decision will be made.

Step 2: Listing Possible Outcomes

After outcomes resulting from an endeavor have been seen, it is very difficult for a decision-maker to maintain objectivity. One usually wants to be objective in the face of his biases. This may be accomplished by first stating the various outcomes which could result

---

*Thus far we have used planning and administration in different ways. The planner could, and some may argue should, be the administrator. However, the planner, for our purposes, is defined as one who works with the administrator in order to provide a group of options with information about each option which will help the administrator make the decision.

in advance of seeing actual results and then assigning biases or, in softer language, preferences to the respective outcomes. This process assures that the decision-maker's preferences are incorporated into the evaluation and at the same time demands that the decision-maker make his preferences explicit.

Step 3: Assigning Preferences

Once possible outcomes have been listed, the decision-maker is able to assign his preferences to these outcomes. Each method of assigning preferences to outcomes has at least one severe limitation. Usually the limitation derives from the recognition that each assignment of preferences has different implications for various target groups. A similar observation may be drawn about assignment of preferences by school administrators. Nevertheless, it remains for a particular administrator faced with a unique set of conditions to assign preferences to possible results of his programs in the most equitable way he knows.

Weighing Effectiveness and Cost:
a Reading Case

A case is presented in this section in order to unify the process elements described thus far and to apply these ideas in a school district context.

Mr. Smith, language arts coordinator for the ABC School District, was asked by a group of primary teachers to modify the first-grade language arts curriculum. After the initial discussion with the teachers, the coordinator indicated that the first order of business would be to evaluate the program as it presently exists to determine if changes were necessary. He also indicated that since the first-grade program was an integral part of the K-2 structure, any proposed changes would require double-checks to uncover subtle implications for kindergarten and second grade.

Processes for Identifying Components
for Relevance and Evaluation

Several primary teachers volunteered to help Mr. Smith. He met with three teachers on several occasions. The three teachers consulted other teachers and Mr. Smith exchanged ideas with some elementary principals and the assistant superintendent for curriculum. From these discussions, several points of tentative agreement about first grade pupils were reached by Mr. Smith and the primary teachers. These points were:

1. Pupils have a vocabulary problem.
2. Pupils have a comprehension problem.
3. Pupils have a social behavior problem in interacting with other pupils and the teacher.

4. More individual attention to pupil problems is required because there are some bilingual children and there is more heterogeneity among pupil backgrounds than was true eight years earlier when the curriculum and teacher's guide were developed.

As an aside it may be pointed out that some primary teachers felt that teachers needed better in-service training in order that they could become familiar with new teaching strategies—especially for bilingual children. The language arts coordinator said that he would gladly hold this alternative for later consideration but that at present they were concerned with evaluating the existing curriculum in order to identify those student needs which were not being met.

After several rounds of discussions and having reached some tentative points of agreement with teachers, Mr. Smith decided to pursue the following line:

1. Determine to what degree kindergarten was developing a vocabulary for children which allowed for normal entry into first grade.
2. Determine to what degree children have a reading comprehension problem and determine if causative relationships could be suggested.
3. Determine to what degree kindergarten was developing social awareness in children so that they could interact with others in the first grade.
4. Determine the number of children with bilingual problems. Determine other background differences.

Mr. Smith spoke to the testing specialist, Mr. Jeffrey, about their evaluation needs. Mr. Jeffrey indicated that answers are not as easy to supply as are questions, but that he would help Mr. Smith and the primary teachers develop evaluations and collect other pertinent information. Mr. Smith also involved the reading curriculum committee in the evaluation effort. This committee, which was chaired by the assistant superintendent for curriculum, volunteered to assist Mr. Smith "as needs arise." Mr. Smith agreed to keep individual members of the committee informed.

Vocabulary Evaluation. Mr. Smith sought the assistance of a reading specialist from a nearby university. The consultant stated that assessment of vocabulary adequacy is difficult in the early years of a child's development for two interrelated reasons. First, there is a great deal to be learned about the vocabulary requirements for a child to perform adequately in a classroom. Second, few tests are available to evaluate primary vocabulary. He was able to suggest the *Preschool Academic Skills Test,* which was developed under Title I, ESEA, in the Pittsburgh Public Schools. He indicated that some information was available for both disadvantaged and non-disadvantaged pupils. Information was also available for the beginning and end of first grade for each of the two pupil populations.

Reading Comprehension Evaluation. Reading Comprehension was evaluated by the *Gates Primary Reading Tests.* The university consultant had suggested another evaluative instrument, but the primary teachers felt that one portion of the *Gates Primary Reading Tests* was more suitable for providing answers to their questions.

Social Behavior Evaluation. A school district psychologist suggested that the best way to assess how well children got along with each other and their teacher was a behavioral check list. A check list was designed by the psychologist and two teachers. Observations were made in kindergarten and first-grade classrooms by the psychologist.

Special Pupil Needs Assessment. A survey form was prepared by the Office of Pupil Accounting. Emphasis was given to identifying bilingual homes, socioeconomic level of the home, and other types of information which could enable the classroom teacher to know more about the child.

Summary of Evaluation

A review of the information gathered from the four sources allowed the language arts coordinator to conclude:

1. Vocabulary is not a problem in the first grade. The bilingual children do not have a vocabulary problem but many of them have problems with pronunciation and therefore are reluctant to use the full range of vocabulary at their visual command.
2. Reading comprehension is not a problem for any group.
3. The social behavior check list indicated that more could be done in kindergarten to:
    a. help the child to complete a task or project;
    b. point out the long-range benefits of sharing things with others;
    c. help the child converse with the teacher; and
    d. engage sulking children in more meaningful activity, especially group activities.
4. The needs assessment survey provided information such as the number of bilingual homes, the number of children in a home, and parental education.

Synthesis of Evaluation Results for Purposes
of Identifying Feasible Program Alternatives

Mr. Smith discussed evaluative findings with the primary teachers. He also consulted with primary teachers from the five other elementary schools. Generally, they were quite willing to revise their feelings about what was needed when presented with information which they helped to develop and consequently felt was pertinent to their concerns.

Together they developed alternative ways to improve three problem areas of the program. Those program areas requiring improvement and the alternatives designed for each were:

Communication: Alternative #1. Conduct regular monthly meetings for K-2 teachers in each of the six elementary schools. Hopefully, this would bring about better communication among primary teachers within each school. *Alternative #2.* Hold a weekend retreat for K-2 teachers at Lake Joseph McDoakes. Hopefully, this would bring about better communication within and among schools.

Social Behavior: Alternative #1. Have the psychologist train kindergarten teachers to work with the pupil behavior check list. Hopefully, teachers would become more aware of individual pupil behaviors. *Alternative #2.* Have the psychologist train kindergarten and first-grade teachers to work with the pupil behavior check list. Hopefully, teachers would become more aware of individual pupil behaviors and more aware of how these behaviors change as the child develops. *Alternative #3.* Allow each K-2 teacher an opportunity to attend a course in early childhood development at a nearby college.

Pupil Needs: Establish a pupil needs-family background file in the school social worker's office. Steps should be taken to update this file for each family each year.

Processes for Weighing Feasible
Program Alternatives

Mr. Smith, the language arts coordinator, asked Mr. Jeffrey, the testing specialist, to help with the development of performance indicators. These performance indicators would assess the degree to which each alternative would be expected to perform if, in fact, the alternative were actually selected. Mr. Jeffrey indicated that cost estimate information was also important when comparing alternatives.

Communication. Mr. Smith, with assistance from Mr. Jeffrey, approached the problem of assessing the two communication alternatives. A performance indicator was developed by the testing specialist based on his meeting with the coordinator. This performance indicator was "number of weighted teacher hours of involvement in curriculum dicussions." Weights would be determined by asking teachers about their interest in being involved in curriculum discussions. They decided that four categories of teacher response would give them adequate information. The form used to elicit teacher responses is shown below:

Teacher Preference Form   April 14, 1970

Teacher Name .... School ....

Do you want to be involved in K-2 curriculum planning and any other activities which might evolve? Please indicate your preference by a check (✓).

No   ☐
Not sure   ☐
Yes   ☐
Absolutely   ☐

Note: All teachers will be paid for after-school hours on the basis established in District Memorandum 16-2, February, 1970.

A weight of "2" would be assigned to each hour of involvement if the teacher responded "absolutely." A weight of "1" would be assigned to each hour a teacher would be involved if the teacher indicated "yes." A weight of "½" would be assigned to each hour of involvement for teachers selecting "not sure." The response "no" would earn a weight of "0" for each hour of teacher involvement.

Mr. Jeffrey and Mr. Smith discussed the weights, indicating that while the weights were not analogous to $2.00, $1.00 and $0.50, they seemed to reflect the way Mr. Smith felt about a teacher's response about willingness to be involved in this program.

Responses from the questionnaire were tabulated by Mr. Jeffrey. He was also able to estimate costs for each of the two alternatives. He found the business manager helpful in estimating costs. Mr. Jeffrey prepared a "performance-cost" table. These data are shown in Table A.

Table A: Communication Performance-Cost Estimates

Alternative	Teacher Hours Weighted by Teacher Preference for Involvement	Cost ($)
1	1,750	1,400
2	2,800	7,400

Mr. Smith was uneasy about making a decision in this instance. He resolved the question to one of assessing whether 1,000 hours of involvement by teachers in communicating with each other was worth $6,000. He introduced another factor into consideration: regular monthly meetings would spread over the school year, forcing teachers to think more often about ways to improve their awareness of other teachers and their problems. The weekend retreat, on the other hand, was highly concentrated and might not have as strong an influence on the teachers. He recognized that $6,000 was also an important aspect of his decision. Mr. Smith selected Alternative 1.

Social Behavior. A performance indicator was developed jointly by the testing specialist, the psychologist and Mr. Smith. It was decided to brief primary teachers in each school and allow them to express their individual preferences.

Results of this poll indicated:

Alternative	Number of Teachers
1	3
2	25
3	6
no answer	2
not sure	36

Cost estimates were also prepared for each alternative. It was decided to express costs on a per teacher basis as well as total cost.

Alternative	Total Cost ($)	Cost per Teacher ($)
1	4,200	116
2	9,000	278
3	10,800	300

Mr. Smith decided to speak to the assistant superintendent for curriculum. They decided to select Alternative #2 and to allow those teachers who want to attend the college course to do so. This, in effect, was a compromise between Alternatives 2 and 3.

Pupil Needs. Only one alternative along the lines of increasing understanding about pupil needs was considered by Mr. Smith. He was able to discuss the problem with staff from the Office of Pupil Accounting and the social worker. They agreed to establish a pupil needs-family background file. The file would be housed in the social worker's office. Information would be entered into the file on forms completed by teachers, the social worker, and the supervising clerk in the Office of Pupil Accounting. The social worker would employ two part-time senior students to update family records and to send information to the Office of Pupil Accounting. The total extra expenditure for a one-year feasibility test of the system was estimated to be $2300.

Summary of the Reading Case

The process by which the language arts cooordinator was able to gather pertinent information related to evaluation, relevance, efficiency and feasibility questions is not uncomplicated. This process involved on the part of the coordinator a clear understanding of the nature of the problem and willingness to communicate and consult with others. The coordinator was able to involve other people in the planning process because he wanted them to influence decisions. While no explicit mention of timeliness of information was made in the reading case, it should be apparent that the decision-maker should possess a masterful sense of timing.

Conclusion

The role of the planner is to systematize and organize information for use in answering critical questions for the administrator and his staff. Systematic identification of problem areas coupled with well-organized data gathering is a preferred method for building specific and persuasive arguments for explaining why additional funds are necessary to allow urban schools to become more effective.

TOWARD A SALARY STRATEGY
FOR URBAN EDUCATORS

Wilbur R. Thompson

If one should poll a representative sample of educators and ask them to
identify the keystone of their arch designs, surely they would respond
with uncommon unanimity that the solution of their problems lies—in
common with most other popular problems of the day—in wresting
more funds away from a stingy public with misguided priorities. One
does not need to take issue with the plea for larger school budgets to
retain a healthy skepticism that simply relaxing the current budget
constraint is both a necessary *and* sufficient condition to achieve
significant improvement in this critical activity. More and more, the
perhaps too clever remark that our conditioned response to virtually
every social problem is to "throw money at it and hope it will go away"
is perhaps all too true.

No attempt will be made here to analyze or evaluate the school
revenue problem: either the "starved public sector" thesis in general,
or the divorce of tax base and service needs among school districts—
prince and pauper school—within the politically fragmented large
metropolitan area. Other papers in this collection, and an extensive
literature in general, perform that function. Rather the argument of this
brief note is that even if school money were less tight, or even when
funds are limited, the civil service salary schedule is just as hobbling to

Wilbur R. Thompson is professor of economics at Wayne State University.

195

the progress of education. As long as the dominant force is toward equalizing salaries between easier and tougher assignments, between beginner and veteran and between men and women (a horrendous issue to raise these days), more school funds will probably permit only limited gains.

A salary strategy is a necessary complement to better funding of education, and it is surprising how little attention has been given to this matter—public attention at least. This writer does not now teach and never has taught school (below the college level) and readily admits that he "does not know the territory." Still, some serious reflection of an outsider, however naive, could serve to shift the focus or change the perspective of the experienced administrator ever so slightly for the better.

Slums and Suburbs

Anyone who has reflected at all on problems of education in our large metropolitan areas is struck by the anomaly of calling for equal opportunity in education while steadfastly resisting any and all proposals for introducing salary differentials into the regional wage pattern. By defending nominal equality in salaries across the spectrum from comfortable posts in new, clean, safe, easy-to-teach-in schools to the nether world of frustrating and even hazardous posts in tough neighborhoods, the educational establishment is, of course, in effect, opening up commanding differentials in the "real wage." (And the teachers "unions" have vetoed all offers to pay premium wages in inner city schools that this writer has seen reported in the newspapers.)

Surely, teachers know much better than outsiders how nominal salary equality serves to starve tough schools and chase the top talent to the orderly schools in the "nice neighborhoods." They are the ones who suffer abuse in the classroom, experience fear in the halls, or have their automobile tires slashed. If we assume that the teachers are second to none in their desire to move toward equal opportunity in education, the defense of their resistance to inaugurating salary premiums in tough posts must lie in their belief that wage differentials are not an operational strategy. ("Good in theory, but won't work in practice.") Surely, advocates of premium pay will admit that there would be false starts, modifications would have to be made with experience, and detrimental, unplanned side effects would have to be cleaned up. Still, how can a history of virtually no experimentation be defended? How can the lack of a series of demonstration programs be rationalized?

The economist can perhaps be forgiven a first reaction of complete incredulity: to the contrary, price (salary) differentials is the most operational decision-making device our civilization has ever conceived for allocating scarce resources (top talent). Simply stated, the salary differential between two schools is optimal when the division of talent between the two is the one desired and when the number of good teachers applying for transfers from the uncomfortable, higher salary place to the more comfortable, lower salary place is roughly equal to the number of good teachers applying for transfers in the reverse direction, that is, willing to trade discomfort for money. (The concept of "equilibrating wage differentials" is discussed in most standard principles-of-economics textbooks.)

Some might even forgive the economist the less charitable thought that the rejection of any and all patterns of salary differentials is traceable in important measure to the (very human) desire to escape confronting a very hard trade-off: money versus comfort. By tying both salary level and choice of post to seniority, the career teacher can count on slow but steady progress toward both goals. But the school system retrogresses just as surely toward educational inequality, as slum schools fill up with inexperienced teachers and/or the transients of the profession and the suburbs attract and hold the better graduates of the system.

Because all of this may seem elementary and appear to be an academic exercise in knocking over strawmen, I offer the following personal experience. Recently, while serving as the outside examiner of a candidate for a doctorate in school administration, I was pressing the candidate to take a position on salary strategy. When he finally "volunteered" the thought that slum schools might improve their competitive position in recruiting teachers by paying premium salaries, one of the examining professors became visibly annoyed that anyone would even consider staffing a school in a difficult environment with mercenaries looking for a "quick buck." He could not seem to see that premium pay would not constrain but rather would enlarge his choice of personnel and open up new options to an innovative administrator. I only wish the logic of the above were obvious and overwhelming.

Is Sex Necessary?

There is, of course, no absolute case in equity to be made for paying men more than women for similar work, including education. But, if male teachers are especially needed and have a distinct role to play—as disciplinarians, father figures, or whatever—and if the outside world offers better pay and more interesting work to men than to women, the schools are in a bind. Education is not free to play the socialist-egalitarian-humanitarian in competition with a total economy which retains large elements of free (and fierce) competition, and still expect to recruit men in significant numbers. Is there some subtle (but not too devious) strategy for attracting more men without unduly violating our sense of equity, not to mention taking on the Women's Liberation Movement? Only one small thought is offered to this end.

The case for operating schools year-round is ordinarily made on efficiency grounds: the heavy fixed costs per unit (per working day) would be cut by about one-third. Loosely put, the extra three months are free. But year-round educational programs could have the invaluable collateral effect of providing summer work for teachers. If, moreover, summer work could be offered preferentially to male teachers or, more generally and defensibly, to heads of families, this would serve as a nutritious substitute for an unpalatable male wage premium. Even if males were not accorded preferential treatment directly, but if summer work naturally appealed much more to male teachers who are typically heads of families than to (largely) single females, a graceful way around the roadblock of equal wage rates would be found.

This same line of reasoning applies to "moonlighting" on evenings and weekend work in adult education, or with dropouts or whatever "human resource development" programs are in fashion. Perhaps our "model city" programs can be linked to our educational structure in such a way as to balance our teaching staffs. To the degree that the educational establishment becomes more responsive to the needs of heads of families, recruiting and holding male teachers will become an invaluable by-product.

Wanted: A Bigger Generation Gap

When we review the time trend in a teacher's salary through his career, we are struck with the anomaly that the terminal salary usually—there are exceptions—is less than twice the beginning rate, and in some places only a little over 50 percent higher. Compare this with the expected career income path of a, say, insurance salesman, whose income will ordinarily triple or quadruple before retirement. If a profession is an occupation wherein serious learning continues throughout one's working life and wherein modest amounts of wisdom that come only with age and experience are hallmarks, then the typical time path of earnings elevates selling to a profession and relegates teaching to casual employment.

The salary structure in teaching does, in fact, suggest manual labor. Work a few years, drop-out, come back-in years later—the salary will be not much different from that earned by the career professional. While this time pattern of earnings may accommodate nicely to labor force participation preferences of unmarried females, its very expediency—responsiveness to the traditional supply of teachers—may well be a major obstacle to tapping new sources of labor: serious, talented career professionals who are or will become heads of families.

Surely one can responsibly advocate higher terminal salaries only by shifting funds—trading them for lower beginning salaries. (Even if we should be so fortunate as to be able to raise salaries all along the time path, we still could choose to give very small or no increases at the beginning end and increasingly larger ones through time; that is, move to a steep time-gradient in remuneration.)

True, the beginning wage may look large in the eyes of many new recruits. But persons with such a high "positive time preference" or "rate of discount of the future" are probably not good risks to become true professionals in socially sensitive endeavors.

Moreover, if one is entertaining an entrapment strategy in the back of his mind, the high likelihood of losing a disgruntled person about the time he becomes experienced and has accumulated family responsibilities should give some pause. The possibility that a disgruntled (underpaid) teacher may not quit is even more disquieting.

Now, to pick up briefly on the main point of the preceding section, the time gradient of remuneration could be made most sensitive to the financial demands on heads of families, and still retain the integrity of reflecting experience, if the salary reached nearly its peak after twenty years of experience, that is, at about the time that the teacher's children were entering college.

"Merit Pay" and "Differentiated Staffing"

"Merit pay" has become such a dirty word in educational circles that a new and possibly related concept has been (self-consciously) brought forth: "differentiated staffing." The teaching profession has, it seems, rediscovered occupational and technical specialization. School administration has long been identified and separated out as a distinctive skill and/or talent; more recently full-time counseling has become routine. Surely, we have always known that we lump under the heading of "teaching" a most heterogeneous mixture of skills: lecturing, counseling, tutoring, record-keeping and miscellaneous janitorial services. But now each of these separate and hopefully separable functions is to be carefully identified, classified and evaluated. What could be simpler than to reward them differentially and, out of a given budget, be in a position to pay more for master teachers by economizing on blackboard cleaning.

As an aside, it is interesting to note that the increasingly specialized medical profession has recently come to wonder whether the integral approach of the old general practitioner did not have some merit, after all. Still, besides increasing productivity and offering potential economies, differentiated staffing has another almost overwhelming attraction: it seems to point to a way of bringing about wider salary differentials in teaching without taking on the "merit pay" issue, and with the support of more objective criteria. Even critics of current teaching practice often agree with the conventional inside position that standards for judging "good" and "bad" teaching are too "nebulous" to make merit pay an operational concept. But, apparently, most would agree that tutoring is a scarcer and more valuable skill than is the grading of examination papers, and *that* in turn is more valuable than cleaning up the classroom.

The great appeal of a concept so firmly grounded in measurable "opportunity cost" is understandable. (The money cost to the school and the real cost to society of commanding the services of a teacher is the value of the alternative goods and services that person could have produced—the *foregone opportunity*.) What could be simpler than to defend a salary of $20,000 or more for a "master teacher" with a Ph.D. in chemistry.

Job evaluation is indeed a most important element in any rational salary structure, but differentiated staffing does dodge the central issue of merit pay. The question there is not should teaching be paid more or less than counseling, but rather should *good* teaching be better paid than *poor* teaching, and should sensitive, sensible counseling be better paid than insensitive or even damaging advice. Hierarchy is not a substitute for competition; structure is not a substitute for process.

Differentiated staffing, as usually described, is a static hierarchical concept. A comprehensive salary structure must address itself to both recognition of performance within rank and to promotion between ranks, and must integrate performance and promotion. How does one progress to "master teacher," that is, acquire a superior function and command a higher salary? Would, ordinarily, the most meritorious "senior teacher" be promoted, opening the way for the "best" next lower rank teacher to move up? If so, how is it that we can time promotion between ranks on rational grounds, but be unable to arrange differential salaries—"merit pay"—to reward talent, skill and effort during the period when that scarce and valuable (and mobile) person is (impatiently?) awaiting promotion. (A period during which a head-of-a-household teacher sees his or her family growing and financial responsibilities mounting, to pick up on an earlier point.)

Often the reader is left to infer, in the absence of direct comment, that a promotion-between-ranks policy has not been thought through and that an educational caste system is implied. Higher degrees in education would most often be critical, if not controlling, in determining role and remuneration. Certainly, the best tutor would not necessarily make a good lecturer, nor would the best lecturer necessarily make a good counselor, nor would the best counselor necessarily make a good tutor—or whatever the hierarchy may be.

But the other side of this coin is that a good teacher may feel forced to become a mediocre counselor because the salary for that work is higher. The only way to avoid this dilemma is to open up the salary range in teaching so wide that, even though counselors earn more than teachers *on the average*, the salary for good teaching is higher than that for mediocre counseling. And we are right back to "merit pay"—judging "good" and "bad" teaching!

Differentiated staffing assumes, of course, differential abilities as well as differential education. Nevertheless, would we have the judging of occupational standing revert to the colleges of education, by default? If I were the principal of a school, I would much prefer experimenting *in the field* with "nebulous" standards, over sanctifying university transcripts. I would prefer *current* evidence from classrooms in which the teacher is a *teacher* to *past* evidence from classrooms in which the teacher was a *student.*

Differentiated staffing commends itself on many grounds: improved classroom quality through greater specialization in both subject matter and teaching techniques (e.g., audio-visual aids); easier recruiting of top talent with wider salary ranges; and economy of lower pay for semi-skilled and unskilled work through use of sub-professionals in the classroom. But as a simplifying substitute for the difficult business of evaluating and rewarding talent, skill and dedication *within* a given function or rank—as a proxy for "merit pay"—it seems, to this casual observer, to be a "cop-out."

THE CYBERNETIC-
ONTOGENETIC APPROACH

Dennis L. Roberts, II

The difficulties of establishing a really homeostatic regulation of society are not to be overcome by replacing one set pattern which is not subject to continual reconsideration by an equal and opposed set pattern of the same sort.

N. Wiener

Probably the most overwhelming imperative that we—humankind—face in this decade of the '70's is the critical question of whether we can master the concept of man living and working together with other men.

To make this a workable reality, we must learn how to make the cities work. Terminology notwithstanding, whether we talk in terms of *urbs, sub-urbs,* or new-fangled *super-urbia,* the root problem is the same: Can we, in fact, create a community in which the manifold interdependencies of people working and living together do not lead to pure, unadulterated chaos?

Mind you, this is not a "challenge" of the type that would be simply interesting and fascinating to consider. We characterize this rather as a *dramatic imperative* of the *we must* variety. Our ability or inability to make the cities work in the '70's is a critical determinant of whether we will even survive to see another decade.

Dennis L. Roberts, II, is president and chairman of the board, Transformind Systems Corporation, and formerly special assistant to the president, Urban Systems Design and Development, Westinghouse Learning Corporation.

If the reader feels that this is possibly an overstatement of the case, we need only remind ourselves that the literature is filled to overflowing with documentation of the symptoms of impending nationwide urban disaster. As S. Barrett notes in a recent issue of *SDC Magazine,* some of the symptoms and problems are:

- Nationwide urban race riots, extensive bloodshed and the destruction and burning of large areas of the metropolitan core.
- Hopelessly jammed freeways forever growing bigger, longer and more numerous, only to result in obsolescence before completion.
- Death-dealing water and air pollution seemingly uncontrollable and getting worse.
- Rapidly expanding slums and deterioration of urban central business districts, fracturing the city's monetary strength— this strength being its only defense against a host of continually growing problems of all types and magnitudes.
- An uncontrolled, chaotic population explosion, its major emphasis taking place in the urban areas projected to contain more than 90 percent of the total population within a few decades.

The problems are many and the problems are real. The problems are technical and the problems are personal; they are educational and sociological; they are psychological, political and emotional. In every case, large numbers of people are affected on a daily basis. As Paul Ehrlich warns: "While you are reading these words, four people will have died from starvation. Most of them children."

In the Douglas Report, the National Commission on Urban Problems tells us again that "The anger of the slums is that of people disinherited from our society." An angry young woman from the slums of East St. Louis told some of the Commission investigators: "You *know* what our slums look like! You *know* we need help there! We have rats, roaches, plaster falling from the walls, we have two-family flats rented out to four and five families with children, and sometimes no bathroom!"

The cities are, at once, hellish and hubs of creativity and excitement. We recall from James Kunen's *The Strawberry Statement: Notes of a College Revolutionary*: "New York is the most exciting city in the world, and also the cruddiest place to be that I can conceive of."

How to diminish or eliminate the hellishness and retain and improve what makes a city great? The problem is enormously difficult, and unfortunately, time is not running out, time has quite run out! The cities are indeed in a race with time—losing miserably—and as Jeanne Lowe notes: "We must run to stand still."

Cycles and Routines

So, what must we do? For openers, we must find ways of getting beyond the *memorandum-report psychosis*. Like the business executive who, upon receiving an idea from a colleague, invariably responds, "Great idea, send me a memo on it," Americans seem to have a thing about commissions and reports. Whatever the national problem or crisis is, we seem to think that the solution is to appoint a commission of "distinguished leaders." The commission invariably performs what it loosely defines as an investigation, the output of which is usually a voluminous report, as if report tonnage were an evaluative index of job effectiveness. This holy report is read by no one, skimmed by a few, and takes its place on the dusty but crowded shelves alongside all the other reports to await another companion—which will be forthcoming just as soon as the next crisis arises.

The data that are already in are more than sufficient to substantiate the fact that this exercise is a poor excuse for problem-solving. Just to mention two specific examples: (a) the Warren Commission Report was little more than a confession of failure. The questions and problems associated with the assassination of John Fitzgerald Kennedy remain unanswered and unsolved; (b) if one wonders about how much problem-solving followed the completion of the Report of The National Advisory Commission on Civil Disorders, one need only read a second report, *One Year Later: An Assessment of the Nation's Response to the Crisis Described by the National Advisory Commission on Civil Disorders:*

> Progress in dealing with the conditions of slum-ghetto life has been nowhere near in scale with the problems. Nor has the past year seen even a serious start toward the changes in national priorities, programs and institutions advocated by the Commission. The sense of urgency in the Commission report has not been reflected in the nation's response.

The report continues:

> The black neighborhoods in the cities remain slums, marked

by poverty and decay; they remain ghettos marked by racial concentration and confinement. The nation has not yet made available—to the cities or the blacks themselves—the resources to improve these neighborhoods enough to make a significant change in their residents' lives.

The final statement of the report echoes what we must know from our own observations: "For a year later, we are a year closer to being two societies, black and white, increasingly separate and scarcely less unequal."

The point here is that scenarios and the organization of intelligence are important and useful if they function as start-up components in a problem-solving system.

Many-Body Problems and Counterintuitiveness

But the problem runs much deeper. For too many years, we have left the solving of problems related to social systems to the whims and notions of politicians, ministers, traditionally trained teachers and do-gooders, a few of whom may be rather well-intentioned, but none of whom are really equipped to generate effective solutions to the massively complex problems that we face in the cities.

Indeed, complexity is the ignored and not understood key. Some time ago, the author was involved in a systems analysis of the education system in the State of New York. In looking at a given community, one discovers that the education system consists of numerous subsystem components, and the number of factors and variables that relate to system performance is large. It is fair to say therefore that an education system is a rather complex system, and engineering improvement in system performance is not a simple task. Simply increasing teachers' salaries all over the State of New York will not necessarily, i.e., with a high degree of probability, result in a more effective education system.

Now, consider that in spite of its complexity, the education system really represents only one component in an urban community system. In addition, there is a transportation system, a health care delivery system, a housing system, etc. The dynamic operation of an urban community system is therefore the result of interactions between and among the thousands of system and subsystem variables and components.

So, we have here what is known in physics as a *many-body problem.* And the real question is: Is there sufficient intelligence available to enable us to solve many-body problems within the context of social systems? In other words, is it really possible to engineer the systematic improvement of a total urban community or a segment of that community, where the number of variables with which we must work simultaneously at least approaches a very large number?

It is not difficult to see why most politicians do not even understand the nature of the problem, let alone have sufficient discernment to discriminate reasonable and workable solutions. Someone should take a fresh look at our selection processes for political candidates. In a later chapter in this book, the author will deal with this problem in greater detail. But let us go on.

The Superficiality of the "Systems Approach"

Now, during the last few years, with the somewhat-less-than-meteoric rise of the so-called knowledge industry, educators who like to sound scientific and scientists who like to sound educated have been doing a great deal of talk about the "systems approach." To begin with, one must allow for and commend the excellent work that has been done by a few people such as Leonard Silvern and Carl Brooks in applying systems engineering techniques to education and training problems.

By and large, however, the systems approach has been rather loosely described as a magical method that somehow dispenses with problems—makes them disappear. This notion is based on a less than accurate conception of both science and systems theory, and seems to rest heavily on the conviction that the use of scientific-sounding terms will produce miracles in social systems. History will attest that this is not the case.

The scientific method, for example, whatever that is, is basically just a way of approaching problem-solving. But to really solve problems in, say, quantum physics, we need to understand the functional relationships between variables, we need to understand relationistic considerations, we need to be able to state the important algorithms and to write down the mathematical representations. This level of analysis is seldom even attempted with social systems.

"Machines a Gouverner"

On December 28, 1948, Pere Dubarle, a Dominican friar, wrote a poignant review of N. Wiener's *Cybernetics* in the Paris journal, *Le Monde*. In that review, Dubarle explored some of the implications of the chess-playing machine that learns and improves its game by experience. He suggested the possible development of a *machine a gouverner,* which would rationally conduct human affairs. A State apparatus might cover all systems of political decisions "either under a regime of many states distributed over the earth, or under the apparently more simple regime of a human government of this planet." Dubarle suggested further that: "The *machine a gouverner* will define the State as the best-informed player at each particular level; and the State is the only supreme coordinator of all partial decisions."

The basic idea behind the *machine a gouverner* is that it collects a considerable amount of information on a particular case, and then proceeds to determine the most probable development of a situation as a function of the average psychology of human beings and other measurable quantities. Now, a number of cyberneticians, including Wiener, would agree that Dubarle's machine does not even compare to the purposive, independent behavior of the human being, and therefore the danger is not great that it would attain autonomous control over mankind. It is possible, however, that such a machine could be used by a man or a group of men to increase their control over others. Or, as Wiener himself points out, there is the danger that "political leaders may attempt to control their populations by means not of machines themselves, but through political techniques as narrow and indifferent to human possibility as if they had, in fact, been conceived mechanically." That problem is very much with us now.

Our point, however, is that we do not propose to replace the current chaos with a *machine a gouverner* a la Pere Dubarle. We would suggest, rather, that what is required is the constuction of a highly sophisticated man-machine system in which the representation for an urban community system is that of a *cybernetic, purposive, adaptive, societal system.*

The Cybernetic-Ontogenetic Approach

The objective here is to create a purposive city system in which all of the subsystem components, education, transportation, etc., are not only harmoniously integrated, but each subsystem is continuously and quite systematically moving to higher and higher levels of effective performance. The net overall result is an urban community system that either constantly seeks higher levels of development or moves closer and closer to a desirable equilibrium state.

One element of such a total plan is certainly municipal government. It can be shown that city government may be viewed as a cybernetic system. For example, Figure 1 shows a simple, conventional feedback control system.

Figure 1
A Conventional Feedback Control System

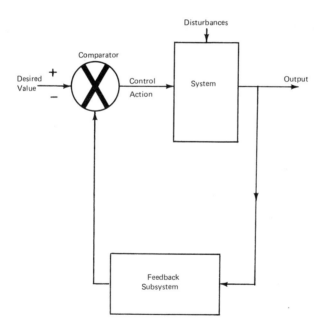

Discrepancies between desired values and measured values result in control action which operates to reduce the discrepancies. An analogous control system suggested by E.S. Savas is shown in Figure 2.

Figure 2
City Government as a Cybernetic System

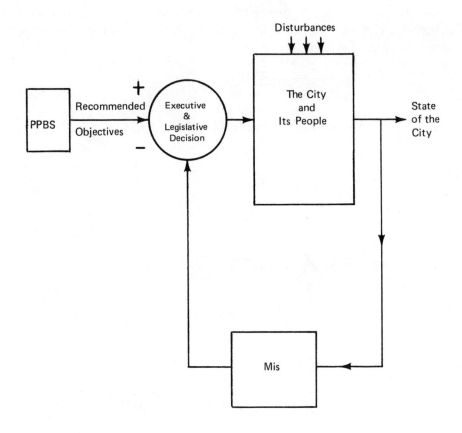

In this analogy, the objectives are set by a goal-setting mechanism represented here as the output of a planning, programming and budgeting system (PPBS). This provides the set points for the city. Feedback is provided by a management information system. Note that if social, political, or economic disturbances can be anticipated, and accommodated by the PPBS, then we can get out of this system a certain degree of feedforward controls.

Savas provides a good analysis of some of the dynamics involved:

The long-time constants and the incredibly involved multi-variable nature of the system require that a very large, very sophisticated, very complicated control device be employed, a device we call government. But it is difficult to keep a large, sophisticated controller tuned up, and there are always component failures, slippage of gears, loose connections, etc. A conventional control-engineering approach to this kind of a problem is to apply minor-loop control and cascade control, although we recognize that complete decoupling of variables cannot be accomplished and that one is sacrificing the optimum that theoretically could be attained by the more integrated total system. Decentralization is an example of minor-loop control. As you know, we have been having some initial troubles in New York City with decentralization as applied to the school system—getting a new controller on-line is always troublesome. Nevertheless, both from the standpoint of cybernetic theory and from the standpoint of good government, decentralization does make sense. Getting decision-making down into the community offers hope of getting more rapid and more effective response of the system to achieve its performance objectives. So, the concept of school decentralization, and of participatory democracy in general, is in accordance with cybernetic principles.

Urban Logistics

The complexity of the task that we are proposing is enormous and fraught with intercomponential relationships and interdependencies. Designing effective education and training systems, for example, is not unrelated to the problem of getting students, workers, businessmen, professors, consultants, etc., safely to and from their centers of activity. The vitality of an effective transportation system and its role in an urban community system must not be overlooked.

In New York City, for example, the transportation system has obviously and distressingly not been constantly adjusted to meet the changing demands of the serviced population. The streets of Manhattan were designed for horses and buggies, and their consequent inability to accommodate limousines and trailer trucks and family cars and motorcycles and, let us not forget, pedestrians is annoyingly reflected in the daily maze of congestion and traffic jams.

During the last 20 years, passenger traffic at New York's three major airports has grown ten-fold. In 1970, 45 million passengers will take airtrips. By 1980, the figure will double. By 1975, every major airport in Southern California will have reached capacity. The solution is not just a simple expansion of existing facilities. Developing an effective solution is a systems problem involving ground transportation, regional growth and planning, political and financial problems, and meshing the system with other components of the urban community. The SCRASS project (Southern California Regional Aviation Systems Study) on the West Coast is an encouraging start in this direction.

Information Theory

Our failure to effectively deal with the urban entanglement is, in large measure, a failure to meet manifold urban needs. Now, if one accepts that a need may be reasonably defined as a state of tension or imbalance which has a tendency to discharge in behavior directed at relieving the tension or restoring the balance, then it can be argued that *homeostatic mechanisms* must be built into the community system components. The understanding of the operation of these mechanisms within the context of a purposive, adaptive system is facilitated by an understanding of such discipline areas as information theory.

Our efforts to solve urban problems should be directed toward the construction of an open, adaptive, purposive urban community system that learns and constantly adjusts to meet changing needs and demands.

Ekistics and Industrial Dynamics

Two interesting efforts at developing a more scientific approach to solving social problems are represented by *Ekistics*—a science of human settlements—extensively applied by the renowned urban planner, Constantinos Doxiadis, and *Industrial Dynamics.*

Ekistics utilizes existing sciences and disciplines to study human settlements in a coordinated, interdisciplinary fashion. The framework for ekistic theory and practice is based on five fundamental elements of human settlements: *Nature; Man,* the basic unit of reference for ekistics; *Society,* the human community; *Shells,* various forms of housing units; and *Networks,* the natural and man-made systems for such functions as transportation, utility distribution and communication.

The industrial dynamics approach to an urban system involves the definition of an urban area as a system of interacting industries, housing and peoples. When conditions are favorable, the interactions between the urban system components lead to the development of the city. As the city develops, and population increases, available land area decreases, and aging processes set in to produce stagnation. As the city moves through the growth phase and into the equilibrium phase, the usual process of development is less characterized by innovation and growth and more characterized by declining industry and aging housing.

Utilizing the industrial dynamics approach, it is possible to organize the growth and goal-seeking processes of the city system into a computer model. The system behavior can then be simulated by the use of a digital computer, which reveals the system's dynamic characteristics. The utility of the simulation is that by modifying the rules that describe how information is used to determine action, it is possible to learn how the behavior of the actual system can be changed.

The Cybernetic-Ontogenetic Approach and Education
How does all of this relate to education? The cybernetic-ontogenetic approach directly relates to the education system in two basic ways:

(a) The politicians and do-gooders have failed to solve urban problems. Furthermore, these groups, acting alone, are just not equipped to deal effectively with many-body problems and complex systems. This means that the education system, if it is to respond to real needs, must begin to generate people and programs that work. This will require the development of new courses, new methods and new techniques for problem-solving in social systems.

Effective ways of problem-solving within an interdisciplinary framework must be developed. The education system must begin to develop what the author chooses to call a *New Breed.* The need is for a new breed of man equipped with the scientific, technological, sociological, psychological, emotional and personal skills to problem-solve in an area that is staggeringly multidimensional and complex. If the education system is itself a failing system, if the educators are continuing to produce graduates who cannot read, how do we move from the level of systems failure to the development of an education system that is even capable of generating the New Breed? This leads us to point *b.*

(b) Just as the urban community can be viewed as a system, the education subsystem can also be dealt with in terms of a systems-analytic approach. But as with the city system, the need is for much more. The author herewith proposes that the cybernetic-ontogenetic approach must be similarly applied to each subsystem component, and in particular, to the education subsystem.

You see, the education subsystem is itself a complex system, and if there is one thing that we have learned from our experience, it is that complex systems are counterintuitive. Most of our intuitive responses are based on experience with first-order negative feedback loops. Negative feedback loops are goal-seeking, whereas positive feedback loops are goal-divergent and have a tendency to exhibit exponential divergence from a point of unstable equilibrium. A complex system such as the education subsystem has a multiplicity of feedback loops, and the internal rates of flow are controlled by non-linear relationships.

So what would appear on the surface to be a solution to an educational problem will usually turn out to be no solution at all; and, in some cases, may even have adverse effects on either or both the short-term and long-term system operations.

Til We Have Built Jerusalem

In a report on the First Annual Symposium of the American Society for Cybernetics, Dr. Frederick Seitz, president of the National Academy of Sciences, made a poignant note:

> Even if we succeed in inducing our society to reaffirm the importance of innovation, there still remains the danger that we will be overwhelmed by the sheer complexity of the problems which lie ahead. It is here, it seems to me, that the field of cybernetics, or what one might call the cybernetic revolution, offers mankind significant hope.

Finally, it must be recognized that our approach to problem-solving in social systems has *always* been wrong. It is more visible now, partly because of the tremendous scale-shift in the magnitude and severity of the problems that we face in the cities. This is a situation that is not totally dissimilar to the conceptual revelations that accompanied the advent in physics of relativistic quantum mechanics.

Every year, the politicians and insincere business and governmental executives play the same game with us; promises, promises, new bills and pills and more rhetoric. But they never really solve our problems. They never really *fix* the education system, and they never really *fix* the cities.

What is suggested by the author's cybernetic-ontogenetic approach is that they really *can't*. The real gut problem is so far beyond them that most cannot even discuss it intelligently, let alone generate and implement effective solutions.

The urgent need, therefore, is for the accelerated emergence of the New Breed: the men who will take existing intelligences and develop even newer intelligences designed systematically to unravel and *solve* complicated problems in complex social systems.

This is the new revolutionary cry. And it must resound and reverberate across the nation *til we have built Jerusalem.*

References

Ashby, W.R. *Cybernetics.* New York: Science Editions, 1963.

Beer, S. *Cybernetics and Management.* New York: Science Editions, 1959.

Bertalanffy, L. Von. *General System Theory.* New York: George Braziller, 1968.

Douglas, Paul H. (Chm.) The National Commission on Urban Problems. *Building the American City: Report of the National Commission on Urban Problems.* Washington, D.C. U.S. Government Printing Office, 1968.

Ehrlich, P.R. *The Population Bomb.* New York: Ballantine Books, 1968.

Ekistics, 24 (145), December, 1967. Athens: The Athens Technological Institute.

Foerster, H. von *et al. Purposive Systems.* New York: Spartan Books, 1968.

Forrester, J.W. *Industrial Dynamics.* Cambridge: The MIT Press, 1961.

Forrester, J.W. *Principles of Systems.* Cambridge: Wright-Allen Press, 1968.

Forrester, J.W. *Urban Dynamics.* Cambridge: The MIT Press, 1969.

Kunen, J.S. *The Strawberry Statement: Notes of a College Revolutionary.* New York: Random House, 1969.

Lowe, J.R. *Cities in a Race with Time.* New York: Random House, 1967.

Raisbeck, G. *Information Theory.* Cambridge: The MIT Press, 1963.

Ramo, S. *Cure for Chaos.* New York: David McKay, 1969.

Savas, E.S. City Halls and Cybernetics. In E.M. Dewan (Ed.) *Cybernetics and the Management of Large Systems.* New York: Spartan Books, 1969.

SDC Magazine, 12 (10), Santa Monica: System Development Corporation, December, 1969.

Weber, M. *The City.* New York: The Free Press, 1958.

Wiener, N. *The Human Use of Human Beings: Cybernetics and Society.* Garden City: Doubleday, 1954.

Wiener, N. *Cybernetics.* Cambridge: The MIT Press, 1961.

Wiener, N. *God & Golem, Inc.* Cambridge: The MIT Press, 1964.

A CYBERNETIC APPROACH
TO EDUCATIONAL FACILITIES
IN THE URBAN ENVIRONMENT

T.C. Helvey

Even the most conservative educators, whose attrition rate seems to be very slow, will agree that education is more than a self-ended task, which every "good" man should pursue, *l'art pour l'art*. They may even agree that education somehow contributes to the happiness of the bearer. But, in general, the impression we as students obtained in our schools a few decades ago was that if we would just memorize historical dates or laws of physics and chemical formulae, if we would learn to use good grammar and spell correctly, and if we would learn the names of kings, presidents and "famous" authors, then education would segregate us from the common man in the street; and if the "schools" would certify this, it would open the doors for us to well-paying positions. And *what else would we want?*

It is gratifying to notice that the trend of the education revolution is much more holistic and systems oriented. This will beneficially influence future teachers, so that not only we "rebels" will preach that education must become an integral and dynamic element of the socioeconomic milieu, which takes into consideration second and third order interactions of cultural, scientific and technological events. The time has passed when a teacher's only contractual task was to develop a nice, basic biology syllabus, to pick a random sample, then rest his

T.C. Helvey is professor of cybernetics at the University of Tennessee Space Institute.

gluteus maximus on his laurels and repeat the same tired stuff year after year. The old argument is, to use the same example, that no matter how the cultural-economic structure of the society changes, all the bones in the birds remain the same, thus it must be taught the "classical" way. This, of course, is nonsense, because if one teaches the bones of the birds only as a glorious inventory of technical terms, then the educational value of this information is negligible. But if the teacher is making these data more meaningful by relating them to Nature as a system, which encompasses human society and its varied dynamics, then the information contributes directly to the growth and maturity of the student who must find his place in an optimized niche in society, along a road of least resistance. Regarding the rapid and continuous change of our socioeconomic environment, education must train modern man to cope with and adapt to this homeodynamism. This approach is valid for all aspects and phases of education, including the bones of the birds.

Admittedly, it is quite difficult to "educate" in the framework of coupled, complex, multi-dimensional systems. First of all, there is the system "student-teacher-environment," which is unduly oversimplified in this form. Then there is the subject matter, which is a dependent variable in the highly non-linear, quasi-random, multi-dimensional matrix of Nature. However, what seems too complex for comprehension today appears simple tomorrow. What was a sacred Elyseum for an exclusive guild of professors day before yesterday, changed to a common playground in colleges yesterday, became a routine subject in high schools today and will move into the grade schools tomorrow. Look at the example of the teaching of calculus. Who expected 20 years ago to see it in the high schools?

Obviously, this trend will continue, and the rate of change in the angle of attack in education depends on the efficiency of teacher preparation. Maybe they won't burn those educators at the stake for heresy who preach and practice the integration of even highly specialized subject matter into the total system of human community.

One of the most severe stumbling blocks to progress is the small number of advanced-thinking teachers. This is understandable because one of the most valuable assets in education is the strong imprint effect of the philosophy and personality of the teachers on their students. Many of today's teachers are under the bias of the teachings of *their* teachers, who got it from *their* teachers. If education were a static, repetitive function, everything would be fine. But human goals, values and interdependencies have changed through the generations, and will do so in the future. Therefore what was emphasized in the schools 50 years ago, and the manner in which it was presented, is not valid today; it will change radically again within the next 50 years.

One would not be surprised if some professional educators and some forward-looking lay school board members would recognize the trend in modern education. This fact would bring into sharp focus the question of the optimized structure of educational facilities. An answer to this question cannot be a prototype, because most interactive parameters can be and are strongly different, depending on the local social, economic and demographic factors. It is obvious that the systems approach to schools in rural South Dakota will have to be different from that of a school in downtown Los Angeles.

But the purpose of this essay is not to design and to provide a blueprint to be copied wherever system oriented teachers are active, but to stimulate thinking along these lines, which leaves much to the imagination and ingenuity of the local persons who are interested in modern education. Some words can be spent, however, on the pros and cons of modelling education.

It is a very un-cybernetic approach to the solution of a problem if we are substituting unknown parameters with assumptions. Those guesses could not be just erroneous, but also misleading in the development of the solution. It is often time-consuming to establish trend values by heuristic considerations; but if the solution requires any degree of fidelity, it is worthwhile facing the inconvenience. Another frequent and, cybernetically speaking, improper attitude in problem solving is the method of reducing the number of parameters, which, in cases like education, may be overwhelming. The argument is that by taking into account only a few seemingly important factors, one can arrive at some sort of a solution, which is given the impressive term, "first approximation." Well, where a "ballpark figure" will do, this could be accepted. However, when decisions are made and implemented based on *a priori* assumptions and a greatly simplified parameter matrix, then inaccuracies will become manifest often in a dramatic manner. Mostly the inaccurate problem solver will get away with it by using some lame excuses, which are generally remote from the exact comprehension of the decision makers, and the project is well underway anyhow. Then the alternative for the decision makers is to hope that by some costly correction the damage could be repaired, although often it is irreparable and irreversible; or, in order to save face, he may say "Well, it is not the best, but let us use what we have rather than to start over again." After all, mostly it is only the consumers' or taxpayers' money that is at stake. And the inaccurate problem solver will use the poor subject as advertising for his services, because the project is *operational*, even if it is far from being optimized. Should he be apprehended for not living up to his responsibilities, his excuse is often, "No one could foresee those events or circumstances." But yes! If he would have spent more time with the use of thorough cybernetic techniques, he could have come closer to optimization. He could have applied heuristics for guesses and developed all possible, even minor, parameters and their second and third order interactions. Then such events as a strike in the steel mill, or a shortage of teachers, or other imponderables with serious consequences could have been taken into probabilistic consideration. Because cybernetic problem solving is based on chance values, there could occur adverse results even if the model is optimized. However, there are now mathematical instruments with which one can arrive at reliable solutions even if the data are unreliable. At any rate, it is beyond doubt that the efficiency of the cybernetic technique, called in some cases "cost-effectiveness," is much higher than the old method, whereby the unjustly called "unquantifiable" parameters are substituted by "hit-or-miss." Yes, even such parameters as human emotions or cultural mixing can be measured—and the values applied to the solution of a problem.

We cannot at this time go into a discussion of the design criteria of the urban educational environment in comparison with that in a rural setting, because this aspect is only one of the matrix planes in a discrete multi-dimensional universe. We cannot even show the four or five dimensional flow-chart here, because if we would single out a given educational microcosmos, like a suburb of Washington, the description of the relevant parameters and their interactions would need much more space than what is available here. All that we can do is to impress and motivate those persons who feel responsible for promoting the best possible education in our society, which is experiencing a population explosion and an austerity program at the same time. Hereby one should bear in mind that the education volume is not only a function of the number of children born, but this figure is significantly augmented by the rapid increase of the number of adults who wish to upgrade a background obtained in an obsolete educational system.

The problems connected with educational facilities require that the meaning of the term "facility" be defined. It can be stated that this term covers the teacher's personality and his knowledge, the paper and pencil, the landscape and the air conditioning of the school building, the comfort engineering of the classrooms to minimize fatigue, the school bus and the lunch, the population characteristics of the parents and the amount of reinforcement they give to extend the work of the teacher, the socioeconomic level of the students and the neighborhood youth structure. All these and many more parameters are inseparable parts of the "educational facility." The development and modelling of a separate single parameter is impossible as long as one requires reliability.

Whether it is the "curriculum" (which is a poor term because it implies that the teacher is hamstrung) or the design of a shelter for educational activities (which means a little more than the term "school"), the goal is to train and adapt man in an optimized manner for life, in its broadest meaning. This idea is not quite new; according to A.N. Whitehead:*

> There is only one subject matter for education, and that is life in all its manifestations. Instead of this single unity, we offer children algebra, from which nothing follows; geometry, from which nothing follows; history, from which nothing follows; a couple of languages, never mastered; and lastly, most dreary of all, literature, represented by plays of Shakespeare with philological notes and short analyses of plot and character to be in substance committed to memory. Can such a list be said to represent life, as it is known in the midst of the living of it?

What this really means for a cybernetician is that EDUCATION is a truly cybernetic system, in which three complex systems are combined; namely, the student, the teacher and the environment. Each of these sub-systems must be thoroughly explored. The lines of communication within the sub-systems, with their inevitable terminal control functions and inductive interactions, must be established before the three sub-systems can be best combined. If this is done properly, and from the system's output, the necessary feedback lines are

*Thanks, John Bremer.

connected to those nodes where automatic error correction (which should include the human components) is most effective, then one can expect good, reliable, goal oriented system operation.

The spin-offs from the cybernetic approach to a system are the properties of self-organization, self-adaptation and self-optimization. In other words, the designer is rewarded by being able to watch his system maintaining, correcting and optimizing itself, with his hands off. Depending on certain design criteria, the homeostatic stamina of the system can be great; thus it would automatically withstand stresses and disturbances from within and from the outside environment. Once it is going, only brute force or proper system manipulation can alter it significantly, and it will counteract, with good efficiency, medium insults from politics or economics. Don't be afraid that after a while such a system may become static, because the dynamic adaptation to a changing milieu is built into it.

The "education" in an urban setting is both an advantage and a disadvantage. The main advantage is the great density and availability of resources; the disadvantage is the significantly greater complexity of the parameters in the state space, as compared with the homogeneity of the rural environment.

In practical application of interdisciplinary and community oriented education, one could symbolize, depict, model, describe, reproduce or substitute various aspects of LIFE and NATURE, and bring them into the classroom. But are those events, people and things in tune with what they represent? Far from it. Therefore the fidelity of the information concerning those spatio-temporal entities which we set out to teach is low. We say, "You see, children, that thing or person I mentioned to you is important to know and it looks, and sounds and feels like this drawing, this model, this record." But it really doesn't. We use cheap, simplified reproductions or models which are easy to explain, even if the mental image in the student's mind is false, and Nature is not like it. For instance, the "atom," that tennis ball around which, on circular wires, little golf balls are rushing in various directions, is not a model for an atom; not even an acceptable approximation. *True, we don't know what an electron looks like. But what is wrong with admitting this to that 6th grader?* There will be a much greater dent in the teacher's prestige when the student advances into college and finds out about all the rubbish he was taught by the li'l ol' lady or the retired colonel, who had acquired a teaching licence.

However, tribute should be paid to those who are the exceptions.

All those pictures, books, etc., are educational facilities. They are mostly static, inaccurate and contain only a small fraction of the necessary number of bits of information which communicate the message from events, people or things to the student for comprehension. The argument, which, in many cases, is valid, is that the teacher cannot bring a mountain range or an elephant into the school; therefore a poor replica must do. But how far is that two-dimensional visual impression from the awareness of the four-dimensional, multi-sensory perception of that cool summer morning in that valley of the mountain range in question?

The new fashion in teaching facilities is not to bring the material to be taught into the school, but to get the students to the natural milieu. There it is much easier, maybe exclusively so, to demonstrate the interactions of seemingly unrelated parameters, which constitute systems output. True, true, one also has to store information and supplement the limited human memory, and for that, at present, the inexpensive and convenient vehicle is still the obsolete, almost 500-year-old invention of Gutenberg, the folded book done with movable type (although today some type is "moved" electronically). But even that can be partially eliminated.

Special congratulations are due to John Bremer and his staff of the Parkway Project in Philadelphia, Pa., who are using the whole metropolitan area as an "educational facility," regarding it as a complex system—with *the student as an integral component.*

Homage should be paid to those pioneers who are successfully experimenting with the "school in reverse," where the students are brought to the "subject matter" in the facility which Nature has provided with great sophistication—those pioneers who try to eliminate the primitive and generally oversimplified replicas to substitute for the real thing.

TRANSFORMING URBAN LIFE AND URBAN EDUCATION

Dennis L. Roberts, II

The young thinkers and doers of the 1970's and some old thinkers and doers have a rather natural and quite justified disaffection with giant corporations, the oft-referred-to military-industrial complex, politicians and educators. The reasons for the disaffection are basic, sincere and deep-rooted; yet, it does not appear that these reasons are genuinely understood by most people.

Briefly, allowing for the negligible exceptions, the politicians are not solving the people's problems, and the educators are not educating. In short, they are not performing. And large corporations and the military-industrialists, on the other hand, pride themselves on the efficiency with which they achieve their objectives; but even if we grant them the argument for efficiency, it is those very objectives that they work so ardently to achieve that are questioned.

The Business of Business

The job before us, therefore, on the one hand, is to transform the objectives of the corporate giants so that money is made in the process of meeting the real needs of the people.

Businessmen should welcome this as a unique opportunity. But, unfortunately, most of them have not yet realized that one of the main

Dennis L. Roberts, II, is president and chairman of the board, Transformind Systems Corporation, and formerly special assistant to the president, Urban Systems Design and Development, Westinghouse Learning Corporation.

reasons the economy lacks luster today is because large numbers of corporate sheep and unimaginative Wall Streeters are sitting around waiting for the business of business to revert to what it *once was*—an "upturn in business."

The fact is, however, that the business of business will never *be* what it *was*. Business in the '70's is an entirely different ballgame, but virtually all businessmen are not aware that this is so.

Institutionalized Failure

Politicians and educators, on the other hand, have a somewhat different kind of problem: even when objectives can be agreed upon, *they generally don't know how to achieve them.* Or, if they do know, they certainly don't *do.*

As we pointed out in our previous chapter in this book, even if one isolates the well-intentioned politicians, the simple fact is that they don't really understand their problems. To expect a solution from these people is fiction; and educators intellectualize a great deal, but the educational system continues not to perform.

What does this lead to? Educators coin clichés and develop devices to explain away or conceal their failures: "These children just don't want to learn." Perhaps 85 percent of a class is three years behind in reading, and there is nothing that can be done about it, so the pass-by-effort device is used to get rid of them and make room for the next group, who will run through the same failure-oriented mill.

In the political area, the underlying assumption is that the serious urban problems in housing, transportation, health-care, sanitation, pollution, education, crime, etc., are somehow a part of life and living. Urban problems are thought to be—like death, taxes and sin—somehow always there. Solving them is seen as being out of the question—a fantasy. So the problems have multiplied every year.

The net result is that this rich and powerful nation has now reached a breaking point. Everyone speculates on whether we will have civil war, open rebellion or revolution. One thing is clear: the business of fooling any of the people any of the time and not really solving their problems cannot continue. For even if the people do not rise up, the problems themselves will engulf us.

The Disturbing Duality

There are those among the readership who may be inclined to feel that this is perhaps an exaggeration. We would suggest that they have been misled by the all-too-prevalent memo-report psychosis and its corollary symptoms. That is to say, the term "crisis" in this country is often taken to refer to whatever situation is capturing the headlines at the moment. As soon as the memos and reports are all written, the assumption is that the crisis somehow disappears.

Admittedly, the phrase "Urban Crisis" has had its share of exposure in the news media. We have not yet done anything dramatic about it, but there are those who feel that the crisis has subsided. As soon as a riot breaks out, we are surprised and stunned. A few people take some token action, and we tell ourselves *that takes care of that.* And we go back to business as usual—until the next riot breaks out. Ernest Erber, in his *Urban Planning in Transition,* describes an important dimension of this problem.

> The rattle of gunfire in the streets of Harlem in 1964 and the incendiary conflagrations that lit the night sky over Watts in the following year heralded the detonation of the social dynamite that had accumulated in American cities, especially in the decades since World War II. The urban problem, no longer confined to the esoteric pages of academic journals, became a daily topic for the press and air waves. The words "Urban Crisis," now capitalized, became part of the common currency of the public affairs dialogue.
>
> The public reacted with renewed surprise and shock at each successive revelation of the extent of inter-group hostility, social dislocation and institutional malfunction. Even those millions of post war relocatees who had moved from the cities—in part in flight from a worsening environment, in part in attraction to suburban amenities—had not suspected the extremity of the cities' plight until the events of the sixties laid bare ever deeper layers of diseased urban tissue—social, economic and physical.

The cities are sick; but they also represent centers of creativity. The real question is, can we cure the illness without destroying the patient? In his book entitled *The City,* John V. Lindsay, mayor of New York, draws a focus on the dual characteristics of a large metropolis:

New York City has more facets of joy and sorrow than any other city. It has the most robust economy in America—and a million people on welfare. It has some of the most beautiful urban neighborhoods in the country—and some of the worst slums imaginable. It has the greatest health facilities in the world—and some of its people die because they do not get treatment. It has more children in its schools than anywhere else—and too many of them do not learn. . . . It has a half dozen specialized high schools that produce the best-educated youth possible, and it has schools where fourteen-year-old children shoot heroin.

It has, in other words, the promise and the danger of urban America: the promise of becoming a still greater city, the danger of falling victim to steady, certain decay.

Confusion

It has become clear that the people on whom we have depended to work out solutions to our social problems are just not able to deliver. Whether this is attributable to a lack of skill and ability, or a lack of will, or a basic confusion over the nature and definition of the problems, the fact is, they don't deliver. Certainly this is quite clear in urban education.

It is important to point out that this fundamental failure even to understand our problems is not confined to the lay public. Large numbers of scholars and professionals who spend a lot of time talking about the problems of the cities don't really understand what is going on.

For example, Edward Banfield, a distinguished professor at Harvard, recently published a book on the urban predicament entitled *The Unheavenly City.*

Banfield claims that urban problems "could not conceivably lead to disaster." He states that some of the problems are "important in the sense that a bad cold is important, but they are not serious in the sense that a cancer is serious."

Banfield gives us the "rising expectations" argument: things are really getting better; they just seem to be getting worse because our expectations are rising. The expectations of some people *are* in fact rising. But "things" are *not* getting better. "Things" are actually getting worse. Our failure to *solve* problems in social systems has for years resulted in severe suffering. As the country developed, population increased, and cities became complex mazes of confusion, we occasionally saw fit to render a little first-aid kind of patchwork treatment. The problems have become enormously compounded.

The problems have become so apparently impossible that the people who should be solving them are beginning to believe that the problems are intrinsically unsolvable. Banfield himself, for example, states that regarding the dropout problem, "there will always be some boys and girls who simply do not have whatever it takes to finish high school."

This is the very same attitude that is used across the country to justify the existence of an education system that produces students who are graduated from high school as illiterates. The educators are not only failing to educate, but also they are *refusing even to admit their failures. They* are failing, but somehow it is the students' fault: they just don't have what it takes!

We have to make a transformation from this failure orientation to a performance orientation. One of the big mistakes that we have made in the socio-political arena is that we have not only tolerated failure, we have also given the people responsible for failures the license to continue perpetrating the injury.

More specifically, in this decade, we will not tolerate the systems failures described above. For years, we have spent billions of dollars on a public educational system that *does not work.* In this decade, parents will insist on performance. And they will spend their money not to sustain a broken-down system but to get performance. And whether getting performance means doing business with a community school, a church school, a Westinghouse Learning school, a General Learning school, a Singer school or a whatever school, the demand is and will be for *performance.*

The question therefore is, can you deliver the goods? If you can, we can do business; if you cannot, we are sorry, but you cannot have the job.

The New Business of Business

As with the failing education system, the people are fed up with our cities in general. In this decade, the people will look less to the traditional politicians and more to individuals and groups who can "deliver the goods." The motion in this direction is already evident.

Private industry has already begun to move strongly into areas such as new-city housing.

Conclusion

We could go on. But the case is clear. The manifold problems of urban education will not be solved by so-called educators. Quite similarly, the complex problems of the cities will never be solved by the traditional politicians and social do-gooders. In both cases, there is often considerably less sincerity, determination and commitment than we would like; even when the *will* is there, we have discovered that the complicated problems that we have asked these people to solve are just *beyond them.* In most cases, they lack the skill and ability and, in general, the equipment to generate effective solutions to complex, many-body problems. And this is what the entire urban predicament is all about.

But, fortunately, there is a rising young group of tuned-in, turned-on professionals who are deeply involved in the utilization of all forms of intelligence, within the context of an economically viable operation, to develop meaningful solutions to the problems that plague the people.

The wisdom of a realistic approach dictates that we fully appreciate the extent to which social problems are political—and they are often extremely so. The mechanics of implementation must be seen as a phase of the solution.

We must be careful not to deceive ourselves. The reality of our predicament is that the urban educational system is not suffering from a few minor ailments which we must one day get around to repairing. The evidence indicates that our urban educational system is a miserable failure. The cities are in the same state. We are not talking about minor problems that make living in the cities something less than comfortable. The problems exist and they are severe. Thus, we must commit ourselves to a program of dramatic change—for nothing less will work.

References

Banfield, Edward C. *The Unheavenly City.* Boston: Little, Brown and Co., 1970.

Erber, Ernest (Ed.) *Urban Planning in Transition.* New York: Grossman Publishers, Inc., 1970.

Lindsay, John V. *The City.* New York: W.W. Norton & Co., Inc., 1970.

Lowe, Jeanne R. *Cities in a Race with Time.* New York: Random House, 1967.

Piel, Gerard *et al. Cities.* New York: Alfred A. Knopf, Inc., 1965.

Changing Functions of
Urban Schools
THE ROLE OF INDUSTRY

Simon Ramo and Leo E. Persselin

Today's crisis of education in the inner city is only one facet of a mosaic which includes problems of poverty, race relations, crumbling tenements and deteriorating tax bases. It is a unique facet, however, in that its resolution can be the prime factor in rebuilding the mosaic.

The urban school of tomorrow can become more than just a place for teaching children in isolation from the realities of the community in which they live. For the individual, the urban school can provide not only more and better education, but also upward mobility through new skills, competencies and understandings leading to expanded employment, enhanced career opportunities and improved social status. For the community as a whole, it can serve as an instrument for restructuring and transforming other public institutions and their services.

If this potential is to be realized, however, an entirely new order of urban education must come into being. To help create this new order of education, a new order of technology is arriving—maybe in the nick of time. It is a technology which will have a profound effect not only upon *how* school is taught in the future, but also upon *what* is taught and *to whom*:

Simon Ramo, industrialist, is vice-chairman of the board of TRW Inc. Leo E. Persselin is a member of the technical staff of TRW Systems Group and an instructor in educational technology at the University of Southern California.

Television and film-based distribution and presentation systems will make it possible for schools at all levels to offer courses which could never be taught before because of previously inadequate resources.

Programmed learning and self-instructional devices will make it possible to offer more complex subject matter at lower grades to students who will advance individually as fast as they are able to learn. Computer-based, individually prescribed instruction will provide lesson-by-lesson, hour-by-hour and day-by-day monitoring and instructional programming for each student.

Entirely new populations of learners will be created—populations of all ages which in the past have been unreachable or unteachable: the physically and mentally handicapped, the culturally deprived and other educationally handicapped for whatever reason.

In the school of tomorrow, technology will greatly broaden today's objective of audiovisual education—"bringing the world into the classroom"—through films, television and other media. At best, this has been second-hand contact with the world, and it has resulted in second-hand education. Technology holds the potential for taking the student out of the classroom and bringing him to the world for learning.

Education will shift away from what is now thought of as the "school" environment for two basic reasons. The first reason is purely economic: it will not be financially feasible to continue building classrooms as they exist today for the burgeoning school populations of tomorrow. The second reason is that technology will make instruction much more effective and efficient if the "school" becomes primarily a source of information—a highly automated instructional data processing and distribution center—while many aspects of learning take place *elsewhere.*

Much of a student's learning could take place in his own home, where he might work with programmed learning materials and electronic data-retrieval devices. Twenty-four-hour communication satellites in synchronous earth orbit could beam thousands of educational channels to millions of rooftop antennas.

Self-instructional centers might be located in neighborhood libraries and other public places whose functions could be expanded to provide a wide variety of resources for independent study. These centers could be served by a nationwide electronic library system—a network providing direct links to the communication centers of universities, institutes of research and other libraries.

Other neighborhood learning centers could be located in rebuilt mills, warehouses and other structures renovated through urban redevelopment programs. These also could be facilities for independent study, which might serve primarily as locales for both large and small group instruction under the guidance of master teachers; individual tutoring by skilled specialists; and expert counseling of all kinds.

Factories, commercial offices, industrial laboratories and other places of business could become community classrooms where students could learn about the real world while the business of that world goes on about them. In effect, *the entire community might become a school for first-hand learning in real-life environments.*

The Role of Industry

The involvement of industry in this educational revolution will be many-faceted. Most in evidence will be an expansion of industry's role as developer and producer of the material resources for education: the computer hardware and software, the audiovisual systems, the self-instructional devices, the space satellites, the electronic library systems and all of the other technical paraphernalia required to transform advanced learning concepts from theory to practice.

Of considerable significance will be those contributions to education derived from expertise gained in other fields. For example, the best of what has been learned about electronic data processing for corporate business administration will be extracted for school administration. Space sciences will be harnessed for space-satellite educational television. New technologies, like those of communication by laser and 3-D displays through holography, will render existing educational audiovisual media obsolete.

Beyond producing material resources, however, industry will play other roles in education which will be substantially new—and a few will be unique. Industry will employ experts in the subjects to be taught, in ways to teach, in the psychology of learning, in the development of educational standards and criteria and in basic educational research.

Industry will assume the role of educator. The "education industry" may well become one of the largest industries in the nation. It is possible to define clearly at least five specific ways in which industry might become more involved both in urban school management and in school teaching.

1. School System Management

Urban education is big business. Several states have budgets for education larger than that of the U.S. Office of Education, and numerous large cities have annual educational expenditures larger than those of many states. The management of large-scale urban school operations imposes requirements on a par with those of the largest business corporations.

Many of the management systems of industry are directly applicable to the large-scale administrative needs of urban school systems. As these needs become more critical and complex with the growth and decentralization of inner-city schools, it will become increasingly cost-effective for industry to take over much of the job of school management.

Financial planning and management; facilities acquisition, development and maintenance; material acquisition and distribution; and personnel administration might all be performed more economically and efficiently under contract to industry than they could be within the school system—while at the same time freeing school administrators to concentrate more of their attention on the vital business of instruction.

2. Cooperative Work Experience Programs

In a cooperative work experience program, academic study is complemented by coordinated on-the-job experience in a business, industrial, or professional setting. The student receives academic credit for his work experience, and may go on to more advanced studies on the same basis as in other programs of instruction.

Productive employment under realistic, competitive, adult-dominated conditions gives good students critical insights into their educational experience. At the same time, cooperative education is attractive to many potential dropouts because of the practical combination of work and study. For all types of students, improved employment opportunities are available as a result of industrial internship.

Cooperative education is the oldest type of formal industry participation in public schooling. Its value and further potential is greatly heightened by the problems of the city and the impact of technology on society at large.

3. Academic Performance Contracting

In academic performance contracting, a school system contracts with a private company to provide instruction to a specified level of achievement within a stipulated period of time. If a student does not reach this level of achievement, the contractor's pay suffers. The contractor may even be required to pay a penalty for each student who fails to reach achievement objectives.

Typically, the commercial contractor is not unduly constrained in his instructional approach. Thus, in accomplishing performance objectives, it is possible for a contractor to use innovative methods of programmed learning, machine instruction, ungraded student groupings, etc., which might otherwise be both slow and difficult in coming into use in the school system.

Performance contracting is one of the newer forms of industry involvement in public education: the first major public school contract was let in the fall of 1969 by a consortium of several school districts in the community of Texarkana, at the Texas-Arkansas border. With a scope of administrative and operational flexibility denied the public school system, private industry may well demonstrate that performance contracting on a profit-making basis can in many situations be significantly more cost-effective than public school instruction.

4. On-the-Job Performance Contracting

On-the-job performance contracting incorporates many of the elements of work experience programs and academic performance contracting. It is unique, however, in that the "student" is actually an on-the-job trainee, a full-time employee of the performance contractor. Also, while the learning program may include basic education and other academic subjects, the primary content of instruction is training for a specific job within the contractor's employ.

The goal of on-the-job performance contracting is to put the trainee to work on a regular basis as rapidly as possible. One approach is for the performance contractor to be reimbursed for instruction only after the trainee is at work on a regular job, and after he satisfactorily remains on the job for a stipulated period of time.

The potential of on-the-job performance contracting has been demonstrated by the dramatic success of the federal government's JOBS (Job Opportunities in the Business Sector) Program. In its first two years of operation, the JOBS Program has resulted in the employment of more than a *quarter-million* formerly hard-core unemployed men and women in the nation's 50 largest cities.

5. Commercial School Operation

School operation as a private enterprise permits a business or industry to combine and maximize the effectiveness of all its varied management, administrative, technological and instructional resources. Because school operation and content of instruction are often related to other activities of a diversified company—e.g., computer training offered by a computer manufacturer—the commercial school environment can be highly motivating. Realistic, job-oriented, attainable learning goals are clearly definable.

In addition to technical training and business schools, some of the newer types of commercial schools include innovative pre-schools and remedial learning centers. Often located in renovated storefronts and lofts, these schools typically offer a supermarket choice of programs designed to fill specific needs. Learning is guaranteed. Unlike public schools, these enterprises cannot fail and stay in business.

Commercial schools can play a vital role in the inner city. Not only can they fill the gaps in public education, but also, in many instances, they might well set the pace for public schooling. As in performance contracting, these schools provide industry with an open arena for demonstrating innovative educational technology.

The five types of industry involvement discussed in the foregoing pages are neither all-inclusive nor definitive. They do, however, present a profile of how the industrial community could play a major role in helping to solve one of the most critical problems of the inner city—the human problem of those who remain jobless, hopeless and permanently poor because all other institutions have failed to give them the education, social acceptance, job skills and work experience which will permit them to become useful, productive and self-sufficient citizens.

Meeting the Systems Requirement

It is quite evident that creation of the urban school system of tomorrow calls for a mammoth reconstruction and transformation of the system as it now exists. Yet, this monumental revolution in education will, in fact, be no more than a single aspect of a technological revolution which will have to be community-wide. The changes in our schools will parallel comparable technological development in every other major sector of the urban community.

Taken within this context, it is clear that the job of creating the school of tomorrow is not only much too large and much too complex, but also much too intimately interrelated with other urban needs to be solved in isolation from those other needs.

Only if reconceived within the context of the city's total needs for all civil and social services—jobs, housing, rapid transit, medical services, urban development and redevelopment—will it be possible for the urban school system to be all the things it must be.

Meeting this requirement calls for the application of the most highly refined skills in systems analysis and systems planning. It is a job for which some segments of today's technological industry are uniquely qualified.

To design and develop the urban school system of tomorrow requires the organization and use of teams of experts in both the technological and non-technological aspects of educational problems. It must include the use of sophisticated techniques for assembling and processing vast amounts of data, comparing alternative approaches, evaluating relative benefits and shortcomings, working out optimum compromises, and making quantitative analyses and predictions where they are appropriate. At the same time, it must take into account judgments based on past experience and the potential of innovations.

The systems experts required to do this job must be true professionals—systems analysts, designers and managers who are well seasoned in inter-disciplinary problems, who know how to relate the many facets of one technology to another and to relate these in turn to all the non-technological, human factors that characterize practical social problems. Many of these professionals are found in industry, because industry provides the large-scale training ground for their development and the massive technical resources required to support their work.

The systems approach to educational planning can provide a

reasoned and total, rather than a fragmentary, look at the community's educational needs and how they might best be met, replacing the confusion and hit-or-miss decision-making of the past with rational, concrete judgments.

Providing the systems expertise for school requirements analysis, supplying the resources for school systems planning, conducting that planning, and managing its large-scale implementation might well be the most important of industry's unique contributions to the urban school of the future.

THE PERFORMANCE CONTRACT:
Turnkey Approach to
Urban School System Reform

Charles Blaschke, Peter Briggs
and Reed Martin

The performance contract is a managerial tool to ensure that results are achieved, yet responsible innovation is encouraged. The approach is simple in concept, although rather complex in realization. With technical assistance, the learning problem is analyzed, and delineation of achievement outcomes required are specified. A request for proposals (RFP) is developed and sent by the local education agency to potential contractors which have demonstrated competent and creative activity in the specific and related fields. The RFP does not prescribe how the job must be done but does establish the performance, financial, administrative and legal parameters of the operation. The RFP requires that the bidder guarantee specific results for specific costs. The confidence that the bidder has in his approach will be reflected in the level of guarantee, social practicability, time and costs. The Management Support Group (MSG), having assisted in evaluating proposals from bidders and aiding in the negotiation stage, presents the strengths and weaknesses of the firms' proposals to the Board, which awards the contract.

The program is conducted with a specified number of students. Incentives are provided in the contract for the contractor to bring each

Charles Blaschke is president of Educational Turnkey Systems, Inc., Washington, D.C. Peter Briggs and Reed Martin are with Educational Turnkey Systems.

child up to specified levels of performance at least cost and to develop a final curriculum and program for which he will guarantee results. The performance contract would require the firm to supply adequate information on programs and dollars spent at agreed upon points in the year. For once, the school would have the managerial tool and flow of information needed to assure that results are meeting policy objectives.

After the demonstration period is completed and all relevant costs, procedures, achievements and performance data have been validated, the performance contract requires the contractor to guarantee an equivalent level of efficiency for the incorporation of the new program into the entire local system. In other words, the contractor accepts the responsibility for providing a reliable, effective, fiscally responsible program; he also specifies the changes upon which success is conditioned. The local education agency then "turnkeys" the instructional program into the school. The MSG may follow through with management assistance services until the school develops its own internal capability to perform the process, usually after the first year of "turnkey" operations.

The Turnkey: Lever for Internal Reform

The turnkey process has been utilized for several years in the field of housing, but its application in education is rather recent. There are significant qualitative differences between a housing and education turnkey project. In the former the concern is a *product,* a house developed by a private corporation, which then "turns the key" over to the owner or the city public housing authority. In education the object of concern is a process which is to be incorporated into an existing institutional framework maintaining high levels of efficiency and effectiveness. Whereas the house, in the former case, meets certain performance specifications, the instructional process, in the case of the latter, guarantees to produce certain levels of performance in the products, which are the students. Even with these differences, some of the reasons for the turnkey process to have been used in housing are analogous to those which make it advantageous in the field of education.

Housing departments in most cities quickly became internalized bureaucracies, creating problems of restrictive codes, archaic specifications, timely deliveries of final products, and increased costs of development and operations. Facing the traditional barriers to innovation, many public housing agencies, under pressures of taxpayers to reduce time and costs, chose to develop performance-type contracts with private builders who would develop new houses or housing developments and then on a turnkey basis turn over ownership to the public authority. In most cases, the private contractor could deal with labor union demands and bypass archaic regulations better than could a government agency. It could also afford to experiment in a responsible and cost-effective manner with the support of the citizenry. If a government experiments and fails, bureaucracy continues to grow; if industry fails, it goes out of business. In addition, where large, but limited, markets were made available through public housing authorities to potential contractors, firms would provide internal research and development resources in seeking innovative solutions, realizing that approaches and sub-systems developed for the first site, a market penetrating tactic, can be amortized in a much larger potential market in the future. The end result was a highly visible demonstration program, which proved to local governments that the existing building codes were obsolete, thus creating political pressures and the leverage for internal reform.

Similarly, as a school superintendent considers the implementation of a new instructional system in his existing school structure, he is faced with administrative and political problems and with the cost of adopting the new system. The performance contract-turnkey approach provides him some answers and a powerful tool for leverage. It gives a school superintendent the basis on which to argue the merits of instituting administrative changes upon the introduction of a new instructional system, which will have been proven in part of his system, thereby increasing its credibility. Additional leverage can be gained by the contractor's alternative levels of guarantee during the turnkey phase. The school superintendent can ask the contractor, for example, to guarantee a specific level of performance within the school system whenever the contractor's program is incorporated therein, *conditional upon specific administrative and managerial changes needed if the level of benefits and the potential of the learning system is to be maintained system-wide.* Hence the school superintendent has enormous leverage when he goes to the school board, the classroom teachers association, or community groups asking for increased dollars to implement a performance budgeting and flexible scheduling system; to train teachers as instructional managers, and para-professionals as teacher aides; or to operate the school on a 12-hour-day basis, etc.

The contractor might be willing to guarantee 90% of the cost-effectiveness demonstrated during the first year's demonstration cycle, if the school system is willing to adopt these changes; if the school is *only* willing to retrain the teachers, then he will guarantee *only* 40% efficiency. Choice is left to the board to select the alternative they prefer—in light of the political, social and economic consequences of their alternatives.

One example of needed changes might be teacher retraining. Many contractors, especially those using self-paced individualized instruction, will utilize para-professionals trained for specific functions, ranging from operating equipment to assisting the instructional manager in administrative chores. To create instructional management capabilities within the classroom, teachers will need to be retrained in attitude, as well as technical proficiencies; and incentives, in many cases, will have to be provided for the new classroom manager to help children achieve as much as possible, given time and costs constraints. The school system will have to adopt some degree of performance budgeting to account for student achievement and costs among the various classroom managers. It might have to consider hiring and training para-professionals to replace some of the professionals who leave through yearly turn-over.

This illustration should point out the need to develop a managerial system and environment that is conducive to the effective application of new instructional technology or learning systems. Therefore, in order to ensure the most effective turnkey of an instructional program throughout a school system, it is necessary to conduct program planning and analysis in the following areas:

Planning Steps

1.   The first basic step is to determine the relative cost-effectiveness of the contractor's program. Because the contractor's program will have been separate from the school with performance accounting procedures, it should be relatively easy to determine the cost-effectiveness of the various program elements, such as the reading program, the work-study program, the math program, the achievement motivation program, etc., if proper cost reporting requirements are specified and fulfilled. To the extent that the first year's operation was

quasi-developmental, the actual allocation of cost will be made more difficult. It is therefore critical that the contractor be required to keep an exact log of specific time allocated to the instructional process and time allocated to the developmental process. Moreover, in the case of the latter, every effort should be made to determine those developmental costs which may be expected to reoccur during the turnkey phase, as opposed to those starting costs which were unique to the specific demonstration cycle and operations. In cases where the accounting for time is not precise, there could be a gross understatement of the start-up costs for the turnkey process, including staff training, development of procedures, etc.

2.   The second step is to determine the cost-effectiveness of the specific school system's relevant instructional program. Allocation of costs is particularly difficult when direct substitution is impossible, e.g., seldom is reading, which lends itself to performance contracting, taught as a separate course at junior and senior high levels; however, one has to make assumptions on the basis of each particular school system's situation. Another judgment is required prior to the analysis in justifying what fixed and variable costs should be included, e.g., if the contractor rents a transportable structure during the first phase but the turnkey will occur in a regular classroom, should the facilities costs be included in the analysis? What school system project administration costs should be allocated to the contractor's performance contract project? The problems are formidable, yet manageable, if proper planning and cost reporting requirements are implemented.

3.   The third step will be based largely upon elements drawn from the analysis of Steps No. 1 and 2. Through cost analysis the actual relationships will be determined between various cost factors, such as salaries, utilization of overhead, student flow and throughput, etc. Over the last two years a general model has been refined which may provide some assistance in determining cost trade-offs and sensitivity analyses. Dubbed the COST-ED model (for COst of Schools, Training, and EDucation), it highlights the critical cost factors and variables in an instructional system and simplifies investigation of the interactions among them.

The analytical concept upon which the model is based appears in Figure 1. Important aspects of the design scheme are: use of "cost per unit of student achievement" as the final summary statistic; relation of all costs to one of a set of "functions" chosen on the basis of usefulness

Figure 1

Design Scheme for
COST-ED Model

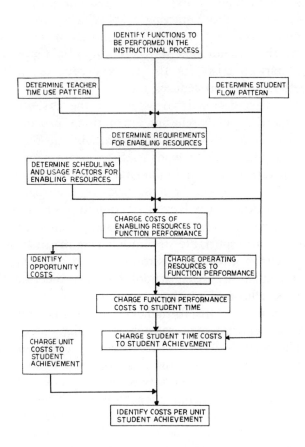

The model relates over 50 isolated cost factors to each other according to the scheme here depicted so that the impact of each on the ultimate "cost per unit student achievement" may easily be identified.

Figure 2

*The Six Modules
of the COST-ED Model*

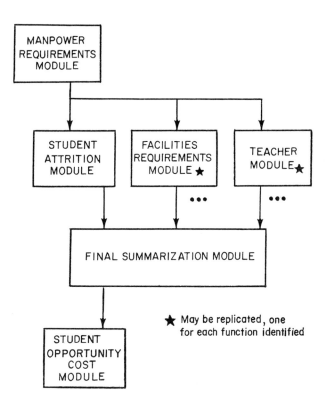

for each application; division of resources consumed into "enabling" and "operating" categories; provisions for the charging of costs on time-dependent and unit bases; and identification of "opportunity costs." The model is designed primarily for use in analyzing the projected economic characteristics of a new instructional system being proposed. Through translation of available budget and accounting statistics into the model framework, however, it may also be employed to discover the underlying economic relationships in an existing instructional system. Figure 2 shows the basic modules which comprise the model, each of which may or may not be used in a particular application, depending upon the organizational environment, the objectives of the analysis, and the level of detail desired.

4.   Based on the results of the COST-ED model or a similar management tool for determining cost analyses of both the contractor-operated program and the existing school system, the various administrative changes and other costs of implementing the contractor-operated program during the turnkey phase into the school will be determined. The results will affect questions such as the following:

a.   Should the contractor's program be made available to all students in specific grade levels or to students in various quartiles, for example, the lowest quartile? The school system should take into account here political implications, such as being accused of implementing a track system in a racially torn school system, or the problem of stigmatizing certain children.

b.   Can the school system justify the expansion and continuation of the contractor's program upon turnkey after the federal funds and federal support are phased out? A properly planned program with specified conditions in the RFP will encourage contractors to develop programs with low operating costs and other characteristics which would tend to allow the school system to operate the program for long periods of time. Key items are the amount of consumable instructional materials, the labor intensity of the instructional approach, the recurring need for inservice and teacher training and retraining, and the obsolescence of equipment and materials plus guarantees of future contracts for both. If proper cost analyses are made and the school is willing to make changes conditional upon the contractor's guarantee during the turnkey, it is very likely that many school systems will be able to justify increased costs incurred during the initial turnkey phases by cost savings elsewhere. For example, if a grade level can be guaranteed in approximately a third of the year, then only a third of the equipment and materials will be required over the entire school year, with an increase of throughput by a factor of three. This will tend to reduce the amortization costs per student achievement, as well as the time involved. If other low cost programs can be provided by the school, such as extended physical education, work-study experiences and enrichment programs, then it is conceivable that the total operating budget can be less after turnkey than prior to it.

Summary

In summary, the turnkey process provides vitally needed leverage for a school superintendent to deal with the requisite costs of administrative charges and political problems created by the infusion of a new instructional and management system through performance contracting. He will have the opportunity to present real and credible alternatives to the school board. The board, in its policy-making position, will know the costs and the benefits of alternative approaches, including the existing public school system, and will understand the conditions necessary for effectiveness to be guaranteed during and after the turnkey. Thus, the turnkey can be conducted in the most effective manner, allowing the school system to realize to the greatest extent possible the levels of performance demonstrated during the first year's cycle.

The turnkey phase is vital if performance contracting is to realize its full potential. Performance contracting is not an end in itself— although it might be thus viewed by corporations seeking new markets and school officials seeking easy answers. Performance contracting is the means to enable our public school system to renew itself by learning what is successful and under what conditions success can continue to be enjoyed.

It is neither wise nor desirable to see our public school system fragmented into endless contractor-operated centers, each competing under so-called performance contracts, with no managerial system to protect the school or the student or the taxpayer. This is what might happen, though, if schools try to jump into this process too quickly. The immediate effect might be the psychological boost that always accompanies participation in a fad, but the long range effect would be to destroy our public schools. For our schools to save themselves, they must adopt a new managerial environment, not just a new technology.

RECYCLING THE
URBAN EDUCATION MELTING POT

Lawrence P. Creedon

Self-flagellation is a mark of the times in public education. It has become commonplace, if not cynically "ho-hum," to observe that the quality of public education—its relevance to today's individual and societal needs, its responsibility for the state of the union and its cost—are of national concern.

The practice of education—whether it be by kindergarten teachers nurturing five-year-olds, or university professors dealing with post-doctoral scholars—is under attack. The criticism is especially severe regarding education in the cities.

In all parts of the nation students are rebelling against the school, claiming it is not relevant to their generation. Parents of minority group youngsters harbor somewhat similar, yet appreciably different, concerns—and are militant in their demands that their children be provided real opportunities for academic achievement. However, they also demand, and as forcefully, that the school organization and curriculum reflect the cultural heritage and values of the particular minority group. Most recently, middle America has been raising the cry that schools "cost too much."

Public education the nation over traditionally has been poured from the same mold. Elementary schools have been organized around

Lawrence P. Creedon is superintendent of schools at Quincy, Massachusetts.

self-contained classrooms. Reading has been taught through the basal reader to three groups: fast, average and slow. Math, and almost everything else, has been taught to the whole class as a single unit, somewhat through the lecture method. In some classrooms, teachers have had two math groups. Spelling has been taught to the whole class in a five-day cycle—from introduction of the new words on Monday, to final test on Friday. Teacher lesson plans have followed the same format, and have been checked by the principal one week in advance. Collaboration between teachers has not been encouraged. Some children have done well in this uniform educational mold, but others—including many living in center-city ghettos—have not achieved at anything like satisfactory levels.

Organizational changes need to come about as the result of faculty (and hopefully student and community) involvement in determining: (1) Who are they as a community of educators? (2) What is their mission? (3) What needs and aspirations are they there to serve? (4) What human and material resources do they have at their command? (5) How should they organize in order to get the job done?

Concern for organization should not be the first order of business. In the five points just listed, organization is where it belongs—in fifth place. However, for the purposes of this chapter, the focus is on organization.

With a variety of organizational options just beginning to emerge in education, and with the legitimate cries of staff, students and parents for more involvement in determining what the school will be, no school system can afford to continue to reflect *one approach* to school organization. Furthermore, school officials must come to realize that what is needed is *not* the tinkering of a few organizational arrangements within the basically rigid existing structure of a school system organized around neighborhood lines. School officials need to realize that parents ought to have the right to send their children to a school that offers an educational program and an organizational design that is *to their own liking.* The old melting pot approach—making all children go through the same kind of education—must give way to an educational system which capitalizes upon and encourages the diversity of the people within the nation's cities.

What needs to be offered within any community are public schools of choice, where programs and organizations can vary to suit the needs and aspirations of students, parents and teachers.

Public schools need to become true community, not neighborhood, schools. In existing neighborhood schools a never-ending conflict goes on between the forces of conservatism on one hand and progressivism on the other. Each pressure group struggles to pull the school in its direction. Why in a nation whose motto is "E Pluribus Unum" is such a struggle necessary? Assuming that common minimum and basic educational goals can be agreed to by all citizens within a given community, why not allow the schools within that community to develop organizational patterns and approaches to learning that can be supported by all members of a particular staff as well as all the students attending the school and their parents who pay the bills?

The public school as a neighborhood school—with neighborhood being defined in geographic terms—should be recycled so that, while it still serves a neighborhood, the neighborhood is defined in terms of common interests and not street address. The several schools of a particular city should reflect the great diversity of interests, attitudes, needs and aspirations of its staff, students and parents.

In some respects the result would not be unlike that which prevails in religious institutions. People do not necessarily go to the nearest place of worship in the neighborhood, but cross geographic neighborhoods in order to form other neighborhoods at a particular place of worship that is based on a sense of identification and community with all who are there.

As public schools move away from the single organizational mold that has characterized them in the past, educators ought to be in the vanguard with those who are exploring alternatives to keeping tax-supported educational institutions contemporary. In a nation that prides itself on its affluence and on its concern for the rights of the individual, students, parents and teachers should be able to choose from among several *tax-supported public schools* the kind of institution in which they, as students, would like to be enrolled; as parents, would like to have their children attend; and, as educators, would like to teach in. The organization of the school—as much as the instructional program—must serve the needs of its diverse urban clientele, reflect the personality of the faculty and have the confidence of the community that supports it.

To acknowledge that there are several emerging organizational patterns through which an instructional program may be offered is to under-state the case. There can be as many different organizational patterns and instructional programs as there are schools. The educators practicing in each school must play a central role in determining the organization as well as the instructional program of the school with which they are affiliated. The breadth of organizational patterns of schools within a single community should, if need be, range from the heavily structured self-contained classroom concept, through the several varieties of departmentalization, teaching teams, non-gradedness and continuous progress, to schools within a school, schools without walls and free schools.

As faculties affiliated with individual schools are allowed to become more involved in forming the character of the school by advancing the goals of the instructional program of the school and by advocating how they ought to organize in order to realize those goals, public schools of choice will become more of a reality.

While being given more autonomy than has heretofore been the rule, it remains reasonable to assume that the parameters of the instructional programs of the schools of a given city or town would fall within an existing learning design developed consistent with a process of systems analysis. The obvious constraints placed on organizational formats should be limited only by the willingness of enough parents to register their children in a particular school. The obvious advantage would be that within a systems approach, framework diversification rather than uniformity would prevail; and student and parental choice in an organizational pattern would characterize the school system, as opposed to conformity to a standardized system-wide organizational structure. Furthermore, the arguments often heard today that schools are either too rigid or too permissive would be tempered as students, parents and teachers chose the school that was organized in such a manner that they could identify with it and through it commit themselves to the pursuit of excellence in education. The end in view would be *public schools of choice for a plurality of publics.*

A heretofore uncommon degree of autonomy would be necessary in order for any given faculty to develop an instructional program and an organizational pattern that significantly differentiated it from other schools. The faculty would need to have some common understanding on learning theory and instructional goals so that they could be instrumental in determining needs in the area of staff, in the purchase of learning materials and in utilization of the physical plant.

Traditionally, classroom teachers have had little involvement in determining who needs to be hired. Faculty members at the building level need to be involved in determining staff requirements. They should share in raising and answering such questions as: Where are the openings going to occur? What are the strengths of the people who are leaving? Do other members of the staff have those strengths so that the particular skill or ability will not be totally lost to students and faculty? What are the known limitations of the existing staff? What skills are needed in addition to those of the present staff? How best can the identified needs be met? Should a one-for-one replacement policy be followed? Would some consultive or part-time resource person meet the identified needs? Would paraprofessionals help? Would a combination of one-for-one replacement, consultive and part-time assistance, plus paraprofessionals be the answer?

Once having assisted in determining who ought to be hired, a building faculty needs to relate the amount of money available for the purchase of staff services to the identified needs.

Every effort should be made to make funds budgeted for learning materials available in a lump sum so that the faculty, working with the leadership offered by the principal and system-wide curriculum specialists, can rank school priorities and commit funds accordingly. These priorities would differ from school to school.

As it is now, funds for learning materials are generally categorized in separate budget accounts, such as general supplies, textbooks, expendable print, and library and audio-visual aids. In addition, and in particular at the secondary level, funds are subdivided by the disciplines and subject areas. In moving to organize public schools of choice, each faculty would need the flexibility, having once identified its own needs compatible with system-wide goals, of being able to commit the funds in its learning materials budget across various categories. For example, if a major thrust forward is planned in reading, then quite possibly all available funds will need to be directed to this particular discipline.

The third category where faculty members need to make a grass roots input is in the area of building alterations that are in support of the instructional program. The same opportunities for faculty involvement in staff and learning materials selection ought to be available for instructional renovations. Teachers need to share in determining what renovations are needed in order to move the instructional program forward, in direct consultation with the particular communities served by the schools.

We shall then be on the way toward utilizing the vast reserve of diverse talents which have been largely ignored in the single-mold approach practiced traditionally in our urban schools.

SELECTING OBJECTIVES AND MEDIA FOR URBAN EDUCATION

Leslie J. Briggs

The current effort to overcome school racial segregation reaches its peak or crisis stage hard upon the heels of a crest of upheaval from the separate but related problem of student revolt and demand for curriculum reform. The first problem involves the question of where students will attend school; the second involves what they will learn and how they will be taught.

While both crises could have been alleviated by doing more about the problems earlier, such periods of turmoil remind us of the necessity to be prepared for both emergency and long range educational planning.

These twin emergencies call for quickly getting the students located in schools, and quickly making needed adjustments in curricula and methods of teaching. As pressing as these immediate needs are, this paper is addressed to the long-range aspect of curriculum planning. The goal is the attainment of curricula which will be free of racism, responsive to the concerns of the students, and directed toward the solution of present problems and the building of a better society. Neither generation—the students' nor the teachers'—has the wisdom to undertake the task alone.

Leslie J. Briggs is professor of educational research and head of the doctoral program in instructional systems at Florida State University, Tallahassee.

It is proposed that a logical sequence of events for the needed long-range planning is something like the following.

Stage 1

Begin in clarifying national educational goals, in broad terms. Such very general goals are often organized under the categories of education for: (a) citizenship; (b) occupational competence; (c) use of leisure time; and (d) lifelong learning as a need in a dynamic society. Such citizenship goals must attend to current social problems; the occupational goals must take account of the changing nature of the jobs people will need to perform in the future; the leisure time goals must involve consideration of values and their place in the learner's efforts to mold society, as well as to adjust to it; and the need for continued learning after formal education calls for a re-evaluation of teaching and learning methods in the schools. This step in the process somehow must involve citizens and students, as well as specialists in planning and prediction, on a nationwide basis.

The above national goals need then to be recast into a local educational policy for the specific urban area, with a broad base of involvement of the entire community—students, parents, employers, government officials, etc. Here attention is given to the nature of the city and the society desired for the future, and the kinds of knowledge the younger generation will need if it intends to achieve such a society. Community action is thus taken to define the place of the urban area in the national picture foreseen for the future. Goals for the city as a whole are translated into functions its citizens will need to perform.

Stage 2

Based on the conclusions from the above two steps, more specific educational objectives for the urban area are defined. Here specialists function to help translate local goals and policy into local curriculum objectives which would achieve the goals resulting from Stage 1. Thus the first stage is the *what* and the second is the *how*. In arriving at the local educational objectives, great care must be taken to permit the student to exercise the maximum decision-making role of which he is capable. This role presumably would enlarge with the age of the learner. A ten-year-old does not have the knowledge to translate his goals into successful paths for reaching them. An eighteen-year-old has more of such capability. Within the broad classes of goals mentioned earlier (citizenship, occupation, leisure time and lifelong learning), attention must be given to the question, "Who is in the best position to select the specific objectives, which if attained by the learner would enable him to reach this type of goal?"

For those objectives which should be specified by someone other than the student himself, who is to do it, and how is he to do it? These questions are addressed to some extent in the closing section of this article.

Stage 3

Once the specific objectives for the local schools are selected, educators can proceed to translate these into curricula, materials and methods of teaching.

Dyer (1968) and Lessinger (1968) have indicated that today's young people wish earnestly to clarify their own values and to obtain the kind of education that would enable them to fulfill the roles they determine in the kind of society they would like to build. Helping them do this suggests a need for radical revisions in both the content and the methods of the curriculum, such as a combination program of work/study/and service. Much learning then would take place outside of school. While the school would provide learning resource centers, discussions and the like, often the reason the learner would appear at school would be to get "checked out" in his progress toward his goals.* Also, it would appear, the medium of television would be employed more widely, both because the medium itself creates dynamic social involvement (McLuhan, 1964) and because timely messages concerning ongoing events can be handled thereby (Dale, 1969).

While some of the more revolutionary educational objectives in a reformed curriculum may at once suggest use of media such as television, work experiences, internships in social roles, etc., selection of media for the tool knowledges and skills may systematically be accomplished by use of any of several models for the design of instruction (Briggs *et al.,* 1966; Tosti and Ball, 1969; Postlethwait *et al.,* 1969; Esbensen, 1968).

For both the conventional and the innovative educational objectives which may result from reform, a new way of structuring the

*Robert M. Gagne, personal communication, February 1970.

curriculum appears needed. Everyday life is not divided up into "subjects" but into functions to be performed. Curricula organized along conventional discipline lines may obscure rather than reveal the real-life value of the content being taught. One type of possible structural change is illustrated in the science project which organizes the instruction to develop intellectual scientific process skills rather than in terms of current (but rapidly changing) science content (AAAS, 1967). One further step could involve focusing upon contemporary problems (pollution) which are amenable of solution by application of both natural and social science.

Stage 4

After the above steps in long-range planning are accomplished, a city could then most appropriately design the school buildings, staff plan, transportation plan, etc., by which a defined *student population* is to achieve *stated objectives* by *selected media* of instruction. Materials and all other learning resources are then designed, developed and improved in effectiveness by the tryout and revision procedures now called formative evaluation.

Stage 5

A plan for continuous (summative) evaluation is then designed to provide a self-correcting (closed-loop) educational system. While current practice often includes "one shot" summative evaluations of a new curriculum, *longitudinal studies* are needed to reveal the longer-term effects of education in relation to the stated goals. Studies like the classic study by Terman for superior students need to be extended to the entire range of students in order to provide continuous monitoring of the effectiveness of the system. While student protest and revolt may reveal some of the most glaring failures of education, a more accurate assessment of outcomes is needed once reform is undertaken. Protests may signal the need for reform, but they do not alone show how it may be accomplished. The latter is everybody's business, and it requires continuous evaluation and program modification.

Who Can Do What to Help?

Specialists of many kinds are clearly needed at each of the above stages for long-range planning for educational reform, and the entire citizenry also needs to be involved. Space permits a few comments on some aspects of needed actions.

The learner himself. Some students are now vocal in protest, but all need to be invited to join in the planning of their educational goals. Flanagan (1968) has indicated that any "systems approach" to education must pay close attention to the learner as a component of the system. The learner's help is needed to change the single word "relevant" to a definition of "relevant for what purpose and for whom?"

Local opinion. It is strikingly evident that local citizens want a voice in *where* their children go to school and *how they get there.* It is less evident that citizens are also prepared to contribute to the identification of what the children should be taught once they get to school. New educational leadership is needed to define ways and means for focusing local opinion more effectively upon this aspect of local determination.

Local opportunities. Even though people are more mobile than earlier, many children are still likely to live and work as adults in the cities in which they were educated. It is, therefore, realistic to expect that job and other opportunities and needs for change in the locality should become input data for determining educational objectives. Thus job descriptions, of both existing and predicted future jobs, are also input data.

Findings of Policy Research Centers. These centers are charged with predicting what society will be like in the future, so that these predictions can be inputs for curriculum planning. These centers thus must estimate the changes expected in the future, and they must recognize that children now in school will help determine the future. Thus the circular action of *present forces, new curricula, school effects upon children,* and *children's effects upon the future* all must somehow be taken into account. While there is a substantial probable error in such predictions, the needed curriculum reforms can hardly be brought about without this forward look as one basis for long-range planning. Automation and other consequences of a dynamic society do complicate the making of future curriculum decisions, but they also call attention to the need for a kind of curriculum that produces problem-solving ability and the ability to control or adjust to rapid change.

Academic and professional societies. These groups traditionally have had a strong influence upon school curricula, but often this influence has reflected more the past history of the discipline than an anticipation of future needs. The focus has too much been upon preserving the structure of the content and not enough upon the social responsibility of the discipline. But new currents are beginning to develop among these organizations of specialists whose help is desperately needed.

Curriculum-development projects. Innovations in both content and method often become introduced into school practice *via* the new curriculum project. Typically, scholars, teachers and administrators, along with the educational technologist, form teams to translate new curriculum theory into classroom practice. These new curricula come into general use through publication of new materials and by special workshops for teachers.

Research in skill development. While much of educational research deals with teaching methods rather than objectives or content, the study of how skills needed for various purposes can be developed can result in suggestions for the detailed content which may be used in the process of cognitive skill development. Research also can offer similar data in the affective and psychomotor domains.

Observation of classroom activity. This is actually a part of the continuous evaluation mentioned earlier. Once a new set of objectives has been defined, it is necessary to watch (and measure and/or record) any unexpected or unforeseen results of presenting the instructional situation and materials. These observations can help to identify new (and attainable) goals, and to note objectives which turn the learners on or off. Revised objectives may then be developed.

Advisory councils to school boards. Typically, the local school boards, being composed of lay citizens, cannot alone effectively coordinate public opinion and school policy. They lack the technical competence to judge *how* the school should implement the desires of the citizens, yet they also may be reluctant to accept the superintendent's judgment concerning this.

It is recommended that special advisory councils or panels are needed at the local level, just as they often function at the federal level for finding solutions to complex problems. Such councils should be composed of a cross-section of the kinds of leadership important in community affairs, and of educational specialists having knowledge in fields beyond the possible training of the school administrator. Such (appointed) councils would be advisory to the (elected) school board, and they would provide information, recommendations and results of special studies to either the board or the administration, upon request. Their function would be to provide studied recommendations on how the educational goals of the city could be attained.

Personal and national commitment. Platt (1969) has suggested that if we as a Nation responded to our current social problems as National Emergencies, just as we responded to the military emergency in World War II, we could avoid many potential catastrophes that appear to threaten us. He outlined how science could participate. Thus if we had the will to take the emergency actions we took then, we could find a way to solve our most crucial problems. This would mean a personal commitment of almost every citizen, and sweeping changes in the rate that governmental actions are taken.

This writer is unable to spell out in detail the techniques and actions that various groups could adopt, given the will to do so, to bring about the needed educational change. But it seems abundantly clear that there are three stages of work ahead: (a) get the schools integrated; (b) make emergency curricular revisions; and (c) undertake long-range planning for educational reform.

Educational technology is a process—not a set of equipment. While it, too, would have to overhaul and enlarge its concepts and procedures to meet the need, it does represent one of the sources of people and know-how that can make a contribution toward the achievement of the needed reform.

References

AAAS Commission on Science Education. *Science—A Process Approach.* Washington, D.C.: American Association for the Advancement of Science, 1967.

Briggs, L.J., Peggie L. Campeau, R.M. Gagne & M.A. May. *A Procedure for the Design of Mutimedia Instruction.* Pittsburgh, Pa.: American Institutes for Research, 1966, Monograph No. 2.

Dale, E. *Audiovisual Methods in Teaching.* New York: Holt, Rinehart, and Winston, 1969.

Dyer, H. Accountability of the Public Educators. In *Technology and Innovation in Education.* New York: Frederick A. Praeger, 1968, pp. 102-112.

Esbensen, T. *Working with Individualized Instruction.* Palo Alto, California: Fearon, 1968.

Flanagan, J.C. Project PLAN. In *Technology and Innovation in Education.* New York: Frederick A. Praeger, 1968, pp. 113-120.

Lessinger, L. Education in a Time of Ferment. In *Technology and Innovation in Education.* New York: Frederick A. Praeger, 1968, pp. 93-101.

McLuhan, M. *Understanding Media.* New York: Signet Books, 1964.

Platt, J. What We Must Do. *Science,* 1969, *166*, pp. 1115-1121.

Postlethwait, S.N., J. Novak & H.T. Murray, Jr. *The Audio-Tutorial Approach to Learning.* Minneapolis, Minnesota: Burgess, 1969.

Tosti, D.T. & J.R. Ball. A Behavioral Approach to Instructional Design and Media Selection. *AV Communication Review,* 1969, *17*, pp. 5-25.

URBAN SIMULATIONS:
New Ways to Teach
and Learn About Cities

Peter House

Urban simulations, in which students participate in developing "real cities," are multi-faceted teaching devices. By focusing on one thing, the city, they can open up for the student a whole world of understanding about the economic, political and social interrelationships that make up our modern life. Since today's concerned student demands that his courses be relevant, these simulations help make both the outside and his classroom worlds more meaningful to him.

For the teacher, urban simulations or games can provide a stimulating framework in which to teach the urban environment, which is essentially a multidisciplinary subject in the social sciences. Urban affairs, current events and social studies are neither government, sociology, economics, nor history courses—they are all of these and more. Simulations synthesize these subjects as they pertain to the urban environment into an interdisciplinary experience for teachers and students.

Moreover, urban simulations set up a "real," dynamic environment by abstractly representing an urban setting in the context of a game. While such simulations may vary in their particulars, they generally have students play various roles or decision-making functions, following game procedures based on already learned concepts. In learning how

Peter House is president of Envirometrics, Inc., Washington, D.C.

cities operate, students ascertain what interrelationships take place in reality, judge the pertinent facts of the problem, and discern the cause-effect relationships. After considering alternative strategies, they make appropriate decisions about their city.

Urban games or simulations differ mainly in how much, if at all, they use a computer to coordinate the interrelationships in the game. Games which use a computer tend to be more comprehensive, while those which do not rely on a computer tend to be more general. Some games are intentionally designed to concentrate on one aspect, for example, economic, of the urban milieu.

A Different Kind of Laboratory

No matter what their complexity, urban games are designed to let the student participate in a laboratory situation, much like a physics laboratory. In both cases, he learns for himself. These games can bridge the gap between theory and experience. The student discovers for himself how learned theory can be related to courses of action rather than feeling that he is being "spoon-fed" by his teacher. Games also give the students immediate responses to their critical decisions, a self-validating method which is not often present in the typical classroom situation.

The teacher's role expands also. In the post-game recapitulations, for example, it is up to him to identify limitations in the game, highlight significant moves made during the game, identify concepts illustrated during the game, and discuss alternative strategies.

New Role for Games

While games and simulations in the business and military fields have a long history, similar techniques in the social sciences are much newer. Social science simulations can be divided into three types: mathematical models which exclude human players, role-playing games in which operations and various win strategies are defined in the model for the players, and systemic games, where strategies and situations are developed by the players within the particular model played.

Led by the economists, social scientists in the research and education fields attempted to particularize and quantify their specialties by turning to purely mathematical simulations based on elaborate computer programs. Mathematical simulations were limited in what they could describe, could not be used successfully in education, and did not explain the social (i.e., human) aspects of a field under study.

Social scientists turned to role-playing and systemic gaming simulations to study and teach about the interdisciplinary aspects of complex social environments. Gaming simulations were designed to teach young persons in primary, secondary and college-level classes.

While some of these games were more like parlor games than interdisciplinary teaching tools, simulations were developed which were better abstract replications of their subject matter. Most of the stronger ones were simulations of a city or urban environment. They have been used in education and training as a step in the planning process or as a means to study the environment to better understand the complex interrelationships.

Urban Needs Encouraged Urban Simulations

Urban simulations as research and educational tools are among the most advanced simulations due to several complementary forces. First, as this country becomes almost completely urban, the need to study, analyze and understand the urban environment increases. Second, a comprehensive method was needed to learn about cities and how they function, since traditional disciplines cannot successfully cope with such a complex environment. Third, the advent of computer technology allowed complex simulations to be designed and developed. Fourth, the growth of city planning departments helped to spur the idea of "the city" as an educational subject. Fifth, the federal government, through grants, encouraged universities to move city planning and urban studies out of the civil engineering, architecture and sociology departments into their own fields of study. Sixth, the federal government, in starting urban renewal and other programs, made the study of the urban environment a necessity.

The foregoing factors were underlined by national events during the past decade. Cities are becoming noticeably less fit for habitation. Traffic congestion, inadequate schools, riots and rising taxes are incessant signs of inefficient urban sprawls and lack of integrated planning. National concern over pollution began with foul urban air and has expanded to cover the environment as an ecological system. Cities again stand out because as entities they are upsetting the natural environment both as consumers of the earth's bounty and as producers of unregenerative by-products.

Some social scientists turned to developing comprehensive, interdisciplinary methods to study the complex phenomena.

Urban Education Changes

Concurrently, with the advent of computer technology, among other reasons, the educational process was changing its emphasis from the traditional rote-learning approach to techniques where the student was more involved and self-motivated in his own learning. Computer assisted instruction, language labs for foreign language instruction, ability group learning techniques and educational games are examples of this emerging trend.

"Urban Affairs" and community project courses are appearing on more course lists in schools across the country. Educators, realizing the importance of topical subjects to effective teaching, are advocating the use of such courses on the secondary level. Some urge their inclusion in elementary school curricula.

On a university level, involvement has been a definite trend in the last decade, albeit most noticeable in an extracurricular fashion. Antioch College is a well-known example of intertwining outside work experience with classroom studies. It is planned at Stevenson College of the growing Oxford-plan University of California at Santa Cruz that each class will spend its junior year abroad in an underdeveloped community.

For educational involvement in the urban environment, simulations seem to offer a dynamic, comprehensive way for students to comprehend the complex interrelationships before they formulate solutions or go out and attempt remedies when they leave school. Gaming and simulation laboratories at the University of California campuses in Los Angeles and Santa Barbara and at Cornell, Michigan State and Clark universities are important examples of the recognition of simulation.

Urban Simulations

The following are descriptions of some of the more sophisticated simulations dealing with the urban area.

The Northeast Corridor Transportation Game, developed by Abt Associates for the Department of Transportation, simulates the Northeast transportation corridor and includes the economic, political and social factors which go into decision-making by state and local politicians. An important feature focuses on regional transportation within a regional political-economic framework.

Another game built to handle metropolitan decision-making using a wide variety of factors is METRO by Richard Duke and others. METRO handles a wide variety of parameters which affect decisions in an urban area. The model leans heavily on early urban renewal and transportation studies by mathematical model builders with considerable experience in modeling transportation systems and land use. Duke added political and role simulators which are quantifiable factors in the urban area. Frank Hendricks and Clark Rogers at the University of Pittsburgh arrived at a similar technique independently. They built a mathematically based computer simulation called the GSPIA game containing a large number of roles. Both models combine mathematical and gaming techniques.

Carl Steinitz and Peter Rogers of Harvard University designed a game called *Urbanization and Change* with many variables to be considered when looking at decision-making in a metropolitan area. Teams are given different responsibilities to perform within a simulated southwest sector of the Boston region. For example, four teams decide the location of industry, open space, recreation, residences and commercial centers. Four evaluation teams make decisions governing local politics, finance, pollution effects and aesthetics. A team responsible for transportation decisions links the allocative and evaluation teams together. Conflicts are negotiated among teams. The game is an excellent approach to teaching the problems of consensus planning in urban and regional development. The model also takes beginning steps toward the inclusion of aesthetic criteria.

The Community Land Use Game (CLUG) developed by Allan Feldt of Cornell University shows a new and different gaming approach. Feldt calls his game a "systemic model," which means that there are neither roles nor mathematical simulation built into the game. Rather, the system is defined, and players become the decision-makers. The players may develop all situations from a blank board. The systemic feature is very important for the simulation of environment systems.

BUILD, a community development simulation game by J.A. Orlando and A.J. Pennington of Drexel University, is a role-playing computer game designed as an educational tool and to assist in advocacy planning of new communities within the city. The model is designed to represent the typical situation of extreme deterioration of housing, services and rapid physical transformation, but with a major emphasis on preservation of community values. *BUILD* is intended to provide a mechanism for persons to actively participate in the decision-making process. The structure is relatively simple, with roles divided into the three broad classes of business, government and people (residents).

The *LOC-series* of six urban games (which deal with locational behavior in the urban environment) were developed by Barry M. Kibel while at the University of California at Berkeley. *LOC-1,* for example, focused on the individual economic decision-maker in his role as selector of economically viable locations for setting up or expanding activities. The game was designed so that these decisions would become increasingly imitative, as opposed to innovative, as the locational process of all the actors matured, and increasingly rational (profitable) spatial patterns would develop over time. A relatively simple board game was employed to simulate the above tendencies. *LOC-5,* a relatively simple game, was designed to portray a political process in a typical urban community. There were two general types of players in the game: the community players (those who placed chips on the game board) and the politicians (those who altered the values on the game board by their decisions). The *LOC*-games can readily be adapted to fit most existing political structures, and the hidden board values can be selected so as to simulate—at least in a rough fashion—any urban area.

The *CITY* series of computer-assisted models developed by my company are further attempts at urban teaching models. The *CITY MODEL* has three interrelated sectors: government, with an executive and councilmen who plan city growth, prepare budgets and set tax rates; economic, in which private property owners and businessmen develop and operate eleven land uses of various densities; and social, in which workers and residents in three socioeconomic classes vote, allocate their time and boycott stores and jobs, played in two-hour rounds simulating a fiscal year. From 50 to 200 decision-makers may participate in running "real" cities of from 250,000 to 1.5 million population, either in a gaming facility or via teletype connected to a computer.

Developing Trends

These models illustrate a trend toward a comprehensive simulation of the urban environment. With development, these models can lead toward an urban laboratory which would not only teach urban concepts but could be used for planning as well, including, of course, educational planning on a broad scale.

While the foregoing simulations are sufficiently complex to be realistic, they are the first and second generation products of an evolving expertise. It appears that future urban simulations for education will probably be of two kinds: specialized simulations focusing on a specific area which will be simpler and thus less dependent on a computer, and general holistic models encompassing an "environment," which will be complex and largely computer-activated. The first type will be designed for short-term learning goals and will have fairly rigid playing procedures. The second type will be reasonably flexible in that the teacher could use them to highlight various concepts and ideas, and easily adaptable in that one discipline (i.e., government) can prevail one time and another discipline (economics) another, thus showing the interrelationship between them.

As a simulation builder, I believe that there are many advantages to simulations. For the student, the advantages are involvement, immediacy and self-motivated experience within a realistic educational experience. For the teacher, there are the same advantages plus comprehensiveness of method and flexibility of approach. The disadvantages would seem to be that, in computer-assisted simulations, an initial fear of computers must be overcome, the "gaming" aspect may be allowed to overshadow the educational purposes, and simulations may take a long time to get their "lessons" across since there are no discernible "right" and "wrong" answers as in conventional educational techniques.

All in all, simulations appear to be the most meaningful and economical use of modern technology to bring the outside urban world into the classroom so that students may later take their comprehension out into that world to solve its problems and change it. That is one of the things education is all about.

TECHNOLOGY IN THE
URBAN EDUCATION MARKETPLACE

Francis A. J. Ianni and Peter S. Rosenbaum

Educational Technology: An Apparent Failure

There has been an audible diminution in the once-shrill claims of the technologist that, given the opportunity, he could revolutionize American education. In contrast to the initial excitement over the promise of educational technology, a pervasive feeling of skepticism is now discernible when this promise is compared with the relatively unimpressive results of technological innovation to date. Nowhere is performance failure so glaring as in urban education, where the problems have been most urgent.

The primary targets of vendors and their spokesmen are the teachers. Their claim is straightforward and to the point. Teachers, both from the standpoint of training and aptitude, are technically and emotionally not prepared for the technological era. Their resulting insecurity, it is felt, gives rise to resistance to innovation and thus blocks the use of technology in the schools. The attack on the teachers is usually followed by a complaint about the fiscal priorities of the consumer population. If education is to be improved, the vendors maintain, someone must be willing to pay for the improvement. If school administrators are not willing or are unable to reassign fiscal priorities, then the federal government should step in with more money

Francis A.J. Ianni and Peter S. Rosenbaum are with the Center for the Study of Systems and Technology in Education, Teachers College, Columbia University.

and subsidize the new developments in technology. If those concerned with education would only think in terms of "value," e.g., the increased efficiency of educational operations, vendors add, the dollar amount would not seem so staggering. Confronted with the possibility that educators may not want their products, the vendors blame the educators for failing to specify their needs, for if they would only say what they want, industry would supply it.

For the potential buyers, on the other hand, the undercurrent feeling about the failure of technology in the schools is simply that so-called *educational* technology has not been designed with the schools in mind.

Of the above explanations, only the last one, the buyer's, do we see as holding the key to the fulfillment of the still present potential of technology in the schools.

Educational Technology as Product Failure

From the marketing standpoint, the fact of 1) the nonpurchase of equipment, 2) the nonuse of purchased equipment, and 3) the use of equipment for purposes other than those intended by the manufacturer, i.e., "misuse," would be seen as a simple case of *product failure.*

From the marketing point of view, the good sense of the consumer is axiomatic; it is assumed; it is that to which the salesman strives to appeal. Accordingly, the fact of nonpurchase implies at least that the potential buyers of technological products do not value them sufficiently highly to justify their purchase. Nonuse implies that the applications of the products confront the user with more trouble than they are worth; hence, use of the product is discontinued. "Misuse" implies that once the user has the product, he can find better things to do with it than those suggested by the manufacturer. From this perspective, the technologist's speculation that the educator is incompetent or irresponsible, that he doesn't know what he wants, that he is not ready for technology, is as unproductive as attributing the sales failure of a new dishwasher to incompetence in housewifery.

The Causes of Product Failure in Urban Education

The manufacturer of home appliances develops his product conceptions within a detailed understanding of what goes on in the home. His products are intended to facilitate certain well-defined, carefully delineated tasks. The same observation could be made about the manufacturer of office products. In both instances, the products are conceived with the hope that they will be clearly recognized by the consumer as *system facilitators* and, as such, will be valued highly enough to be purchased at the price offered. Examples of system facilitators are numerous and obvious—copying machines, adding machines, dishwashing machines, sewing machines, etc. A product which is intended by its manufacturer to be functional but which is not seen by its prospective buyer as facilitating some process in which he is in some way engaged is a product that will not be purchased.

Consider the non*purchase* of educational equipment. Typically, the promotional campaigns for technological products have promised improvements in various aspects of education, but we argue that these putative benefits have in general not been seen by the educational consumer to be significant enough to justify the expense. We do not know whether the incidence of product failure in education exceeds the norms established in other markets, although we suspect that it does. To whatever extent industrial performance in education has been atypical, we would identify this atypicality as the failure of industry to understand the systems in education that technological products might reasonably be expected to facilitate.

Consider the non*use* of equipment. A very great deal of technology has indeed found its way into urban schools, although only in the lower price ranges and with scarcely the good will that a company generally likes to attribute to its clientele. In many instances the installation of technological innovations has resulted from bequests in the form of federal or state aid, or both. In other instances, certain types of apparatus became fashionable and, when not unreasonably expensive, were acquired out of a quite natural desire to be up-to-date. Much more rarely, buyers discerned a meaningful application and bought the equipment.

There are many reasons why equipment that finds its way into city schools is not used there. First, equipment acquired through bequest may fall into disuse for much the same reason that the proverbial gift from one's mother-in-law finds its way into the darkest recesses of the attic. Second, equipment bought for mere prestige value does not have to be *used* to achieve its purpose. Third, the nonuse of products intentionally purchased for an advertised application may arise because of the purchaser. When the use of the product does not make life easier, and provides no compensatory rewards, then, inevitably, the device ends up in the closet.

Finally, consider "misuse." Have you ever used a stapler for a paperweight or bent paperclips to hang Christmas tree ornaments? These experiences suggest that, from the user's point of view, there is no such thing as misuse of a product. There is only *his* use, which derives from his needs and his ingenuity in finding ways to improve life as he has to deal with it. Misuse is a misnomer, although the discomfort of the technologist with the use of his products for other than intended purposes is readily understandable. For one thing, this circumstance creates for him a great deal of uncertainty about how to maintain and broaden his market base, for, from the product planner's vantage point, misuse has to be viewed as synonymous with nonuse and as resulting from the same causes.

In the broadest sense, product failure in educational technology can be traced to the mistaken marketing assumption that the educational market is an abstraction known as education, as somehow apart from the administrative, supervisory and instructional staffs of the schools and their respective patterns of activity. The potential success of any educational product can be measured in terms of the extent to which this product does in fact improve the circumstances, the facts of life, of the school environment. In our experience, the typical process has been to take a piece of equipment designed for military, industrial, governmental, or other functions and to "find" or "invent" uses for the device and its attendant support systems in a new market called education. This has often been done with a certain flair for inventiveness and even some real concern for the essential uniqueness of the educational system; but it has missed the fundamental point of systems design which holds that the adequacy of a subsystem depends largely upon its compatibility with the global system in which it is to be integrated. The basic question should be "what are the uses to which education can put technology" rather than "what are the potential applications of technology in the educational system."

Systems in Education

The most productive approach to the analysis of systems in education is to imagine a series of behavior patterns institutionalized over time as the logical outcome of seeking to maximize personal, social and, at times, educational goals. The educational system can be viewed, in short, as a complex code of behavior, a structured set of rules of the game which regulate all activities within that system. What are the systems like in education? Three elements are illustrative of the systems defining urban education.

1. Contingency structures in the schools. Extrapolating from a fundamental precept of psychological learning theory, the activities of both teacher and learner are conditioned by the emotional conse- quences associated with the performance of these activities. Another way of saying this is that the alternative selected from a set of different courses of action is inevitably that course of action valued most highly by the actor. This observation is very significant, for it suggests that the value systems and the domain of possible actions governed by these value systems are *the* critical factors in determining the successful entry and use of a new instructional tool or technique.

For example, there exists a textbook called the *Harbrace College Handbook*, a handbook of English grammar, which is used in college freshman composition courses. This book is far and away the best seller in the field, with yearly sales, it is rumored, of better than a quarter of a million copies. This book has been a huge success for more than twenty-five years. The book is a well-designed product in many ways, but one alone foretold its success. The author organized his book in categories corresponding to the major classes of composition errors, and he provides a letter code, e.g., *sp., frag., agr.,* etc., which was pasted on the inside cover along with associated page references. The genius lay in the system of classroom use. English professors, interested profession- ally in literature and literary analysis, impatient with grammar and the necessity of devoting classroom time to its discussion, could now simply identify errors on students' compositions with the code symbol and instruct the students to correct these errors at home with the help of the handbook. (Teachers really *do* favor self-instruction, provided this doesn't mean that they will lose their jobs.) Introductory composition in colleges has become a different course as a result of this innovation and, needless to say, no significant handbook since has omitted this feature.

What are the values associated with teaching activities in urban education, and how are these values related to the outcome of deciding among alternative courses of action? How can these values be appealed to for the purposes of systems innovation? The answers to questions such as these are clearly essential to any product design strategy.

The values of the urban child, apart from those of the urban teacher, are also important, for the nature of the student's responses to an innovation will be a dominant factor by which the teacher will decide whether the innovation is a blessing or a curse. If the students seem to be constructively engaged and are not disrupting any aspect of classroom life, that's favorable; discipline problems, confusion and chaos are unfavorable.

A learner's degree of involvement with his assigned activities is widely considered to be the preeminent predictor of whether the student will learn what the activities are supposed to teach him. Learner values are central to this degree of involvement, for the learner's attitudes toward his work depend upon how he perceives and interprets the consequences of undertaking courses of action in his immediate learning environment. Important in this regard is the fact that gold stars and letter grades are frequently not seen as worthwhile incentives by large numbers of students, notably those from urban minority groups. Hence, these outcomes can do little to promote a favorable attitude toward such intrinsically unappealing activities as drill and practice. However, numerous experimental projects, using such incentives as money, options, enjoyable activities such as movies, juke boxes, free time, games and others, as well as incentives in the form of intrinsically engaging learning activities such as photography, have produced changes in students' behavioral development that are obvious to the naked and untutored eye. Because of the instructional power (in the sense of water behind a dam) that derives from cleverly conceived incentives incorporated in an effective contingency management system, a comprehensive description of educational systems would have to contain a delineation of existing contingencies in the school environment in order to be considered complete.

2. *Child-rearing antecedents of learning.* If we rule out, for the moment, the many correlative studies of intelligence and family background or child-rearing practices and personality, little systematic study appears to have been given to the child-rearing antecedents of cognitive behavior and even less to the development of teaching strategies based upon such knowledge. And yet, if we consider learning as resulting from an exploration of alternatives, and one of the functions of teaching as the economizing of random activity in such choice, then any attempt to encourage such exploration through

teaching either by machine or by teacher must take into account the fact that the propensity to explore is heavily conditioned by the cultural context within which it takes place. That is to say, every culture and every subculture within it produces predisposing factors which develop or inhibit the child's drive to explore and to consider alternatives. An adequate urban pedagogy, then, must understand these factors and develop an instructional strategy that builds upon or vitiates the predisposing factors.

3. The social and cultural environment of the city. The present mood of so-called diagnostic teaching, which places strong emphasis on the individualization of instruction, posits certain optimal conditions for instruction: specifically 1) that the teacher should operate within a system which identifies and exploits the experiences and encounters which predispose a child to learn, 2) that the information to be transmitted must be based in a careful structuring of knowledge that is optimal for comprehension and that is presented in the properly programmed sequence, and 3) that the system must comprehend the nature and pacing of rewards and punishments. Here again the systemic context becomes a critical factor. Obviously, such cultural elements as the degree of intellectual stimulation the child receives from his family, the value his subcultures place upon learning, and the richness of his cultural environment will influence his predisposition to learn. The structure of knowledge and the mode of presentation are heavily dependent upon the complexity of society. For example, our own society instructs the young by abstracting—telling out of context—while the instructional mode in primitive societies is one of showing by action. Understanding the influence of these systemic elements is important to the improvement of the teaching-learning confrontation.

A proper exploration of each of these and other areas would, of course, require enough search strategy and generate enough data that computer technology would be essential to an adequate treatment, but this is not what we have in mind; rather, as we proceed to develop a conceptual scheme of systems in education, producing in the process a blueprint for a new model for urban education in schools and communities, we should also proceed to extract performance characteristics for a new technology which will optimize the values we may posit for the system. We must assume from the outset that none of our present techniques, approaches, or equipment is safe from obsolescence and then ask the tandem questions of what it would mean to optimize educational systems and how technology can best serve these ends.

Finding the Systems in Education

The successful identification of the systems in education has eluded most of those who have pursued it. Most who have failed, have failed by virtue either of insufficient effort or incorrect assumptions about the defining characteristics of the market. The prescription for a more productive approach is straightforward: Go find out. With hope that the educational technology industry will take this step, we would offer some advice on the positives and negatives of different sources of information about education.

In the past, industry has relied quite heavily on the intelligence generated by the professional staffs of the schools of education. Although these schools are identifiable with public elementary and secondary education—it is in these schools that the personnel of the public schools acquire their preparatory professional education—there is some risk that would have to be attached to the indiscriminate use of the information obtained through these sources. For better or worse, most professional school of education educators know relatively little about the everyday life of the public school classroom, in the sense of feeling intuitively the priorities that are felt by public school personnel. The school of education staff is not, in any significant measure, part of the fabric of public school education. Professors of medicine are medicine as a profession, but professors of education are not education. The exception to this admonishment arises when the school of education is itself the projected market, in which case tactful queries may elicit valid and useful information about the workaday lives of the people who inhabit this environment.

Perhaps the best advice received by industry in the past has been that provided by the academic technologists. Certainly, their opinions would be much less biased by vested interests than those of the professional educationists. Also, their technical competence, coupled with their familiarity with certain aspects of education, makes the academic technologists useful in preparing specifications that can readily be translated into hardware and software systems. However, they do not know education intimately. Moreover, they are inventors as a rule, who, because intellectual freedom of creativity is a necessity of their trade, oftentimes overlook the special constraints under which product development proceeds in a competitive market situation.

The safest and potentially most productive route is to go directly to the schools, as businessmen, and find out what they are like and what is important to the people who populate them. The first thing that such an exploration will unearth is that "the schools" are actually different groups of people with different functional responsibilities and problems.

1. Teachers. Teachers are the people whose best exemplars lead the hardest life in the schools, with the possible exception of the students. Teachers work enormously long hours, mostly under emotionally trying conditions. In varying degrees, teachers see themselves as being hounded by principals and supervisors, shortchanged by administrators, threatened emotionally and sometimes physically by students, undermined by parents, betrayed by politicians and hampered every step of the way in the execution of their responsibilities by arbitrary administrative rules. In schools that have problems, these are the facts of life for teachers. The priorities and behavior patterns of teachers take their form within this framework of conflicting forces. These forces largely determine how the classroom will be managed and what procedures will be followed. They determine how available time will be utilized. They determine the form of viable instructional systems. And, consequently, they form the systemic framework in which technological system facilitators must be conceived.

The teacher's experience with technological innovation has not, in general, been a good one. Teachers have seen a variety of educational revolutions pale because the strategists focused on dramatic but piecemeal attempts to improve some part of the educational system. For examples, one might study the very promising curriculum revolution of the 1950's and 1960's, and the teaching machines, from the simplest roller operated programmed instruction device through computer assisted instruction. Teachers are unimpressed by the interpretation of educational technology as a revolutionizing force for the learning process in urban areas and, indeed, the realist would have to conclude that no technological innovation for classroom instruction in the urban schools is particularly promising if it does not take into account the systems relations defining the teacher's role in such environments.

2. Principals. The one computer technology that seems to have taken root and thrived is automated scheduling of classes and room assignments. This eventuality could have been anticipated because the application facilitates what is perhaps the major managerial chore for which the principal is responsible, although there are others. By the same assumptions, interest in grade report generation could have been anticipated. On the other side of the coin, the relative unattractiveness of automated record keeping cannot be viewed as surprising since detailed record keeping is not viewed as a vital school function and, consequently, the automation of the procedures associated with this function would generally be assigned fairly low priority. New technological applications for the urban school setting that would be attractive to principals are numerous, as an extended visit to the schools would surely reveal. For example, particularly in urban schools, principals are harried by their inability to communicate rapidly with school personnel. A well-designed school communication system would facilitate many administrative processes which are now executed in a manner analogous to sending mail from Boston to Washington by stage coach.

3. Superintendents. To the superintendent, cost savings are quite possibly more important than labor savings. In the rapidly escalating battle between the community and the personnel of the school, the superintendent must both lower costs and raise costs, both of which are hard to do. And he must soothe conflicting emotions. He will avoid any alternative that so much as hints of pressure on the tenuous equilibrium between the servants of education and the subscribers. The superintendent will always balance cost against its effects on school personnel and the community with respect to both financial and emotional considerations. Although the superintendent can be the buyer of technology, he is himself rarely the user. Typically, he is a user only of office products.

4. Community. Directly through taxes and indirectly through influence on school personnel, the community is a major force in public education. Although the home educational products market shows some promise of developing, the residents of the community, because they pay the bills, are most important in their roles as subscribers. The extent to which the school is providing what the community wants will often determine the amount of money that will be available for expenditure on educational products. The story is told of a school superintendent who was able to convince his community to pass a school budget—by guaranteeing that the students in his school would offer their seats on the bus to elderly persons. Knowledge of community interests is essential to market development in education in general, and this is even more true with regard to urban education.

5. *Academia.* Academia, although not a part of what we think of as public education, nonetheless influences public education. Sprinkled through the academic world are a few educational engineers who can interpret such developments as psychological findings about learning or the analytic techniques for quantifying and modeling systems in terms that can prove relevant to public education. Often, these people will express their thoughts in a convincing manner and, as a result, will generate intellectual waves that occasionally reach down to the schools themselves. A major example is the research done on operant conditioning, which has led to the not astonishingly successful development of such products as teaching machines and programmed texts. Sometimes styles of this sort endure for years; more often, their duration is fairly short. It is thus important to understand academic fashions well enough to pick out the significant.

6. *Students.* As purchasers of products, students don't count for very much. Even when they themselves are buyers, e.g., the purchase of textbooks in college, their options are few. However, the ease with which a teacher will be able to manage the operations of the classroom depends very much on student behavior. Thus, the behavioral and value systems which characterize students in educational settings—in urban situations very little is known about such things—will determine many features of what the teacher will see as a system facilitator and also the prospects that a product once purchased will be used.

Particularly at the college level, students are acquiring a more direct influence on the way in which educational funds are spent, and the direction of this development should be watched and its significance ascertained.

A Caution on Changing Systems

No piece of gadgetry is successfully introduced into the schools without concurrent changes in the behavioral organization of the school, in the role of the teacher and in the functioning of the institution. This is because the very introduction of something new into the system irrevocably alters the domain of possibilities over which the values of school personnel operate. A successful innovation often comes to dominate the local environment within which it is to be used. As a consequence, a new pattern of values and priorities begins to emerge. Thus, it is important to ask the converse of the question put so often by educational technologists about the potential applications of technology in education and to ask rather about the undesirable side effects. For example, under certain proposed schemes, it would be argued that the advent of certain technological innovations will drive up the cost of teachers with only dubious compensatory benefits, an effect not to be accepted lightly or without meditation. What is suggested by such possibilities is that systems innovators should root their work in an ecological frame of reference in order to assure that actions taken in the present will reflect, to the best available knowledge, the most probable educational priorities of the future.

Conclusion

What we are proposing here is that industrial product designers might profitably explore a range of questions couched in a conception of urban education as a system, as a dynamic set of changing behaviors which can be holistically conceptualized; and then they might proceed to develop a technology that grows out of the needs of this system. This awareness is now developing slowly in education. What is necessary is some theoretical and engineering framework within which to project this new approach. It is only in such a context that technology can be meaningfully developed and applied, both as a product and as an advance in education.

Failure to accept these suggestions as imperatives explains in most cases technology's inability to make any drastic change in urban education to date. In urban education, as elsewhere, no one is going to build a better mousetrap until we find better ways of catching mice.

ESTIMATED COSTS OF COMPUTER ASSISTED INSTRUCTION FOR COMPENSATORY EDUCATION IN URBAN AREAS

D. Jamison, P. Suppes and C. Butler

Introduction

As this paper goes to press, a number of institutions in the United States will have acquired several years' experience using computer assisted instruction for compensatory education in both urban and rural areas. Our purpose in this paper is to discuss, on the basis of this experience, the short-term potential for using CAI in urban schools. Our discussion will focus almost entirely on the drill-and-practice programs developed for grades K through 6 in elementary arithmetic and beginning reading at Stanford University's Institute for Mathematical Studies in the Social Sciences. The reason for this focus is that the curricular content of these courses has already undergone a number of phases of development, and is now in a position to be readily implemented by any of a number of different computer systems.

Before proceeding to that discussion, however, we feel it important to place in context the potential role of CAI in the urban schools. Research over the last four or five years has given us rather systematic evidence about three aspects of that urban context. These are:

1. Information concerning the costs and effects of a number of compensatory education programs, primarily those financed

Dean Jamison and **Patrick Suppes** are at Stanford University. **Cornelius Butler** recently completed his doctorate at Stanford.

by Title I of the Elementary and Secondary Education Act of
1965.

2. Information concerning the relationship between school
    inputs and various measures of school performance; this is
    information obtained primarily from the data in the 1964
    Equality of Educational Opportunity Survey.

3. Further information from the EEO Survey concerning the
    state of inequality of educational opportunity by social class
    and race.

We shall discuss each of these briefly in turn in order to place in
perspective the potential role of CAI in urban compensatory education.

For a number of years, over a billion dollars a year has been spent
by the federal government on compensatory education. The reasoning
behind this large expenditure is that, as President Nixon (1970) put it,
". . . the most glaring shortcoming in American education today
continues to be the lag in essential learning skills in large numbers of
children in poor families." Unfortunately, however, as the President
goes on to say. ". . . the best available evidence indicates that most of
the compensatory education programs have not measurably helped the
poor children catch up." The President's assessment is shared by a large
number of members of the academic community. For example, Arthur
Jensen (1969) begins his well-known article on IQ and scholastic
achievement by asserting that "Compensatory education has been tried
and it apparently has failed." Jensen then supports this assertion by a
number of references to studies by the federal government. H.
Piccariello (1969), in concluding a large-scale evaluation of 1966-67 and
1967-68 Title I funded reading programs, found that in these programs
a child had a 69 percent chance of no significant change over a peer in a
control group in terms of his reading ability and, given that he did show
a significant difference, that he only had a slightly better probability of
having that difference be positive rather than negative. The programs
that Piccariello evaluated were those that had been funded at a higher
than average level.

There are, however, two lines of argument against those who
would conclude from such studies that we have accomplished little or
nothing by our Title I programs to date. J. Hunt (1969), in a rebuttal to
Jensen, argues that the instances of compensatory education being
examined by Jensen (notably the Head Start program) were not

appropriate types of compensatory education. Hunt argues that, in this case, compensatory education did not succeed because it was not tried. If instead of the type of play school that Head Start seemed to represent typically, the students had been given intensive drills in cognitive skills, Hunt feels that there would have been enduring gains in achievement on the part of initial underachievers. Hunt's arguments are supported by Professor H. Kiesling's (1970) study of a number of successful compensatory education programs in California. Kiesling's approach was to examine in detail those compensatory education programs in California (funded by ESEA Title I and California Senate Bill 28) that had proved very successful. What he hoped to do was to isolate characteristics common to all those programs that would differentiate them from less successful compensatory education programs. What Kiesling found was that there are three aspects of the successful programs that appear over and over again—(1) thorough planning and program coordination, (2) thorough inservice training of teaching personnel with respect to local instructional problems, and (3) individualization of instruction. The implication of Kiesling's finding is simply that, while compensatory education may on the average in the past have been unsuccessful, there is no reason to continue the average practices of the past. We should instead tailor our future compensatory education programs around those that have *shown success* in the past. Kiesling then presents a number of paradigmatic compensatory programs for both reading and arithmetic and provides a detailed cost analysis of those programs. We shall return to his cost and effectiveness estimates in a later section of this paper in order to compare the more traditional compensatory education techniques that he considers with computer assisted instruction.

A reason that compensatory education may have been a failure on the average, other than, as Kiesling argues, that generally it was incorrectly organized, is that what goes on in the schools has very little effect on achievement of students. Arthur Jensen in the article previously cited is implicitly making this point when he argues that the reason for the failure of compensatory education for black students is that they have been equipped genetically with a lower IQ. The importance of IQ in learning is, he argues, sufficiently large so that additional schooling resources devoted to disadvantaged students do not show a large or lasting effect. The U.S. Office of Education report on the *Equality of Educational Opportunity* prepared under the leadership of James Coleman (and popularly known as the Coleman Report) also comes to the conclusion that what goes on in the schools is of secondary importance compared to what happens to the child outside of school. The Report's somewhat discouraging conclusion is that various school inputs such as teacher skills and classroom facilities have relatively little impact on the achievement of the child. These conclusions have been subject to vigorous debate in the four or five years since their initial publication; for an overview and rebuttal to this literature, see Coleman (1968). Nevertheless, since publication of the Report there has been an increasing consensus that the input factors in the schooling process, as traditionally defined, have a good deal less effect on the outputs than had been thought previously. This has caused a focus of attention on outputs and what causes outputs to change instead of, as before, simply trying to improve schooling by increasing the quantities of traditional inputs.

While the somewhat pessimistic findings of the Coleman Report concerning the potential of affecting student performance by changing school inputs would seem to argue against large-scale expenditures on something like computer assisted instruction, there are good reasons to believe that the range of inputs considered in the Report was not sufficiently broad to enable us to say anything definite at all about important changes in instructional technique. For example, in their criticism of the Coleman Report, Bowles and Levin (1968) assert: "The findings of the Report are particularly inappropriate for assessing the likely effects of radical changes in the level and composition of resources devoted to schooling because the range of variation in most school inputs in this sample is much more limited than the range of policy measures currently under discussion."

A third important aspect of the context into which CAI would be put for compensatory education in urban areas is the widespread inequality of opportunity for students in those areas. Various notions of the meaning of the word "inequality" and the extent of its existence are examined in some detail in a recent study by Stephan Michaelson. Michaelson's results are summarized in a recent paper (1970). Michaelson used data gathered by the Coleman Survey for one large eastern city—which he calls Eastmet—and argues very persuasively that there is large-scale inequality in educational resources devoted to blacks as opposed to whites and, within either racial group, an increasing level of resources devoted to children of increasingly high social class. An important purpose, clearly, of CAI in an urban context would be to reduce these racial and social class differences in access to educational opportunity.

In our preceding comments we have briefly surveyed what is now known about the effects of compensatory education, about the relation of educational inputs to educational outputs, and about the extent of inequality of educational opportunity in the urban United States. We conclude that while there does exist large-scale inequality in access to educational opportunity, we now know enough to be able to provide a reasonable level of compensatory education for those who have been subject to discrimination in the past. While from the Coleman Report we have probably learned that varying the levels of traditional educational inputs probably scarcely affects the level of output, we cannot conclude from that Report that new compensatory techniques—either of a conventional variety or utilizing a technology such as CAI—would be ineffective. In what follows we shall report on some of our previous experiences to show, on the contrary, that the arithmetic drill-and-practice program developed at Stanford University has proved to be effective as a compensatory education device. While it has not produced the very dramatic achievement gains that the best programs surveyed by Kiesling have, its cost on an operational basis in the relatively near future appears to be markedly less. These cost projections will be discussed in the final section of this paper. Before turning to a more detailed discussion of CAI we would, however, like to discuss requirements for providing the financial resources (on the order of $100 per student per year) that would make its introduction possible on a wide scale.

Financing CAI for Compensatory Education

Kiesling (1970) estimated that his paradigm compensatory education programs would cost between $212 and $354 per student per year, depending on whether an appreciable amount of the compensatory program had to be carried on outside the regular classroom. In the final section of this paper we estimate that the cost of providing arithmetic CAI to a student would be about $50 per year; to provide both arithmetic and reading would cost a little over $100 per year. These figures represent increments in the cost of educating a student that amount to appreciable fractions of the initial amount spent. In a time of tight budgets in general, and particularly for school systems, it is important to address the question of where the money will come from.

A very natural possibility is to reduce the amount of time the student spends in contact with a professional classroom teacher. One to three hours of the child's school day could be spent on organized play, unorganized play, watching *Sesame Street*, listening to music, sports, etc. These are all activities requiring only a paraprofessional monitor (perhaps a mother working half time, or a college student) and having a large student-to-monitor ratio. The students would be faced with frequent decisions about how to spend their own time, and encouraged to follow their interests.

Simple and obvious as such an approach to cost reduction appears, it would no doubt entail major and difficult administrative restructuring. We bring it up here for the following reasons:

1. The Coleman Report and subsequent related research consistently suggest the ineffectiveness of traditional school inputs in producing scholastic achievement. Yet few people seem willing to act on the implication of those results—that *cutting back on these traditional inputs is unlikely to seriously impair production of scholastic achievement.*

2. In order to increase our understanding of how school inputs affect achievement, we need both to vary those inputs downward as well as upward and to provide means for altering the mix of inputs to include new technologies.

3. The most important reason is the one we began this section with: Education's budget is stationary and compensatory education, costly. *Only by cutting back on some school inputs can we increase the level of others;* it is incumbent on those who propose any compensatory education program to face this problem squarely.

Another approach to financing CAI or other new technologies of education is to monitor and evaluate with much greater care the programs supported under the Elementary and Secondary Education Act of 1965, especially Title I. For the short term, effective use of these funds seems to be the most realistic possibility for a major implementation of new educational technologies.

Operational CAI in New York City:
Cost and Effectiveness

Our purpose in this section is to present results from an ESEA

Title III funded ($2.5 million) program in CAI in New York City. The New York system used an RCA Spectra 70 computer that served 192 student terminals located at 15 elementary schools in Manhattan, Bronx and Brooklyn. About 6,000 students were involved and the curriculum used was a commercial successor of the elementary arithmetic drill-and-practice program developed at Stanford University's Institute for Mathematical Studies in the Social Sciences. A detailed evaluation of this project may be found in Weiner, *et al.* (1969) and an extensive discussion of the complexities of implementation is given by Butler (1970). Here we shall simply present a summary view of the cost and performance of this particular system in order to place in context the next section containing our projections for the short-term future.

This analysis will derive tentative cost-effectiveness values for the experimental and control groups according to three different sets of assumptions which are summarized as the median case, the best case and the worst case. To obtain cost estimates on a per-student basis we make separate estimates of overall system cost and utilization rate. The effectiveness of the system is considered only in terms of arithmetic achievement test scores. Use of a single measure of this sort has obvious shortcomings; we feel, nevertheless, that the information it provides is the best single measure of system effectiveness. It should be noted that use of this single measure is likely to understate the overall benefits from using the system because improved achievement in one area is likely to increase motivation and achievement in other areas; see Levin (1970).

Cost of the New York CAI System

We will present only summary cost information here; a detailed breakdown and justification of these costs may be found in Butler (unpublished). We present two separate cost figures—those actually incurred in the 1968-69 school year and those anticipated for 1970-71. The cost reductions included for 1970-71 are only those felt very likely to be possible, and our cost-effectiveness estimates are based on this cost. Table 1 presents a cost summary.

Since the total projected cost for 1970-71 is $428,000 and the system serves 192 terminals, the per terminal cost is $2,230 per year. We shall indicate in the final section of this paper that available technical advances can reduce this cost by about 50 percent.

Table 1

Costs of New York City CAI System[a,b]

Category	1968-69 (actual)	1970-71 (projected)
Hardware	190	190
Curriculum	20	20
Administrative staff	80	52
Paraprofessionals	60	75
Telecommunications	130	70
Teacher training	15	13
Miscellaneous	20	8
TOTAL	515	428

[a] Costs are in thousands of 1969 dollars.

[b] Costs of classroom space and students' time are not included.

Utilization of the New York CAI System

Median case. The rate of utilization in the median case is based on expected system use in 1970-71. This rate assumes that the elimination of familiarization problems of the first year of operation, plus the publication and circulation of the first year's student performance data showing the benefits of CAI, will effect a rate equal to the highest rate achieved in the first year by one school, 25 pupils per terminal per day.

Best case. The rate of utilization in the best case includes the same assumptions as for the median case. It assumes also that a significantly higher rate will be attained when all schools can establish an optimal utilization schedule at the start of the school year. In the year's activities analyzed in this study, technical problems of the CAI system prevented the schools from using the system every day, until February. At that time school administrators were reluctant to create new schedules that would use all of the available system time. (Administration of the urban school is notably inflexible and even more so in a system trying to regain equilibrium after the longest teachers' strike in its history.)

Utilization rates in the best case also take into account the fact that students will be able to complete lessons in a shorter average time, and that therefore more lessons will be completed. This expectation is based on the following: (a) the students will be more familiar with the terminals and the structure of the lessons, and (b) teachers will improve the degree to which their in-class instruction will precede the related CAI lessons, thereby reducing the number of incorrect responses and time-outs by students.

In the McComb, Mississippi and Waterford, Michigan projects, the average daily utilization rate is above the 30-pupil rate chosen for the best case in this study. Both projects use a curriculum and a student terminal virtually identical to those used in the NYBE CAI project; the "next" students are in the terminal room before the prior students finish their lessons, thereby keeping all terminals in constant use. Utilization rates as high as 60 per day have been attained in Ohio by using the terminals after school hours. At the present time in New York the paraprofessionals return one group of students to their classroom before escorting the next group to the terminal room.

Worst case. The utilization rate for the worst case is the rate attained by the clustered schools in the first year of operation (18 pupils per terminal per day). The rate assumes the opposite of the assumptions used to derive the rate for the best case; i.e., the significant student gains of the first year will not be an inducement to schedule a larger number of students; the nonrecurrence of the political events of 1968-69 will not permit better planning; the ability of the system to accommodate 192 terminals simultaneously from the beginning of the school year will not encourage a schedule of maximum utilization; the increased confidence of teachers to integrate the in-class and CAI parts of the curriculum will not reduce the average length of a lesson, or the schedules will not take advantage of such reductions by scheduling more students.

Student Achievement in the CAI Group

Median case. Student achievement gains for the median case, shown below, are based on the assumption that the amount students learn increases with the amount of their instruction, and that appropriate testing instruments, properly administered, will indicate such increases. It is also assumed that, over the time periods we are considering, student gains increase linearly with the increase in the amount of instruction. In the median case it is assumed therefore that a pretest-posttest interval of nine months would demonstrate student gains 80 percent greater than those actually observed in the NY project with a five-month test interval.

Best case. Student achievement data from CAI projects in California and Mississippi that used a similar curriculum to that used in New York City form the basis of this study's best case values. The Mississippi project used the Stanford Achievement Test; in New York City, the Metropolitan Achievement Test was used. Tables 2 and 3 show achievement data from these schools. The CAI schools of the California group were also tested in the previous year. Although comparison of the results for these schools in the two years is impossible, for reasons indicated by Suppes and Morningstar (1969), significant improvement for the CAI students in 1966-67 in comparison with the 1967-68 results is clearly indicated.

For the best case, therefore, the identical result reported by Suppes and Morningstar (1969) for the contrasting student populations in Mississippi and California will be used. On the basis of a 15.3-month achievement gain in a seven-month test interval, and also assuming a linear increase in student achievement with an increase of test interval, an increase of 19.8 months would be produced in a nine-month test interval.

Worst case. Student achievement gains for the worst case will assume that a nine-month test interval would indicate the same student gains as were indicated using a five-month test interval. Such a failure to produce further student gains could be attributed to the teachers' failure to continue to select appropriate CAI lessons for the students, or to a deterioration of the environment in the terminal rooms, or to a reduction of student enthusiasm in the CAI mode of instruction. (Each of these assumptions is contrary to present indications in the project.)

Student Achievement in the Control Group

Median case. The value used for student achievement in the median case is based on the assumption that the gains that would be demonstrated using a nine-month test interval would be 80 percent greater than those demonstrated using a five-month test interval, i.e., a

Table 2

Average Grade-Placement Scores on the Stanford Achievement Test: Mississippi 1967-68[a]

Grade	Pretest[b]		Posttest		Posttest-Pretest		t	Degrees of Freedom
	Experi-mental	Con-trol	Experi-mental	Con-trol	Experi-mental	Con-trol		
1	1.41 (52)	1.19 (62)	2.55	1.46	1.14	0.26	3.69[c]	112
2	1.99 (25)	1.96 (54)	3.37	2.80	1.42	0.84	5.23[c]	77
3	2.82 (22)	2.76 (56)	4.85	4.04	2.03	1.26	4.64[c]	76
4	2.26 (58)	2.45 (77)	3.36	3.17	1.10	0.69	2.63[c]	131
5	3.09 (83)	3.71 (134)	4.46	4.60	1.37	0.90	3.43[c]	215
6	4.82 (275)	4.36 (160)	6.54	5.48	1.72	1.13	5.18[c]	433

[a] Data from Suppes and Morningstar (1969), p. 342.
[b] Values in parentheses are numbers of students.
[c] p < .01.

Table 3

Comparison of MAT Arithmetic Computation Raw Scores Earned by Students in the Eight Schools Matched by the Board of Education [a]

Grade	Pretest							Gains						
	CAI			NCAI				CAI			NCAI			
	N	Mean	SD	N	Mean	SD	P	N	Mean	SD	N	Mean	SD	P
2	82	16.71	6.02	79	18.44	5.97	N.S.	82	7.15	5.12	79	3.50	4.51	<.01
3	106	17.49	6.14	98	19.96	6.17	<.01	106	12.92	5.65	98	9.31	5.34	<.01
4	190	25.32	9.16	93	31.36	8.60	<.01	190	8.02	6.35	93	6.10	6.75	<.05
5	208	15.75	8.24	49	21.61	10.16	<.01	208	7.57	6.71	49	2.89	8.09	<.01
6	136	22.77	10.02	23	35.34	7.63	<.01	136	4.28	7.99	23	2.69	7.44	N.S.

[a] Data from Weiner et al. (1969), p. 24.

gain of nine months. (The 80 percent increase is the same as that used in the median case for CAI plus Traditional Instruction [TI] and is derived from the same assumptions as used in that case.)

Best case. The student achievement value used in the best case is based on the assumption that a control group more closely matched with the experimental group would have achieved larger gains than the control group used in the experiment. (In every grade the mean pretest score for the control students was higher than that of the corresponding experimental students, thus providing the control students a smaller range of potential improvement, as indicated by the standardized test.) The best case for TI students will assume a gain of ten months, or one month more than the gain used in the TI median case.

Worst case. The worst case value for TI student achievement is based on the assumption that the control group selected was provided a more intensive mathematics program because of the awareness of the control schools that they were part of the experiment. This is precisely what occurred in one school in the California CAI evaluation conducted by Suppes and Morningstar. The worst case value for TI student achievement will be eight months, or one month less than the gain used in the TI median case.

Table 4, below, summarizes the achievement gains to be expected from having CAI in addition to TI as opposed to simply having TI.

These achievement test scores from New York City are averaged across all students participating, not just those needing compensatory education. Data in Suppes and Morningstar (1969) clearly indicate that CAI does relatively more for low-performing students; thus the median information in Table 4 would probably tend to understate the expected value of CAI for compensatory instruction.

Cost-Effectiveness Data for the
New York CAI System

We are now in a position to combine the cost and performance information discussed thus far. Immediately following Table 1 the annual per terminal cost for 1970-71 operation in New York City was estimated as $2,230. The best, median and worst case figures for student utilization of the terminals were 30, 25 and 17.75 students per terminal per day. Table 5 summarizes this information and combines it with data from Table 4 to obtain estimates of cost per month of achievement gained by use of CAI. We emphasize that these costs

Table 4

Achievement Gains from CAI[a]

Group	Median case		Best case		Worst case	
	5 month[b]	9 month[c]	5 month[b]	9 month[c]	5 month[b]	9 month[c]
(1) CAI + TI	8.4	15.1	8.4	19.8	8.4	8.4
(2) TI only	5.0	9.0	5.0	10.0	5.0	8.0
Achievement gain: (1) - (2)	3.4	6.1	3.4	9.8	3.4	0.4

[a]Achievement gains are measured in months of achievement.
[b]Actually measured gain.
[c]Projected gain.

cannot be extrapolated to achievement gains much larger than those shown in Table 4.

The cost-effectiveness figures in Table 5 obviously do not in themselves enable a school decision-maker to decide whether to implement CAI. He must also have an estimate of the value of improving low performers' arithmetic scores and estimates of the cost-effectiveness of alternative compensatory education techniques in arithmetic. It is beyond the scope of this paper to discuss the value of improving arithmetic scores. However, the study of Kiesling (1970) previously cited does contain estimates of performance as well as cost for alternative compensatory techniques, and we feel it would be worthwhile to mention his findings here.

Kiesling surveyed the most successful compensatory programs in California, including in his study projects that ". . . exhibit gains that are approximately double (at least) the expected gains (in cognitive achievement test scores) for children from the same background . . ." (p. 3). For the median case of the New York City CAI project, the gain with CAI was about two-thirds again the gain without it; thus the CAI project was slightly less successful than the programs Kiesling surveyed. On the other hand, its cost per student per year is only about one-third Kiesling's estimates of the cost of replicating the projects he studied.

We conclude that the New York City CAI program in elementary arithmetic is a highly cost-effective compensatory education technique.

Future CAI Costs

There are two quite different lines along which CAI technology is evolving. One is that of a small low-cost computer serving a small number of student terminals (5-20) at a single location. The other is for a single high-capacity computer to serve a large number (several hundred or more) of terminals over a broad geographical region.* Bitzer

---

*A critical aspect of the economic viability of the latter approach is the cost of communication. Current methods of communication between computer and terminal make use of an individually strung wire (for very short distances) or use of voice-grade phone lines to carry a number of multiplexed signals from teletype terminals. We at Stanford are considering an alternative to these communication techniques: use of geostationary communication satellites. Use of satellites is particularly attractive for long distances and therefore for rural schools, since cost is independent of distance up to about 10,000 miles. On May 18, 1970 we made our first experimental test using a satellite to distribute CAI. Nine terminals at a single elementary school usually served by a phone line were run through NASA's ATS-1

Table 5

Cost of One Month's Achievement Gain with CAI

Terminal utilization rate (students/day)	Cost/student/yr.[a]	Cost of the one month's achievement gain		
		Median case	Best case	Worst case[b]
30	$ 74.00	$12.00	$ 7.50	$185.00
25	89.00	14.50	9.00	223.00
17.75	124.00	20.00	12.50	310.00

[a]These cost figures assume that the terminals are unused during the summer; if the terminals are used during the summer, these figures should be about 25 percent less.

[b]The worst-case cost estimates are so high because the nine-month estimated gain of CAI + TI over TI alone is only 0.4 months.

and Skarperdas (unpublished) have made estimates of the cost of a future high-capacity CAI system that they call PLATO IV. Their design is for a 4,000-terminal system having an initial cost of $13.5 million. They estimate that PLATO IV would achieve a cost of approximately $.34 per student contact-hour (about 10 percent of the cost per contact-hour of the New York City CAI system described in the preceding section, although they assume about three times the utilization rate obtained in the New York project). Problems of finances, communications, curriculum preparation and utilization must be overcome before PLATO IV becomes a reality, so what we would like to discuss here are cost reductions feasible in the very near future.

The system we shall describe is at the other end of the spectrum from PLATO IV; it is small, special purpose, has simple terminals, and utilizes existing curriculum. The first CAI system of this type was produced by Computer Curriculum Corporation (CCC) of Palo Alto, California late in 1970. It is an eight-terminal system that is used for drill and practice in arithmetic (grades 1-8). While this particular system is special-purpose for arithmetic, similar but slightly more expensive systems are being designed for drill and practice in reading, and for tutorial work in foreign languages.

The CCC arithmetic system has two practical advantages. First, it is a "stand-alone" system in the sense that the computer requires no operator but can be simply placed in a classroom and plugged in. Normally all eight terminals would be located in close proximity to the computer, although, at some additional cost, provision can be made for remote location. Second, the system is low in cost. Let us now detail the cost of this system for comparison with the costs given in Table 5 of the preceding section. We should emphasize that the initial purchase cost and the maintenance cost are current price quotations from CCC.

The selling price of the system is set between $30,000 and $40,000 and the monthly maintenance cost is $250 ($25/teletype + $50 for the central processor). The (conservatively estimated) lifetime of the system is eight years. We can obtain the imputed annual cost, p,

---

experimental communication satellite with no difficulties. In many respects the future cost of satellite communication facilities depends on complex administrative and political decisions more than direct economic or technical considerations.

of the system from its initial cost, I, its lifetime, n, and the prevailing annual interest rate, r, by means of the following standard formula:

$$p = [\frac{r(1 + r)^n}{(1 + r)^n - 1}] \ I.$$

We have I = \$30,000 or \$40,000 and n = 8. Table 6 shows p for I = \$30,000 and several different values of r and for n = 10 as well as n = 8.

Table 6

Imputed Annual Hardware Cost

of CCC Arithmetic System[a]

System lifetime (n)	Annual interest rate (r)		
	.05	.10	.15
8	\$3,650	\$4,640	\$6,690
10	3,240	4,890	5,970

[a] If I = \$40,000 instead of \$30,000, values in this table must be increased by one-third.

Table 7 gives an estimate of the total annual cost to a school district of using the CCC arithmetic system under the assumptions that n = 8 and r = .10. Table 7 has the same format as Table 1, though entries that appear in Table 1 have been omitted from Table 7, if we believed their value to be close to zero. The estimates of costs for paraprofessionals and teacher training are based on the estimates of Table 1 scaled down proportionally to an eight-terminal system.

Table 7

Total Annual Cost of CCC Arithmetic System

Category	Annual Cost	
	I = $30,000	I = $40,000
Imputed annual hardware cost	$4,640	$ 6,190
Maintenance (12 mos. @ $250/mo.)	3,000	3,000
Paraprofessionals	1,500	1,500
Teacher training	500	500
Miscellaneous	300	300
TOTAL	$9,940	$11,490

For a sale price of $30,000, the total cost per year is $9,940 (it would be 15 percent less with a ten-year lifetime and 5 percent interest) for a per terminal cost of $1,240 per year. With a utilization rate of 25 students per day and no system use during summer school, the system costs $50 per student per year for instruction in a single subject matter.* This is only slightly more than half the $89 per year that the New York City system costs; as that system already only costs about one-third as much as alternative compensatory systems of about the same quality, it appears that CAI can markedly reduce the cost of compensatory education in the near future.

*Use of the system during summers would reduce this per-student annual cost by about 20 percent. The possibility (as yet unproved) of having 12 or even 16 terminals run from basically the same system would further reduce costs.

We believe that the assumptions made to compute the annual student cost of the eight-terminal system are conservative. Improvements in technology in the next five years can be anticipated, and there is every reason to think that the cost of CAI relative to other forms of instruction will continue to decrease.

As in the past, so today the manner, style and substance of education is a subject of great controversy in our society. In this paper we have not attempted any deep-running defense of CAI, but have restricted ourselves to certain sharply defined measures of achievement and the associated costs of producing such measured achievements. We believe that CAI provides an unparalleled opportunity for moving some of the past and present controversies about education from the arena of great generality to one of data analysis and confrontation of theories with facts. However, we cannot pursue these matters in greater detail here.

References

Bitzer, D., & D. Skarperdas. The Economics of a Large Scale Computer Based System. Unpublished, undated paper of the Computer-based Education Research Laboratory of the University of Illinois.

Bowles, S. & H. Levin. The Determinants of Scholastic Achievement: An Appraisal of Some Recent Evidence. *J. of Human Resources*, 1968, *3*, 3-24.

Butler, C. A Systems Analysis of an Urban Educational Innovation. Unpublished paper, 1970.

Butler, C. A Political Systems Analysis of a Federal Innovation Model. Unpublished Ed.D. thesis, Stanford University, 1970.

Coleman, J. The Evaluation of Equality of Educational Opportunity. Santa Monica, Calif.: The Rand Corp., P-3911, 1968.

Hunt, J. Has Compensatory Education Failed? Has It Been Attempted? *Harvard Educational Review*, 1969, *39*, 130-152.

Jensen, A. How Much Can We Boost IQ and Scholastic Achievement? *Harvard Educational Review*, 1969, *39*, 1-123.

Kiesling, H. A Study of Successful Compensatory Education Programs in California. Internal Rand Corporation Document, March 1970.

Levin, H. A New Model of School Effectiveness. Stanford Center for Research and Development in Teaching, May 1970.

Michealson, S. Unpublished paper.

Nixon, R. Special message to Congress on educational reform, March 3, 1970. Quoted in *The New York Times*, March 4, 1970.

Piccariello, H. Evaluation of Title I, mimeographed paper, 1969.

Suppes, P., & Morningstar, M. Computer Assisted Instruction. *Science,* 1969, *166*, 343-350.

Weiner, M., *et al*. An Evaluation of the 1968-1969 New York City Computer Assisted Instruction Project in Elementary Arithmetic. Division of Teacher Education, City University of New York, July 1969.

THE COMMUNITY COLLEGE
IN THE CITY

Murray H. Block

Of primary importance in the planning of Manhattan Community College, or any urban community college, is how to reach out to become part of the surrounding neighborhood. Although America is fast becoming an urban nation, many of its institutions are deeply rooted in an agrarian past. In the minds of the majority, a college is still imagined as a rural retreat designed for that quiet interlude between youth and adulthood. Cast in the light of contemporary urban conflicts, however, this kind of institution, as well as the attitude that engenders it, no longer seems appropriate. Many educators today feel that the place in which to study the human condition is in its midst. Manhattan Community College is certainly "in the midst of it"; or, in today's parlance, we are "where it's at."

We have a mandate to reach out into the community to find the "ought-to-be student," the dropout whose capabilities are sufficient but whose motivation is not. It is the responsibility of an urban community college to remotivate these individuals, retrain them if necessary, so that each can become a more fulfilled individual, a useful citizen, and a productive member of the community. One device now being discussed is the establishment of pre-admission counseling outposts throughout

Murray H. Block, formerly president of Manhattan Community College, is deputy of the chancellor for campus relations, State University of New York, Albany.

the metropolitan area. In an adaptation of techniques used in alcoholic and drug rehabilitation centers, these outposts may be manned by former dropouts whose own backgrounds would enable them to best reach this vast but unshaped human resource. Other outposts for recreation and special research would further expand the college into the community.

We are also eager to explore the opposite side of the coin—why not have the community establish outposts on our campus? Opportunities for courses in continuing education are almost unlimited. The idea that a person trains once in his life for a single career is no longer valid.

So long as the college truly wishes to be sensitive to the needs of local business and industry, then why should we not involve local businessmen directly? Why not bring them in as guest lecturers, as advisors and consultants? Why not give business leaders a role in training the students they will later hire as their employees? Why not foster a continuing program of field trips into neighboring plants and business offices? Local governmental agencies, in the same way, could have reciprocal arrangements with the college.

The college can "use the neighborhood as a laboratory." This refers to the development of a continuous program of student involvement in the neighborhood, and strongly implies that the college think of itself as an important vehicle for social change.

While reviewing the growing variety of urban problems, the nature of urban students, and the varied community the college must serve, we have determined that new ways must be explored and developed for the presentation of information. It is true that the college must have schedules, and courses must be programmed. Semesters must begin and end. But the precise allotment of hours to specific activities can greatly vary from student to student. Many will be working during the day and studying evenings. Others who will work nights will wish to study during the day. Some will have no predictable pattern, such as those who will be employed on shifts that change periodically. The latter group has always been precluded from higher educational opportunities because of the rigidity of class schedules and semester dates.

It is therefore essential for the new Manhattan Community College that we provide our students with what we have come to call the *24-Hour Learning Center.* This is visualized as a new kind of educational center—not a student union, library, cafeteria, or classroom building, but a combination of each. It may be thought of as a campus in miniature, with facilities for quiet study, research, socializing, recreation, eating and perhaps even napping. We are hoping that the center would always be open—available to students 24 hours a day—so that a maximum number of working students may have access to higher education.

Properly designed, this center will lie at the heart of the campus both physically and symbolically. Easy accessibility for students, faculty and community will do much to ensure its success. More important, this will be the facility that all students, regardless of their schedules or academic discipline, will have in common.

We are concerned that this college do a good job in providing physical education opportunities for students and community members. On our small site, this obviously becomes quite a challenge. There is general agreement that physical education at Manhattan Community College must be given new and non-traditional emphasis. The small city site makes it obvious that the big sports favored by many other colleges—football, baseball, track and field—are inappropriate. The size of our site is not the only reason for the inappropriateness of such sports. Urban Americans have few, if any, opportunities of pursuing such activities after leaving college. College programs that encourage passive rather than active participation in sports fail their students in preparing them for the future. The emphasis at Manhattan Community College must be on "doing" rather than on "watching others do." The emphasis must be on individual participation rather than on varsity sports. Energies must be redirected toward sports that can be carried on in a healthful way throughout life. Handball, squash, tennis, bowling, swimming, bicycling, badminton, dance and gymnastics are especially appropriate.

The effects of this thinking on the design of future facilities is quite interesting. These ideas suggest a physical education facility similar to an urban health club. Informal use and easy accessibility will be paramount concerns to the students whose time between work and study is quite limited. Athletic facilities, normally developed in generous amounts on large campuses, will necessarily be concentrated for effectiveness at Manhattan. Some facilities, such as bowling alleys and squash courts, can be placed underground. Others, however, require more prime space, and the college will attempt to develop its external spaces high above the ground in a series of open areas for athletics, as well as for roof garden and lounge facilities. This we can truly envision as becoming a Campus in the Sky.

In the spirit of reaching out, we hope that our college can develop joint programs with the City for public park use in return for community use of college facilities. It is also suggested that the "outpost" principle be applied to the physical education program, with a facility being developed, along with other colleges, outside the City, perhaps in the Catskills, designed to broaden the experience of urban students. Thus, the college's physical education program could be expanded to include camping, hiking, fishing, skiing and other popular seasonal outdoor sports.

It is clear the "community" in Community College refers to several different communities in the case of Manhattan. Our college must relate itself productively to each. In addition to providing a source of students, these communities will be a source of jobs for students while they are in college and after their graduation. These communities also form an enriching source of faculty and guest lecturers. They require that imaginative continuing education programs be developed by the college. Finally, and perhaps most important, they place Manhattan Community College in a vital and growing context and insure the college a decisive and prominent role in shaping the City's future development.

URBANIZATION AND MEDIA:
A New Sense of Community

David W. Martin

Nostalgia for rural and small town life has been a persistent theme woven into portrayals of America by the mass media. In books and motion pictures, on radio and television, the rural countryside dotted with little villages—complete with spacious skies, amber waves of grain and purple mountains majestic above fruited plains—has been the traditional source and locale for "the good life."

On the other hand, the incunabula of all our problems labeled "social," the repository of evil, the great contaminator, has been the city. The perspective provided by the media of urbanization is that it is the most insidious of social diseases, only curable, if at all, by frequent and liberal doses of bucolic.

Representative for me of our predilection to see and define beauty in rural towns and ugliness in urban conditions were two events involving university students. The first was a mixed media presentation woven about a folk song "This Land Is Your Land," popularized by the folk singer, Pete Seeger. The first run-through of this song was illustrated by the students with a series of photographic clichés of

David W. Martin is professor of sociology and health education at the University of Texas, School of Public Health. Previously he was director of the Urban Semester Program, Institute of Urban Ecology, University of Southern California and professor of education at the same institution.

"beautiful"; the second run-through was vivid in contrast, showing all that is purportedly ugly, contaminated and polluted in "our land." Significantly, almost all that was beautiful was rural, and all that was ugly was urban.

The second event occurred in an exercise used in an urban studies program to illustrate how media can both assist and influence our perceptions of the city. We sent students to a designated part of the city within a small area. The students were provided with cameras and deliberately ambiguous assignments. They were to return with photographs of sights which were "beautiful" or "ugly" in this area. The results were not surprising. A significant number of photographs testified that "beauty" in the eyes of the beholders was defined by flowers, trees and grassy expanses.

More important, however, than any beautiful or ugly definition of physical phenomena determined by our rural, small town predilections are the differential modes of social relations associated with the rural-urban dichotomy. As Anselm Straus states in his study of how American novelists have perceived New York City:

> The stereotype of rural life embodies notions of close kinship and friendship ties, of intimate and satisfying face to face relationships, of stability, simplicity, honesty, integrity, concern for associates, and other attributes of tightly knit groups.

> . . . in the urban environment all classes alike suffer from certain of its brutalizing or destructive features (states Lewis Mumford). This severe criticism is couched in a vocabulary built around such terms as loneliness, strangers, artificiality, front, facades, exploitation, surface, superficial, unnatural, boredom, apathy, routine, dehumanizing machine, meaninglessness, purposelessness. Explicit or implicit in this lexicon is a rural-urban contrast, with the city coming off the loser.[1]

Some of the most significant changes occurring in an urbanized area or society are, of course, in the ways in which people relate to one another. Dysfunction occurs when norms for behavior and institutional

1. Anselm Straus. Urban Perspectives: New York City, in Anselm Straus (Ed.) *The American City: A Sourcebook of Urban Imagery.* Chicago: Aldine Publishing Company, 1968, pp. 8 and 10.

modes developed *sui generis* from rural, small town existence are applied to an urban situation which represents quantum variances in population density, and social, economic and political complexity.

That all of the phenomena delineated by this lexicon exist in the urban milieu is, of course, all too apparent; however, to suggest that they are *caused by* the city borders on the absurd. It is even possible that the city, instead of being a causal agent, may rather be an ameliorating factor protecting people from the full impact of phenomena which are the result of factors other than urbanization occurring in our society.

Anyone who believes that the repository of friendliness or neighborliness is in rural, small town America never has moved from the city to the country or village where he can exhibit no prior relationships, no kinships and little sharing of local norms such as dress, haircut, dialect, or life style. The hostility, the strangeness, the loneliness, the alienation that occurs in rural America under these conditions makes life in an apartment in mid-Manhattan seem like an exercise in communal living. The most shattering portrayal of such rural, small town American "friendliness" occurs in "Easy Rider," one of the first films to break the tradition of the rural American as folk hero and to transform him, instead, into a vicious and brutish villain. It is possible that this film may portend a general shift of the origins of our heroes and villains in much of the media.[2]

Interestingly, one of the major themes of "Easy Rider" is movement; and when one analyzes the sources of the problems attributed to cities by urban critics like Lewis Mumford, one discovers mobility and change as both symptoms and causes of these urban problems. Behind both, however, is an even more important phenomenon, industrialization, which Leonard Riessman considers a big factor in the process of urbanization. He notes that a contemporary urban area is quite different in both quality and quantity from the historical "city," to say nothing about the rural differences.[3]

2. It should be noted, however, that "Easy Rider" does continue the tradition and valuing of rural America as a physical focus of beauty as well as suggest in its treatment of a rural commune created by urban young people that "getting back to nature" is the embodiment of the "good life." Significantly, in this generation the individual Thoreau-by-Walden Pond has become a group "thing."

3. Leonard Riessman. *The Urban Process.* New York: The Free Press, 1964.

The most important defining features of rural, small town norms of behavior are their dependence for being learned, applied and enforced upon face-to-face, intimate, primary group relationships. When this personalization is broken down by conditions of urbanization, these norms tend to disintegrate; anomic behavior becomes endemic, and it is almost defined as normality. Martin Shubik cogently delineates the problem and poses a key question:

> Taking a few crude calculations we observe that if half a day a year is needed to maintain contact with a relatively good friend, there is an upper bound of seven hundred persons with whom we could have much personal interaction. How many cases can the judge handle? How many patients can the psychiatrist treat? Is personal interaction becoming a luxury that modern society cannot afford, or are there new social forms and institutions that will foster and preserve it?[4]

The social forms and institutions of rural, small town America were mostly embedded in a tightly knit, personalized concept of community which emphasized physical proximity; but this kind of community is a disappearing facet of urban life, and attempts to return to it, restore it, or even retain it may be futile. In fact, such action may be dysfunctional, as it could divert our efforts from creating new social forms and institutions that may make personal interaction possible and viable.

Essentially, any sense of community is dependent upon the communication of shared values, opinions, perceptions and similar ideas. In traditional communities, where intimate, face-to-face relationships were both valued and possible, such was the mode of communicating these shared aspects of living; however, in a mass society, regardless of the possible desirability of this intimacy, it is unachievable. Therefore, it is to the mass media we must turn to discover the means of creating a new sense of community significantly apart from sheer physical proximity. If in the process many more of us are cured of our rural, small town nostalgia and if we discover that this means there is beauty other than in the "country," our future may be the better for it.

4. Martin Shubik. Information, Rationality, and Free Choice in a Future Democratic Society. *Daedalus,* Summer 1967, *96* (3), p. 774.

The viability of the mass media in establishing a community has been partially demonstrated in the study by Morris Janowitz of the community press in the Chicago metropolitan area. Janowitz found conclusive evidence that local newspapers were serving to increase cohesion in neighborhood areas. The emphasis upon the "local" aspect of the newspaper, however, indicates a persistent small-community bias, because in these local newspapers there is still an emphasis upon the man next door, the people on the next block, the neighborhood school and the local shopping center; avoided is the vital recognition that what the man 20 miles away in the central city may be doing could be far more important than the next door neighbor's activities.

As far as other mass media (i.e., the metropolitan press, television, radio, magazines, books, etc., which provide coverage over the totality of national and international affairs), they, too, tend to be defective in being complete and viable instrumentalities for creating a new sense of community, as the communication that occurs—with some singular exceptions—is essentially only in one direction. Approximately two percent of our population write and produce magazines, newspapers, radio and television materials, and books; the other 98 percent, in a very real sense, make up a "silent majority" insofar as making their opinions known outside of their traditional primary group communities. This group is composed of the passive, apathetic participants in the new urban, mass community.

This passivity or apathy of listeners and viewers of the mass media has been a continuing concern of many social observers. Typical of the charges is that of Paul Lazarsfeld and Robert Merton:[5]

> Scattered studies have shown that an increasing proportion of the time of Americans is devoted to the products of the mass media. With distinct variations in different regions and among different social stratas, the out-pourings of the media presumably enable the twentieth-century American "to keep abreast of the world." Yet it is suggested, this vast supply of communications may elicit only a superficial concern with the problems of society, and this superficiality often cloaks mass apathy. . . That the mass media have lifted the level of

5. Paul L. Lazarsfeld & Robert K. Merton. Mass Communication, Popular Tastes and Organized Social Action. In Bernard Rosenberg & David Manning (Eds.) *Mass Leisure.* New York: Free Press, 1964, p. 464.

information of large populations is evident. Yet, quite apart from intent, increasing dosages of mass communications may be inadvertently transforming the energies of men from active participation into passive knowledge.

Quite obviously, then, the key to utilization of the mass media as foci for the creation of a new urban community resides in the possibilities of establishing means for and modes of active participation within the mass media. Some of these means and modes already exist, and they may presage future forms for the creation of the new community.

The most traditional forms for eliciting active participation of the media consumers with each other and with the producers have involved the use of "letters to the editor" columns of newspapers and magazines. As far as substantially increasing the number of active participants, however, the results of these columns are miniscule, especially in increasing consumer awareness of participation. The most significant developments with regard to the creation of mass media forms of active participation by citizens in an urban community have occurred within radio and television in the form of so-called talk shows, which have become so ubiquitous that their format needs no description.

Conversations—particularly those involving the ordinary listener and not celebrities—are the essential ingredients of this type of programming. Talk shows had their beginnings early in the history of radio. Who was "first" is difficult to establish, but the "when" and its first full flowering occurred in the early 1930's, and involved an ex-taxi driver in New York named Lester Kroll, later to become John J. Anthony, host of the "Original Good Will Hour," who interviewed anonymous couples with marital difficulties who were willing to reveal, to the extent the mores of the time would permit, "who did what to whom at home."[6]

The other ingredients of talk programming, the broadcasting of telephone calls over the air, occurred as a generalized phenomenon in the early 1950's. Again, who was "first" is unimportant as well as difficult to determine, because for many years prior to talk becoming consciously and deliberately programmed, individual announcers often

6. Sam J. Slate & Joe Cook. *It Sounds Impossible.* New York: Macmillan Company, 1963, p. 131.

put telephone callers on the air, initially by simply holding the telephone close to the microphone.

This utilization of talk as a focus for a program, however, was first on the after-midnight programs broadcast to insomniacs, night workers, old people and the generally lonely.

By the mid-sixties, talk radio could be heard nearly all of the time, as it had even spread to television, where talk programming often combines a host announcer, a panel of guests, and studio audience participation, as well as telephone calls.

Why talk programming developed first on radio rather than television, and why it blossomed first on night shows appealing to the alienated is suggested by a 1955 study made by McPhee and Meyersohn as to the utilization of radio by residents of cities with television channels. Those people who were the most alone—in solitude—listened most to radio programs involving social interaction because these programs furnished them with feelings of kinship, concern and vicarious participation.[7] Talk radio, of course, provided the social interaction. A soap opera also involves such interaction, but it does not offer the possibility of personal and direct involvement as the talk show does: the kind of confrontation that is suggested in this story about an early (1954) talk show conducted by Bob Jones over WCOG, Greensboro, North Carolina:

> All types of people telephone "Party Line," and because they are not asked to give their names, some frank talk results. "Now I'm an old man," said one quavering voice, "and I say Eisenhower is the greatest President we've ever had." A few minutes later an answer came: "All I want to know is what has he ever done?" "I'll tell you what he's done," said a female voice shortly after. "I had two boys in Korea and only one of them came home, but Eisenhower brought my other boy home. And don't forget what Roosevelt said about not sending our boys overseas and then look what happened." Moments later a husky baritone called: "I've just got one question," he said. "What ever happened to Franklin Delano Roosevelt?" Then he hung up.[8]

7. William N. McPhee & Rolf Meyersohn. *Futures for Radio.* New York: Bureau of Applied Social Research, Columbia University, 1955.

8. Argument by Telephone. *Newsweek*, May 10, 1954, *43*, p. 92.

The very mass of the audience hearing the pronouncements of fellow citizens is important, also. It is one thing to grumble about the property tax to a grand total of seven—one wife washing the dishes, one dog scratching a flea, one cat sleeping on a chair, three gold fish and a parakeet—and another to have that opinion heard by 50 thousand people, including many who may be in a position to do something about that opinion.

It would be an error to attach, as many do, the major significance of this exchange to the content of what is said. What is most important is that in a short time[9] four people had their opinions heard by thousands of people. Since our focus is upon the possibilities of the media for the establishment of a new sense of community, and since the probabilities suggested by the research are that these callers are more often the lonely, the alienated, one can easily see the function of talk radio in community development, particularly in the inclusion of the heretofore excluded.

Another factor in providing listeners with an opportunity to be heard on the mass media is the extent to which media appearances in our society establish prestige for individuals and groups. Any sense of community is dependent upon the degree that one is given status and prestige by participation within it, and when talk radio or television furnishes this, a reinforced sense of community will occur. As Lazarsfeld and Merton point out:

> Recognition by the press or radio, or magazines, or newsreels testifies that one has arrived, that one is important enough to have been singled out from the large anonymous masses, that one's behavior and opinions are recognized enough to require public notice.[10]

Prior to talk radio and television, this prestige was bestowed only on the few.

There are those social critics who focus their primary attention upon the content of citizen participation in conversation media, and

9. In an unpublished study participated in by the author for a major talk station, we found that the average time per call was 3.3 minutes.

10. Lazarsfeld and Merton, *op. cit.*, p. 461.

they sometimes lose sight of the significance of that participation
regardless of content.

> All there is for most of the day and night on this station
> is an announcer, a phone and some poor, lonely,
> disaffiliated citizen who harasses and is harassed by the
> well paid radio man.[11]

Another critic comments:

> The hot line show is one of the most discredited forms
> of radio programming. What could be more unedifying
> than know-nothing listeners phoning in their philos-
> ophies to know-it-all disk jockeys?[12]

Some of the calls represent participation that many regard as
kooky. The policy book of a station that at one time programmed
conversation radio entirely, recognized this problem:

> People who feel moved to complain about conversation
> radio say that it is a crime to let people spout their
> meaningless ideas, their ignorances and misinformations,
> their prejudices and their hatreds, their petty problems
> and ambitions on the radio.

The answer to this charge, of course, particularly important to
citizens in a mass society, is provided by John Stewart Mill in his essay
On Liberty:

> If all mankind minus one were of one opinion, and only
> one person were of the contrary opinion, mankind
> would be no more justified in silencing that one person,
> than he, if he had the power, would be justified in
> silencing mankind.[13]

---

11. Marjory Potts. Talking Radio. *The Realist,* August, 1966, p. 5.

12. The Cool Hot Line. *Time,* August 23, 1968, p. 48.

13. John Stewart Mill. *On Liberty.* London: Parker, 1859.

To the question, "Why should this be so?," John Locke gave four reasons: (1) If an opinion is silenced, for all anyone knows it might be the truth; (2) even a wrong opinion may contain a bit of truth to assist in the discovery of the whole truth; (3) if the commonly held opinion is really the truth, it will not be adhered to rationally unless it is tested and defended; and (4) for a commonly held opinion to maintain its vitality, its force, it must be challenged from time to time.

In contemporary discussion of this issue, no better case for free expression *for everyone*—not just newspapers, or magazines, or television, or paid radio commentators but for average Joe Citizen—can be made than this excerpt from the report of the 19th Commission on Freedom of the Press:

> Freedom of expression can never be made a costless immunity by shackling hostile response, for response is also expression. Free expression is destined not to repress social conflict but to liberate it. But its intention is that the level of social conflict shall be lifted from the plane of violence to the plane of discussion.

> Liberty is experimental, and experiment implies trial and error. Debate itself could not exist unless wrong opinions could be rightfully offered by those who suppose them to be right.

Within the framework of our search for a new sense or a generation of community by the utilization of media, the notion of lifting the level of conflict from the plane of violence to the plane of discussion is especially crucial.

It has been long recognized in the arbitration of disputes, be they marital, labor-management or international, that peaceful settlement is possible as long as communication channels remain open. When they close, the risk of violence becomes high. In a mass society, any and all communication channels which can be opened to the people should be cherished and maintained.

The price of inarticulateness—of wanting to be heard but no ears listening—can be violence, even riots. In part, the prevalence of disturbances in our Black ghettos can be attributed to feelings that if the white power structure will not listen to what Blacks are saying, maybe it will listen to what Blacks are doing—even if it includes burning, looting and killing. In 1967, Los Angeles, despite continuing resentment, little alleviation of ghetto conditions, and the longest hot, humid summer in the history of the area, had no riots. Nor have any riots occurred since this period. Obviously, there is no concrete empirical evidence to establish a relationship between the absence of riots and the presence of conversation radio, but Southern California had three radio and two television stations devoting some or all of their programming to conversation radio. Blacks do listen, call into these stations, air grievances, and comment on other people's ideas; and while it may not be possible to prove, it certainly is reasonable to hypothesize that the discussions of issues over conversation radio made a contribution to racially "cool" summers in Watts.

One of the researchable areas yet to be embarked upon is the extent to which in an urban environment the existence and usage of communication channels open to disparate social, economic, political and physical populations are effective safety valves for the release of pent-up frustration, alienation and associated phenomena.

On the other side of the possibilities on conversation radio for Black rage being articulated is the expression of racism. The bigots, of course, make their calls, and they are a part of the urban community. There are many people, including those in control of media production, who insist that only people with "reasonable" ideas be heard. Usually "reasonable" is defined as agreement with their prejudices. These people would prevent the bigot from being heard. A more reasonable position and one based upon what the research in communication and attitude formation indicates, is that bigots should be heard if only to remind people that bigotry still exists; that it is a force to be reckoned with in our society.

Too many people today live encapsulated lives, listening only to others who agree with them, and interacting only with those who confirm their ideas. This includes both the person committed basically to the democratic ideal and those espousing authoritarianism of both the left and the right. It is all too easy to assume that the fight for freedom is secure; listening to talk radio and television is a constant reminder, however, that an "escape from freedom" is still being sought by many; the struggle for democracy is not over.

To risk having the statement of a bigot or an authoritarian reinforce the attitudes of others like him is probably more conducive to the development of democratic attitudes, if it assists in alerting the vast majority of citizens with democratic beliefs to the clear and present dangers of bigotry. It is the authoritarians who are most violently opposed to the concept of two-way radio as if they sense in it a threat to their existence.

In the course of research on talk radio in which the author participated, samples of the vituperative letters written to one station were examined. One was left with a vivid impression of tragic personalities, some of them sick, most of them rigidly bound to an egocentric and prejudiced view of the world. These people are probably the most in need of being brought within the confines of a community which embraces the democratic ideal of divergent ideas: the only ideal which, in the author's opinion, will make a self-fulfilling urban community possible.

Actually, the dangers of converting people to bigotry or author-itarianism if expression of such attitudes are permitted on the mass media are slight on the basis of research which indicates that mass communications are much more likely to reinforce existing attitudes toward such problems as racial prejudice or religious intolerance rather than convert people to different points of view, particularly if these attitudes are ego-involved and central to the person's self-image.

Interestingly, research in mass communication has also found that, on the whole, people are most disposed to attend only to those communications which are consonant with their own beliefs and attitudes, and to be inattentive or disregard conflicting beliefs and attitudes.

The evidence accumulated by the author and fellow researchers from an extensive content analysis of conversation radio seems to contradict these findings as applied to this type of programming. Listeners were listening to and did not disregard opinions which differed from their own. Our findings were that the talk generated exhibited all of the qualities of dialogue between and among members of a pluralistic community. The dialogue seemed rather balanced between callers who disagreed with the opinions of the communi-castor,[14] those who agreed with him, and those who were neutral.

14. What to call them? As Jessica Mitford said (Hello, There: You're on the Air. *Harpers,* No. 232, May, 1966, p. 49):

There is as yet no universally accepted appellation for the host on

The range of percentage of callers who agreed with the communicastor's opinion varied between stations and communicastors from 16.3 percent to 48.3 percent; the range of disagreement was from 0 to 23.4 percent; and neutrality (defined as either no discernible opinions or requests for information) went from 13.8 percent to 58.7 percent.

A substantial proportion of the calls on these stations' conversation programming represented situations where a listener expressed an opinion but the communicastor did not reciprocate with his own views; he simply allowed the listener to present his. The percentage of calls in this category range between 18.1 percent and 24.8 percent. Conversely, a situation where the caller expressed no opinion but the communicastor did was relatively rare, and varied between 0.9 percent and 3.8 percent.

The data we gathered seemed to negate the expression within segments of the mass media—indeed, the general attitude of the public—that conversation radio is where controversy and vituperation rule:

> The principal ingredient in any successful hot-line show is the personality of the host, and often the more opinionated, the better.[15]

This reputation, of course, was fostered by the publicity given to a few of the communicastors who, indeed, did thrive on invective:

------

these programs. "Commentator" or "moderator" is not quite accurate. "Talk jockey" is disliked in the trade as being somewhat derogatory, too flip to describe the serious role some are trying to carve out for themselves. No doubt in the near future, with the American genius for upgrading status through the use of high-sounding titles, somebody will come up with "conversation engineer," "talk counselor," or "spokestonian." In the absence of a distinctive title, I shall steer a safe middle course and call them "talkicians."

Jessica Mitford notwithstanding, in this paper they shall be referred to as communicastors.

15. The Hot Hot-Line. *Time*, June 18, 1965, *85*, p. 93.

Insult, like any other minor act, attracts its not-so-artful practitioners. Currently, the bluntest instrument of them all is a Los Angeles broadcaster named Joe Pyne, who has become simultaneously the industry's hottest property, and as a *New York Times* critic, Jack Gould, recently said, its "ranking nuisance." On his interview shows, Pyne often addresses callers and guests as "stupid," "jerk," or "meathead." An epileptic was once asked, "Just why do you think people should feel sorry for you?" Pyne's standard lines run from "Go gargle with razor blades," to "Take your teeth out, put 'em in backwards and bite your throat." Says Pyne of himself: "I'm not a nice guy, and I don't want to be."[16]

Joe Pyne quickly developed a number of imitators, some of whom attempted to out-do him in obnoxiousness. It is the personal belief of the author that this "matador syndrome," which was the Joe Pyne style, as expressed in the policy book of one conversation station, is dysfunctional to the utilization of media for the creation of a viable community:

The Matador Syndrome

The audience—any audience—is always hungry for the kill. The aficionados appreciate the cape work; the rest of the people come for the sword.

The . . . radio audience is accustomed to a blistering pace; it has learned to expect a quick end to boring calls. They share management's frequent impulse, expressed as "Shut him off," "Wrap it up," and "What a drag." The listener rightfully expects hopscotching from interesting topic to interesting topic. This pace and diversity is one of our strongest weapons against the competition.

Keep your sword sharp. The audience comes for the spectacle, the popcorn, and artistry, but mainly for the kill.

16. Killer Joe. *Time*, July 29, 1966, *88*, p. 30.

Regardless of how management intended this directive, the most common interpretation of this analogy between conversation radio or television and the bullring is that communicastors are being urged to slash the audience to ribbons, blow them off the air, or get out the knives. Americans typically have long employed invective, vituperation and loud voices to rid themselves of opponents, and it has been appropriately noted that this behavior seems to be the last refuge, short of physical violence, of an individual bested by the rationality or the reasonableness of his opponent.

To the extent that interactive radio and television can avoid this rather infantile reaction to conflicting ideologies and instead assume an attitude toward its listeners or viewers as co-participants rather than passive partakers, then these media can be important ingredients in the establishment of a necessary, new urban community. However, they must treat the audience better—as something more than escapists or people attendant at a perpetual circus. This has been a persistent attitude of most mass media producers toward their consumers:

> . . . all these media look at man with the eyes of an adolescent Plato, rather than the eyes of Aristotle. They think of him coming to the movies or sitting before the television screen, not in a mood to think . . . but rather in a mood to suspend his critical faculties, to give himself to the story, to identify with the characters and experience vicariously what they do, to forget for a while the problems of his daily life and the aspirations which he may hold for art and society.[17]

There is some evidence that conversation radio and television may generally assume a more enlightened view of their audience than most other programming. At the worst, they are schizophrenic in their view of listeners and viewers. The same station whose policy book proclaimed the "Matador Syndrome" in another section stated:

Maxim: We must meet the people on common grounds.

17. Wilbur Schramm. *Responsibility in Mass Communications.* New York: Harper and Bros., 1957, p. 282.

No's: Never talk down to a listener; never talk
                over his head.

Yes's: Listen to the caller. Understand the
                listener. Respond to the listener.

and later:

He (the communicastor) must meet the caller as an
absolute equal at the start.

If this attitude were the one that prevailed, the likelihood of
participant, interactive radio or television having more of an effect
upon its consumers would be substantially increased.

Another quality of this use of media which contains a potential
for being more influential upon its audience than other uses is its
personal quality. There is abundant evidence from communication
research that greater effectiveness in changing attitudes and opinions
occurs as the media become more personal. Essentially this means that,
other things being equal, a newspaper story is not as effective as a
personal conversation. Conversation radio and television can be
hypothesized, therefore, as being somewhere in the middle between the
effectiveness of conventional radio and personal conversations.

There seems to be another important reason for such effectiveness.
As has been suggested earlier, people tend to be highly selective of the
content of the mass media: should someone be against capital
punishment, it is extremely unlikely that he will listen long to a
program devoted to the pro-arguments. On the other hand, in
conversation radio or television, he will be more likely to listen to
arguments for it, in the expectation that someone else in the next few
minutes may call in with a rebuttal; indeed, *he himself knows he can*. It
is quite likely that, being exposed to more arguments for it, he will
change, or perhaps modify, his position; at least he may gain respect for
the arguments of the opposition—no small victory in a democratic
society, and especially important for any formation of a new sense of
community.

Every community has "opinion leaders": those people who can,
in a sense, on the one hand, give some new directions to cultural
behavior, but who, on the other, simply are able articulators of the

ingredients of the desires and needs of the masses. The extent to which personages in the mass media are viewed as more than entertainers is suggested by the names Ronald Reagan, George Murphy and Shirley Temple Black, to name a few from one state. Our research revealed with regard to conversation radio listeners a high frequency of callers who ask either for an opinion from the communicastor, or confirmation by the communicastor of the caller's own opinion. This tends to establish the role of the communicastor as an opinion leader in the mass media community. If he is, then much of the research findings with regard to such opinion leaders is applicable.

One of the functions of an opinion leader is to mediate between the mass media and those people associated with him. Studies of opinion leaders indicate that they are much more voracious devourers of the mass media than their followers. In our research involving radio communicastors, a constant theme of their participation in conversation radio was the necessity of "keeping up." Representative comments were:

> The most stress on me is the amount of reading I have to do. I am forced to read at least ten times as much as the ordinary person. I must keep up.

> You really feel like you're going back to school again. This job requires re-education, constant reading and listening.

If the communicastor is an opinion leader, then from other studies we begin to appreciate his relative importance. These studies show that, contrary to common beliefs, most people do *not* obtain their information directly from newspapers, television, radio and other media, but rather *through contact with their opinion leaders*. This suggests that the communicastors may have more of an information dispensing function than the news staffs on their own stations.

Another facet of the opinion leader is his basic conformity to group norms. This does not mean that he cannot hold divergent views, but it is doubtful if he could remain an opinion leader should the totality of his views run counter to those of his followers. This implies, at least, a *modus operandi* for successful participant radio and television in a democratic society. A democratic society, particularly a massive and complex one like ours, means the existence of not one group, but many, for we are basically pluralistic. Should a station attempt to employ communicastors of only one political or social ideology, following only one set of forms, then it will tend to attract one group of listeners whose norms correspond to the norms of the station. It may remain solvent, but it will not be successful. For those who would become concerned about the ability of a conversation radio or television station to become a powerful force for a particular brand of social and political ideology, we would predict it has contained within itself the seeds of its own destruction.

On the other hand, for those concerned about the possible contribution of the participant media to complete conformity, they may not have really listened. It is discussion, argument and debate that make this medium intrinsically interesting and captivating—especially to those who are call-in participants rather than passive consumers. In conventional uses of mass media, the opinions and attitudes expressed are essentially those of the power structure producing them; and there is a widespread belief (with little evidence, it may be added) of those in this power structure that affirmation of the status quo and avoidance of controversy is safer and more lucrative. By and large, the participants in conventional radio and television behave accordingly.

Conversely, the participant media, with only the guidance of the canons of good taste and libel laws, can offer programming covering the entire spectrum of political and social opinions and attitudes. They can become both bastions and supports for divergent thinking which the evidence of history so clearly indicates is desperately needed for the preservation of freedom and the progress of civilization.

With this ability to appeal to widely divergent interests and needs, conversation radio and television avoid the problems of other programming, whose producers are always in the predicament of deciding whether to utilize programs which are designed to appeal to specifically different groups in a society and, therefore, at a given time serve a minority; or whether to utilize programs designed to appeal to as wide an audience as possible and therefore leave unmet the needs of minorities and individuals. As many of the analysts have observed, what results in most programming is a sense of compromise which leaves both minority and the majority unsatisfied. The creation of a new urban community, with its pluralistic base, demands media which can give expression to divergent needs, attitudes and values.

At the same time, however, there is the opportunity for the ventilation of divergence; there is also an opportunity for another phenomenon important to the creation of a viable community to occur: the reduction of the gap between private attitudes and public morality, this reduction having been something conventional media programming has done only haphazardly and much too timidly.

What is this gap, and how does it occur? Essentially, this gap is the difference between what the social norms—the standards of behavior in a society—*really are*, and what the social norms are *believed to be*, or are said to be. Of course, all societies change; and when they do, changes in the norms of that society are always involved. A case in point in our present society are the norms involving abortion. There is neither time nor space here to analyze why this norm is changing, but essentially the rigid enforcement of our abortion laws has become almost impossible because these laws are no longer expedient for a substantial number of individuals. Many find this norm oppressive; consequently, what occurs is increasing laxness in the application of the norm. There is both a substantial increase in deviant behavior and the surreptitious tolerance of such deviance.

If such a gap only involved one set of social norms in a society, the amount of dysfunction accruing would probably be slight; but this is not usually what occurs. Instead, what happens is that because private toleration of deviance occurs in one area, many people take the attitude, "Well, if it's really all right to indulge in this deviance, it must be all right to indulge in another, and another, and another." The end is a disintegration, or, at least, the dissipation of the strength of all societal norms, and the society is in danger of collapse.

The gap between private attitudes and public morality occurs only as long as those involved do not take a stand publicly. When, however, the private deviations are exposed and publicity is given to them, people begin to range themselves *openly*, either for or against the norm. There is much more pressure exerted in favor of a unitary rather than a dual morality.

Conversation radio and television encourage such stands; and because there are no tabooed subjects (provided the canons of good taste are met) a punch toward this unitary morality is exerted which provides a substantial societal adhesiveness. It is important in this type of programming to preserve this freedom from taboos precisely because it is within a tabooed context that duality of morality occurs.

Other media can provide, of course, the publicity for the widespread disregard or private violation of a public norm and in this way perform a valuable function; but it is participant programming that permits the ordinary citizen—who ultimately in a democracy must make the decisions—to take his own personal, public stand for or against a given norm. This public stand, then, becomes more viable, and much more resistant to change.

Another function of community is to provide within it opportunities for the mutual assistance of its members. In this regard, the mass media—particularly those fostering and encouraging active participation by its consumers—can perform significantly. The media can become clearing houses for action by the community. Citizens can bring their human problems to the media, whether they be trash removal, alcoholism, drug addiction, delinquency, inadequate street lighting, suicide, or marital discord. Note that there is emphasis here upon *citizen* delineation of the problem and not upon the role of the media producers in reporting it. The individual who reports the violation of air pollution requirements by a nearby factory to a television or radio station is going to be much more interested in the ultimate resolution of pollution problems than the passive viewer who watches the results of what some reporter found.

Members of a community also have intensely personal problems, and even here the media can play a role. There are those who decry the fact that people are willing to bring very personal problems to a public medium; however, that they do is certainly no indictment of the medium, but rather an indictment of the society that has spawned people who have no one to turn to but a sympathetic, assisting voice on the radio. The detractors then usually respond that this may be true, but radio is taking advantage of personal misery for commercial ends. Thus they betray a singular lack of knowledge as to how our social system operates, by their assuming that, because one makes a profit, no sense of altruism can exist. Most doctors may be impelled by public service, but they are not disinclined to accept a fee for their services.

Most of the problems people bring to conversation radio are not unique, and many other listeners in the audience suffer in common. Misery loves company, but usually the miserable have to share it first with others. While there is no research to substantiate this position, it can be predicted that many in the listening audience may have found help beyond solace in the personal predicament of others. Certainly it is well known that, when agency referrals are made in the course of a phone call over talk radio, many more than just the suffering caller take advantage of the referral in subsequent days.

Little is known about the efficacy of what amounts to public therapy to make a judgment as to its worth; however, some research indicates that having juvenile delinquents talk to a tape recorder run by housewives, truck drivers and other untrained lay people seems to make a difference in reducing delinquency among these juveniles. There is also evidence that group therapy which contains elements of a public medium has proven its worth as a therapeutic tool by innovative psychiatrists. It is doubtful if it can be much less efficacious than private, extensive (and expensive, it may be added) psychoanalysis. Even if this does not occur, the usefulness of participant media programming in functioning as a referral agency to marriage counseling services, Alcoholics Anonymous, social welfare agencies, psychiatric clinics, the Suicide Prevention Center, etc., is obvious.

Probably the most important function the media can serve in establishing the new sense of community demanded by the urban milieu is to provide for the individual citizen a new sense of power in being able to effect change. As alienated individuals in a mass society, many people feel virtually helpless in the grip of the nameless, faceless abstractions who seem to control their lives. It is a rare citizen who has never called a public agency and been given "the run-around" by bureaucrats who are unperturbed by a lone and irate householder. Many of the public organizations that run our mass society themselves have become masses.

It may be that the mass media utilized in participatory, interactive modes can become the instruments for effective interpersonal contact among "leaders" and "members"; they also could be the reply to the "perhaps" in this statement of the President's former advisor on urban affairs, Daniel P. Moynihan:

> Clearly one of the most powerful forces right now . . . is the diffusion of middle-class attitudes concerning partic-ipation—"I want to take part," "I want to help decide," "I want to be heard"—these are animating more and more people, but perhaps the number of people who can be heard is limited.

The numbers of people who can be heard may in reality be only limited by our inability to escape the perceptual bonds of our rural, small town origins and effectively utilize the mass media in the innovative ways demanded by urbanization.

NEEDED: A NATIONAL
URBAN SERVICE

Lloyd Rodwin and Michael Southworth

Most people are familiar with their own neighborhood and with the customary paths they travel, but the rest of the city is strange and sometimes even dangerous turf. To be sure, with limited time and energy, we can never profit from more than a very small chunk of the world in which we live. Nonetheless, we know far less about that world than we could, and we explore and enjoy it less than we might.

Stephen Carr and Kevin Lynch have suggested that "the educative city" of tomorrow should take more deliberate advantage of the urban experience. It "would invite exploration and reward it; it would encourage manipulation, renovation and self-initiated changes of many kinds. It would contain surprises and novel experiences, challenges to cognition and action."* Indeed, if we were really to exploit the educative potentials of the urban environment, the options before us are exciting to contemplate.

*See S. Carr and K. Lynch. Where Learning Happens. *Daedalus, Journal of the American Academy of Arts and Sciences,* Fall 1968, 97 (4), pp. 1277-1291. In addition to the stimulus provided by this perceptive article, we have greatly benefitted from suggestions received from Stephen Carr, Hilbert Fefferman, May Hipshman and Kevin Lynch.

Lloyd Rodwin is head of the Department of Urban Studies and Planning of M.I.T. **Michael Southworth** is an NDEA Fellow and research associate in the Laboratory for Environmental Studies, M.I.T.

How could the city be opened to exploration and discovery? Three recent experiments suggest some of the ways in which this might be done, perhaps by a new Urban Service. One of the experiments, the "Summer in the Parks Program," sponsored by the National Park Service .during Summer 1968, was designed to acquaint Washington, D.C. residents with the variety of open space in the region. Through its Surprise Trip Program, urban youth who had rarely been outside their own neighborhoods were taken on daily junkets to different areas. Each day more than 1,000 children and teenagers were bussed from recreation centers, block camps, or church centers to new places. At each, a different program had been developed around unique features of the area. One day, for instance, the youngsters could float a raft to an island with tree houses, where they then took part in crafts and nature activities. On another day they might go to the Chesapeake & Ohio Canal, learning how to fish, and how to clean and cook their catch. The impact of the program did not stop with the trips, for many youngsters returned on other days and brought their parents with them.

During Spring 1968 the Boston Redevelopment Authority tried another such experiment: an eye-catching outdoor information center enabled pedestrians to make better use of the wide variety of things to do in the Park Square section of Boston. Films, slides and sounds conveyed contrasting images of the city; recorded messages reported daily events; large picture maps and directories of local activities aided orientation; teletype printers gave instant news; a computer-like machine printed out answers to a variety of questions on the city. Information told about nearby places and Boston's history, culture and physical organization. But besides imparting information, the center's fanciful form made a lively urban place that gave people a reason to stop and talk. It became a place to meet, to chat, to pass the time of day. Several visitors even remarked that for the first time they had felt at home—welcome—in a strange city.

Still a third effort, Philadelphia's new experimental Parkway High School, illustrates what can be done within the public school system using the city as the classroom. The program's philosophy is that people learn best when their education is self-directed and when it involves the world around them. Classes are ungraded, the course requirements are loose, and many teachers are provided by business and industry. Students travel around the city from one source of learning to another, for there is no schoolhouse. Zoology and anthropology, for example, are taught at the Philadelphia Zoo, biology at the Academy of Natural Sciences, statistics and business management at the Insurance Company of North America, law enforcement at the Police Department, and industrial arts at an auto repair shop.

These ventures (and others elsewhere) have made the city and its surrounding areas more interesting and "educative." Although such efforts are encouraging, numerous other exciting possibilities are still seriously neglected. Lack of funds is one stumbling block. The main obstacle, however, is that we have not recognized the potential for enjoyment and education which cities hold. The country long ago grasped such opportunities in the natural world by creating the National Park Service. Each year the Service gives millions of travelers a chance to appreciate some of the finest natural and historic parts of the country. Through its efforts diverse places such as Grand Canyon, Everglades and Mesa Verde have been preserved unspoiled, while at the same time encouraging tourism and the sharpening of regional identity. Besides protecting such places, the Park Service has pointed up their unique features by means of interpretive trails, wayside exhibits, films, and even revival of colorful ceremonies, music and crafts. One of the most admirable features of the Service has been its staff of applied naturalists, who have become skilled not only in resource management, but in helping visitors appreciate natural and historic phenomena. Partial evidence of the success of the program is that, in the last year alone, the National Parks played host to almost 175 million visitors.

This success could be matched in urban regions. Just as the National Park Service has planned parks to help travelers discover the ecology by first-hand observation, an equivalent Urban Service could expose people to the intricate functioning of the city by highlighting the many places and ways in which the mind and eye can take an interesting journey. However rich the world of nature, the urban environment provides even greater potentials, for it is a living museum of our culture. Features in the city which are now often hidden or confusing could be highlighted and made more meaningful. Also, following the same high traditions of the park ranger corps, cities could build up over time a professional staff to help interested residents or visitors to learn and to enjoy themselves as they move about the city.

For example, an Urban Service could greatly increase exposure to the city by making the transportation system more usable. Frequent orientation information is needed to simplify city travel—signs, maps, computerized orientation machines. Besides encouraging travel, the Service could exploit a variety of other means, including viewing devices, cut-away sections, push-button sonic messages and film loops to tell about local activities and history. Paths could be planned that wind through the city, exposing aspects of the environment related to special interests—history, industry, architecture, ecology—and to specific groups, including children, teenagers, visitors and old people. Entire transportation networks, such as railroads, highways or bicycle paths, could be designed as enjoyable educational networks; factories, parks or historic places could be included as parts of that system. Private firms throughout the region might participate by providing information along the street about their own activities and by making it possible for passers-by to see what is going on inside. They could open their doors to the public, at least on certain days, for demonstrations, lectures, tours or even work-training courses. The public costs need not be large; indeed, most of the expense might be borne by the participating firms as the best kind of advertising.

There are a variety of other ways in which the Urban Service could promote educative activities for all ages. Large operable outdoor models of the water, power and transportation systems could allow participants to learn mathematical principles of flow and capacity. Outdoor replicas of the city and region could help one grasp the region more clearly, like Madurodam, the popular miniature city near The Hague. Some settings might emphasize the sensual impact of environment; sounds, images, color and light could be changed in quality, with participants determining the optimal conditions for each impression. Different people's conceptions of the city could be presented and compared in order to encourage people to see the environment in new ways. Other possibilities are outdoor observatories with telescopes for viewing both stars and city, orientation games that could be played in the city, signs in several languages, and neighborhood gardens and zoos where maintenance is shared by residents.

A city with a port or river might transform it into a living museum with displays and events that are not fixed, but constantly evolving over time. A river could tell its story through boat trips, outdoor dioramas, or special exhibits at landmarks. Underwater TV or other sensing devices might communicate what is happening beneath the water. Walk-through models of a harbor and region could show the historical development of the waterfront. An historic ship could be reconstructed and docked at various points to serve as a center for ecology education, as well as for fun, food and drink. Similarly, bridges, islands, industry and people who use the river have stirring sagas to be told. From them one could learn about past and present uses of the river or about the many forms of plant and animal life that depend upon the river—their perils, conflicts and symbiotic relationships.

How to Promote the Educative City

The problem in achieving the educative city will be to design a simple mechanism that will encourage these efforts, while allowing maximum local options and initiative in adapting the idea to each area. No completely satisfactory model exists for the type of organization required to make this program work. As we have intimated, the National Park Service in the Department of the Interior comes closest to what we have in mind, but it is too centralized to encourage much local experimentation. It also operates chiefly on federal property and works primarily outside urban areas. Nonetheless, its experience is relevant because of its ecological perspective and the high traditions of its service.

With a permanent staff of about 6000 and yearly expenditures of about $170 million (1970), it manages 277 areas, including 107 natural and recreational parks and 170 historical areas—totalling in all about 30 million acres. Established in 1916, its primary functions have been to preserve areas of unique natural beauty or historic significance, to develop public understanding of such areas, and to provide for public enjoyment of them. The Service offers assistance to states for public park and recreational facilities, and it sponsors grant-in-aid programs in preservation planning, acquisition and development of historic properties. Recently, matching grants-in-aid have even become available to historic properties owned by private groups. Thousands of part-time and seasonal jobs have also been created for young people by the Service's Job Corps program, whose role is to help the Service meet increasing demands for recreation facilities, historic preservation and maintenance of natural areas.

For the Urban Service that we envisage, however, a decentralized program is needed to ensure expression of regional and local diversity. Although a national agency would be necessary to provide incentives and leadership and to overcome some of the financial and jurisdictional hurdles, the individual programs would be designed and run by local agencies. At the national level, the program might be administered by the Department of Housing and Urban Development, or by other agencies concerned with new development, open space, recreation and education (e.g., the Departments of the Interior and of Health, Education and Welfare). The national agency's main functions would be to set general policies, and to provide matching grants-in-aid, loans, training and technical advice to the local participating agencies.

In addition, state enabling legislation might be drawn up to authorize city or regional governmental agencies or Urban Service Corporations to develop programs and raise funds. Their main functions would be to develop sites and programs of unique interest and educational value, and to encourage and coordinate area-wide participation of local public agencies and private organizations. Agencies which receive public assistance might be encouraged (or required) to reach cooperative agreements with the local Urban Service agency. As in the case of urban renewal or economic development programs, it might also be desirable, at least at the outset, to utilize the device of the public corporation in order to avoid financial, administrative and jurisdictional restrictions.

Direct incentives to local participation would primarily be federal matching grants-in-aid, plus fully repayable loans at federal rates of interest plus a small added amount (say ¼ of 1%) to cover administrative costs. Several indirect incentives might also be effective. For example, in many areas space could be leased to concessioners to operate outdoor museums, provide guide services, food or information. Franchise fees could then be used in support of the program. Thus, over 200 concessioners now operate shops, restaurants, camps or guide services throughout the park system under terms set by the Park Service.

Another indirect incentive might be to modify city ordinances to require major new construction projects to make educative contributions to the city. The building and zoning ordinances, for instance, might permit special development opportunities, such as zoning variances, for exceptional efforts to create sites and activities of educative value to the city. Perhaps certain construction projects or other environmental programs supported by the federal government could even be required to provide opportunities for visitors to the site to learn about the projects or about the section of town in which they are located.

Railroads, automobile associations, airlines, chambers of commerce and tourist bureaus have found it to their advantage to cooperate with the Park Service by advertising the National Parks and Monuments, because it helps sell their services while enhancing their public image. Similar cooperation could be anticipated if there were an Urban Service. In very special cases private organizations could be given assistance to develop the educative or historic quality of their property. Such a method is now used in the oldest areas of San Juan, Puerto Rico, where homeowners are given maintenance grants for preserving the historic character of their homes.

At the start, to get things moving on a modest basis, we suggest amending existing legislation covering various community assistance programs (for example, Model Cities, and certain programs of EDA, OEO and HEW) to allow supplementary grants for those communities interested in experimenting with educative city environments. During the first few years, the number of interested communities would be limited and political pressures for participation in such grant programs would be minimal. This would provide an opportunity for the program to prove itself. To enhance the prospects of success, the federal agency should encourage the assistance of top designers, ecologists, psychologists, as well as other professionals in the formulation of local policies and experiments, especially during the early period.

At this point it is difficult to estimate the costs of such a service. In fiscal year 1970, we are spending about $168 million on the National Park Service, about $75 million of which is for historic preservation, new acquisitions and construction of roads, trails and buildings. The remaining $93 million covers management and protection, maintenance and rehabilitation, and general administration expenses. Compared with most other federal expenditures, this program is relatively modest. For instance, expenditures during the same period will be nearly $6 billion for highways and about $1½ billion for urban renewal and low and moderate income housing programs. Costs of education and manpower training will be almost $8 billion; about $3 billion of this is allotted to manpower training, and the Head Start and Follow Through programs alone will receive $400 million. Nonetheless, we suggest that for the first three years, a very modest sum of approximately $25 to $50 million for grants on a three to one federal-local matching basis and perhaps $100 million for completely repayable loans would suffice to get the program underway and give us ideas as to future costs.

The Risks and the Benefits

There will be some difficult problems, of course, in trying to make such a program work. The American mania for labelling and packaging everything could seriously betray our aims, as might dull or obtrusive projects. We do not wish to create a city that gives the impression that everything is explainable or that the city is simply a machine for learning. It is important to preserve—perhaps even to heighten—opportunities for discovery and mystery in the environment, while still making many of its complexities and disorders more manageable.

Some might argue that the city is already too stressful and informative—that addition of educative elements would overload our senses or would further invade individual privacy. In some places, such as busy commercial streets, this could be true, but in many more areas, adding information could reduce confusion and monotony. Nevertheless, information-free places should be designed into the system. After all, quiet spaces, especially in the center of the city, are as important to learning as exposure.

Another of our concerns is that the city might become a giant propaganda machine—an environment not unlike the streets of Chinese cities today, with their street-corner plays, billboards, loud speakers and parades—all preaching the cultural revolution. A strength, however, of the decentralized organization we have proposed is that it would minimize such dangers by encouraging individual expressions and wide-ranging local experiments.

In short, we concede that an Urban Service carries risks. But our hopes far exceed our fears. An Urban Service is hardly a panacea for the problems that plague our cities: clearly, physical and social changes are necessary that would not be directly affected by this program. We would contend, however, that an Urban Service merits support because it could enable great numbers of people to profit from the educative potentials of the city.

One of the many advantages of such a Service is that it would make more available the diversity of experience that is so important to individual development, particularly in the early years. Although television serves this function in some sense, that experience is vicarious; direct exposure or activity is far more vivid and telling. By encouraging encounters with new situations, an Urban Service might particularly benefit people who come from places that now lack variety or opportunity—suburbs, urban slums, depressed regions, even central cities.

An Urban Service might also help to compensate for some of the weaknesses of formal education. For many of the young, school is often dull and unrelated to their interests. The rigidity of most schools discourages the involvement of students in a personal way, at their choice, in discovery of the world. Conventional education is often too specialized, focusing disproportionately on preparing students for jobs and for college rather than for living. An Urban Service would extend education outside the walls of schools and museums and beyond the years of formal schooling. Learning would be firsthand, personal and enjoyable. The student would be free to learn what interests him from whatever sources he chooses; he could set his own pace without fear of competition. People would be reached who now have no access to formal education. Moreover, such an emphasis could help to offset some of the negative forces of poor schools, homes, or neighborhoods by providing other avenues for learning.

As the work week shrinks, the Urban Service might also assist the already crowded cultural and recreational institutions to accommodate the new leisure interests. This role will be all the more valuable as cities grow—as the need develops for alternative uses of leisure which do not require extensive investments in land or expensive trips to distant places. The "Summer in the Parks" program previously mentioned did this very successfully in outdoor spaces throughout Washington, D.C. by means of a variety of events—children's theaters, art workshops, sports exhibitions and instruction, concerts featuring both local talent and celebrities, the National Capitol Open bicycle races and an Indian pow-wow. For each event talented local designers created settings to give the park a festive mood appropriate to the occasion. These activities might be enhanced in still other ways. For example, the Service might have a staff of street people—guides, musicians, story tellers and actors—whose role would be to make the city streets more delightful.

City information systems, such as we have described, could also provide a relatively economical way to brighten the image of a whole region without massive physical changes while achieving other valued ends at the same time. Along with designing elements for learning purposes, they could be made to heighten visual order and sensory delight. Use of public transportation systems, for example, which is now usually a stressful and dreary experience, could be made far more enjoyable. Why couldn't the routes of highways, commercial strips, sidewalks and railroads function as more than channels of movement and contribute positively to the travel experience?

Directly or indirectly, an Urban Service would nourish critical evaluations of the city and help to bring about constructive changes. By making the interdependence of man and environment more explicit, the consequences of poor management are less apt to be overlooked. Egregious mistakes could even be underscored: giant air pollution or noise gauges, visible over large areas, could blacken as pollution or noise reaches danger levels; major polluters could be identified along highways. Similar mechanisms might be devised to show the effects on natural life of pesticides, contaminated water or the filling of wetlands. Along with exposing the mistakes in environmental management, solutions could be made known by exhibiting places where good environmental decisions have been made.

Future plans—including conflicting views— could be demonstrated outdoors through models, pictures or mock-ups. These could be evaluated by the public and would stimulate lively discussion. The continual decision-making process within the city could also be illustrated along with the consequences of the decisions on how the city looks and works. Manipulable models and maps might even encourage testing the consequences of alternative public policies that affect the environment.

In sum, benefits of an Urban Service could be broad. It would reach almost everyone—rich and poor, young and old, resident and visitor. Business would be helped. New opportunities would be created, many of which might provide jobs and learning experiences for the disadvantaged. It would foster natural pride in the city, concern with improvement, and outside interest including tourism. Most importantly, it would satisfy the natural and universal itch to find out about other people, places and things.

DEVELOPING A NEIGHBORHOOD CLINIC WITH COMPUTER AND TRAINING TECHNOLOGY

Stephen Schacher and David Bryson

Introduction

The delivery of urban medical care is a problem badly in need of organization. Because physicians require long periods of training and apprenticeship, restructuring of health delivery requires restructuring of the training and utilization of health manpower.

This chapter describes an urban health system in which professional responsibility can be developed in individuals trained in less than two years. Much of this training involves automated, sequential decision making. This type of man/machine interaction should prove to be important not only in medicine but in other technical fields as well, where computerized decision logic may help to provide services and personal education to urban residents.

We hope that decision makers in urban education will see generality in our specific approach to urban health. Viewed broadly, we describe how previously untrained people may very rapidly, by means of simulation techniques, be given major responsibility in an area in which the requisite sensory, logical and motor skills are frequently complicated.

We describe below a plan of medical care for urban patients, and the computer and training technology required for implementation.

Stephen Schacher, M.D., is a special student at Massachusetts Institute of Technology. David Bryson, M.D., is manager, Behavior Systems Division, Westinghouse Learning Corporation.

The provider of care is a non-M.D. clinician who executes decisions which are made by a comprehensive, computerized information system. In addition to improved health, advantages to the patient include treatment without delay by a familiar person, and initial and frequently total care within his own neighborhood and sometimes even within his own residence. A special advantage for physicians and hospitals would be a lesser utilization of these services by patients who do not in fact require them.

The plan differs from most others aimed at the urban health crisis in the full clinical responsibility delegated to a non-physician and in the deliberate and frequent use of an information source in the presence of patients. But while our clinician has no direct human supervisor, the information system is a constant source of specific guidance and direction. "Look over the shoulder" it actively does, though the "behavior" of the information system to a user would seem much closer to that of a colleague/consultant rather than a supervisor/ delegator.

The information system differs from most medical information systems in that it operates in a step-by-step (sequential) fashion, telling the clinician the next best action to take (e.g., ask about nausea, check for tissue swelling, administer electrolytes by mouth and enter change in patient status in one hour), rather than only rendering a single, final opinion after a cluster of patient findings are entered in parallel. It differs also in the range of disease states it considers; existing computer aids to medical decision-making are dedicated to single areas of diagnosis, such as congenital heart disease, renal disease, thyroid disease, etc. Our system considers all common diseases, but only to points which remain within the diagnostic and therapeutic capabilities of the clinician.

We propose that the system be set up in open and free competition with the existing suppliers of ambulatory care—the emergency room and out-patient departments of urban hospitals. Patients may by-pass the local clinic and go directly to the hospital if they so choose—no administrative links attempt to shunt self-limiting illnesses away from the hospital. Free competition between the two systems should result in greater satisfaction for patients, for physicians and hospital personnel, and for the payers of medical bills.

The paper is arranged as follows: 1) principles of clinic operation; 2) principles of information system design; and 3) principles of clinician training. A final section will list some good and bad features of the total plan.

Principles of Clinic Operation

1.   *Neighborhood clinics are headed by neighborhood clinicians.* The neighborhood clinician has managerial authority over a team of medical technicians and supportive personnel. The information system constantly imposes decision constraints on the neighborhood clinician, and thus his clinical decisions are relatively minor. In contrast, his managerial decisions are major, and he allocates clinic resources in relation to such unpredictable matters as patient cueing, emotional emergencies, employee illnesses, etc.

2.   *Self-limiting and non-serious illnesses are treated at the neighborhood clinic; other patients are sent to the hospital.* Conditions treated at the neighborhood clinic include common childhood illnesses, minor burns, strains, gastroenteritis, superficial lacerations, some uncomplicated lower respiratory infections, nearly all upper respiratory infections, uncomplicated malnutrition in infants and the elderly, some acute intoxications not requiring washing of the stomach, and some rat bites. Doing so could relieve the hospital emergency room of 60% to 80% of patients, who now use this facility as their "family physician." The operational definitions of "self-limiting" and "non-serious" would be conservative and prudent, so that illnesses of uncertain nature, as well as those obviously requiring physician intervention, would be directed to the most accessible hospital.

3.   *The neighborhood clinician is an expert at executing the decisions of the medical information system.* With high precision, the neighborhood clinician can perform specified aspects of physical examination and can elicit and interpret the verbal responses to specified aspects of the patient's history and chief complaint. He knows how to input this information, as well as simple laboratory and radiological findings, into a computer terminal at the neighborhood clinic.

4.   *X-rays are taken and interpreted by a non-physician radiologist.* We have concluded that the visual skills required for the interpretation of routine x-rays require a category of personnel separate in training and function from the neighborhood clinician. This person takes routine films requiring no special patient preparation (no barium swallows, no IV pyelograms, etc.) and can detect fractures, lead lines in

bones from paint eating, and make simplified interpretations of chest films and abdominal films. He knows how to state the findings in a format which the neighborhood clinician can enter directly into the computer terminal. Certainty of his findings, as an obvious fracture or a questionable fracture, would dictate that physician services and the skills of an M.D. radiologist are required.

5. *Certain laboratory tests are performed in the neighborhood clinic.* A highly automated clinical laboratory is operated by a technician. Tests include urinalysis, complete blood count, blood sugar, routine blood chemistries and examination of stools or parasites. Of particular importance would be the culturing of throat and urine for the presence and type of bacterial infections. This would allow for retrospective adjustments (start, stop or change drug) in patient therapy, and since culturing is rarely performed in the emergency room, would also yield important epidemiological data. The low cost of multichannel analytic devices may generate more information than the computer actually calls for in a single patient at a single time. The information system also may call for electrocardiographic information in certain patients. Information here would bear only on the decision: send to hospital/don't send to hospital; and thus special discriminations in EKG interpretation would be excluded from consideration. It is probable that a separate remote access computer system would automatically scan, interpret and print out the results of EKGs taken in the neighborhood clinic, and thus the only task of the neighborhood clinician would be to feed verbal printout of the EKG system into his own information clinic.

6. *Certain drugs are prescribed in the neighborhood clinic.* Under the prescription of the information system, the neighborhood clinician dispenses a variety of therapeutic agents consonant with the scope of the neighborhood clinic. The low incidence of medical emergencies precludes the dispensing of drugs by intravenous injection—all internal medications will be delivered either by mouth or by intramuscular injection. Such common agents as antibiotics, tranquilizers, vitamins, non-narcotic analgesics and topical steroids would be prescribed. However, certain common medications, because of potential danger of overdosage or idiosyncratic reactions, or because of the severity of the underlying disease, would not be available. Among these are digitalis, systemic steroids and antitumor agents. Our position on narcotics is that they should not be a part of neighborhood clinic

operation. Any patient who develops acute pain of sufficient intensity to require morphine is certainly an emergency case in need of a physician. Phenobarbital might be administered to such a patient before ambulance boarding.

7.   *Emotional problems are welcomed in the neighborhood clinic.* The term "crock" is used disparagingly by some physicians in describing patients who present themselves at the hospital with no bona fide physical illness. Aside from the fact that patients cannot interpret the significance of their complaints as can physicians, the need for reassurance from an authoritative figure is real. Such patients are often mistreated in the hospital in the hope that negative reinforcement will weaken the tendency to return. By design, the neighborhood clinic staff views warm words as good medicine for everyone, and can deal with sexual problems, illness or death of a family member, or any other emotional situation likely to cause suffering and the incapacitation of a patient. The neighborhood clinician dispenses support and advice in the best tradition of a family physician. The neighborhood clinic is equipped to handle emotional emergencies in all but the most violent categories. Thus a strong tranquilizer administered intramuscularly and physical restraint would be a standard procedure, available if required. In emotional matters, the neighborhood clinician operates independently of the information system—he manages patients as well as resources. The neighborhood clinic should in no way be expected to crack the problems of chronic alcoholism, addiction and psychiatric illness.

8.   *Care of pregnant women is not a function of the neighborhood clinic.* Pregnant women should be seen by those physicians who will be responsible for the delivery and care of the newborn. Trivial illnesses with no medical implications for the state of pregnancy, as a common cold or a laceration, could provide input acceptable to the information system.

9.   *Home care is provided for patients unable to come to the neighborhood clinic.* House calls are made for those patients who are too incapacitated to come to the neighborhood clinic (with the qualification that the patient is probably not seriously ill and in need of a physician), for those who cannot come because of young children at home, for those who are recovering from recent hospitalization and are not being seen by a visiting nurse from the hospital or who develop an

unrelated illness, etc. While in a residence, the neighborhood clinician will be without direct access to his information system, and thus as much information as possible will be determined and processed by telephone before departure. The neighborhood clinician may direct staff aides to transport any person into the neighborhood clinic if he expects that direct access to the laboratory and the information system will significantly improve his services.

10. *Return visits to the neighborhood clinic are scheduled.* For patients treatable at the neighborhood clinic, the final printout of the information system typically contains two statements: a treatment statement and a follow-up statement. The follow-up requested might be only a few hours as part of the decision-making process, but more usually a definite entry is made in the patient's record to return in x number of days for continued care—removing stitches, changing bandages, checking on healing, weighing after prescribing nutritional supplement, etc. If two neighborhood clinicians are provided for each clinic, one could hold office hours while the other makes house calls.

11. *Forms are filled out after patients are treated, rather than before.* The neighborhood clinic takes seriously the truism that administrative functions are less important than relief of patient suffering. Any person who enters any neighborhood clinic will be cared for, regardless of indigency or lack of it, and regardless of any geographic or other type of requirement.

12. *Dental problems are beyond the scope of the neighborhood clinic.* An important component of urban medical illness is poor dental health. Our approach is not applicable to dental problems because, unlike medical problems, the bulk of dental work required by urban populations is not minor. Complex diagnostic skills and especially complex manual skills are required to provide orthodontia, periodontia, and the replacement of missing and hopelessly decayed teeth.

Principles of Neighborhood Clinician Training

1. *A simulated information system is a major feature of neighborhood clinician training.* The first group of neighborhood clinicians would begin training before the actual information system is developed. The trainee would work at a simulated terminal, and a human instructor, remote from view, would produce printouts which would rule on the acceptability of trainee input and would request the

trainee to perform the next desired test. From the start, the trainee would develop experience with the capabilities and limitations of his objective companion. Conversely, results from the information system simulation would be important input to the team producing the actual information system, since these results would help to identify the capabilities and limitations of human trainees, especially with regard to maintaining effective communication with a restricted input code.

2.   *Simulated patients are a major feature of neighborhood clinician training.* A multimedia interactive device should be able to simulate a wide variety of visual and auditory features, such as general appearance, rapid breathing, splinted breathing, color of skin, gait, arterial bleeding, type of cough, regularity of heart sound, etc. For tactile skills, such as palpations of the abdomen, live actors will be required. An important rule in all sensory discriminations is that the trainee has considerable experience with input at the level of direct reality (actual sounds, actual sights, actual touches) before he is given any symbolic scheme of classification (this sounds irregular/that sounds regular, this looks enlarged/that looks normal, this feels hard/that feels soft, etc.) We think that the cerebral entry for a sensory classification should be in the dimensions of the sensation itself, rather than a symbolic representation of it.

3.   *The neighborhood clinician is trained to think of illnesses in terms of what is done for them, rather than what caused them.* Physicians are trained to go through two mental processes—one for diagnosis, and then a separate one for treatment. In the training of neighborhood clinicians, diagnosis as a formal intermediary preceding treatment is eliminated. The rationale for this is that the information system is completely competent to handle the diagnostic process, and the emphasis on treatment will make the neighborhood clinician even more oriented towards results.

4.   *The neighborhood clinician is given particular training in the elicitation and interpretation of verbal reports of illness.* Many of the patients seen in the neighborhood clinic will be inarticulate with respect to medical terminology. Psychological barriers to communication, such as attempts to please or attempts to conceal, will also be prominent. The trainee will be given the multidisciplinary skills to enable him to be an effective buffer between the language of the patient and the language of the information system.

5.   *The neighborhood clinician is trained in behavioral skills.*

The trainee is exposed to sensitivity training, managerial techniques, group therapy, supportive psychotherapy, family dynamics, simulated psychotic episodes, acute emotional troubleshooting, etc.

6. *The neighborhood clinician is trained to execute the therapeutic decisions of the information system.* The manual skills related to therapy required by the neighborhood clinician are few, and include superficial suturing of wounds, intramuscular injection and the splinting and wrapping of sprained joints. Suturing would be learned on a material with physical properties similar to the skin; other manual skills would be learned on self or another trainee.

7. *The neighborhood clinician is trained to view his services more in terms of benefits for individuals rather than benefits for the public health.* The neighborhood clinic exists to treat neighborhood illnesses; and, in so doing, the neighborhood clinician develops and maintains a personal relationship with his patients. Thus the trainee comes to view preventive and public health ramifications of his services as a beneficial side effect. He is taught the public implications of such problems as venereal disease, drug addiction, the avoidance of un-wanted pregnancy, or rat holes in an apartment, and how to bring the proper city agencies to bear on these problems. However, his self-image is essentially that of a single individual attempting to relieve the suffering and improve the health of another single individual.

Principles of Information System Design

(The following principles are adapted from Gorry,* with the exception of the system's emphasis on treatment rather than diagnosis.)

1. *The information system is designed to be shared.* All neighborhood clinics in the same city would use the same data base (time sharing). Such sharing would not introduce impractical delays for any user, i.e., input-output delays in the step-by-step examination of a patient would be insignificant (real time).

2. *The information system makes sequential decisions.* The information returned by the computer to the user at any decision node is the "next best test." "Test" means any action which will generate information bearing on the next decision, such as a question to the

*G. Anthony Gorry. Strategies for Computer-Aided Diagnosis. *Mathematical Biosciences*, 1968, *2*, pp. 293-318.

patient, a physical inspection of the patient, a laboratory or x-ray procedure, or a therapeutic trial of a medication. For example, if the initial input is "6-year-old, abdominal pain, no current medications," the computer's initial response might be any of the following types of requests: previous appendectomy? (past history); has the patient vomited? (present history); are bowel sounds present? (physical exam); obtain abdominal film and determine if small bowel loops are distended (clinical test). After the result of the above test is inputted, a second test is requested and again the result is inputted. Eventually the "next best test" is to perform no further test but rather to make a final disposition.

3. *In deciding upon the next best test, "costs" are considered by the information system.* "Costs" include discomfort or potential danger to the patient, the inconvenience of time delays ("watching and waiting"), and possible dangers of treatment or non-treatment. In general, the cost of sending a patient to the hospital who will not, in retrospect, need physician care is much less than the cost of sending a patient home who is in fact in need of a physician.

4. *In arriving at a final decision, the information system chooses a diagnosis, but prints out treatment and follow-up care only.* The final printout (disposition) is consonant with a ˙fundamental principle of neighborhood clinician training, namely, to think in terms of "what should be done for this patient," rather than "what disease does this patient have." In the final internal action leading the information system to a "most likely diagnosis," all the diagnoses which are being strongly considered are multiplied by the cost of each being wrong. The diagnostic category which then emerges with the lowest cost is chosen and the disposition is printed out. The information system does not distinguish between diagnoses having the same disposition. For example, it would not distinguish between appendicitis and ruptured ovarian cyst, since *both* require a surgeon. It also would not make distinctions between conditions in which treatment and follow-up care at the neighborhood clinic are identical.

5. *When the decision-making program is initially installed in the information system, all diagnostic probabilities and all costs are estimated by medical experts.* Accurate disease profiles for urban populations do not exist, and thus estimates are required initially. Certain parameters of costs are subjective, such as the inconveniences of delay and the unpleasantness of tests. These will have to be weighted

into the program after considered judgment and program trials.

6. *The accuracy of all dispositions recommended by the information system are at some future time fed back into the computer, thus updating probabilities and costs.* By so doing, the information system is able to reflect transitory variation in disease incidence in the neighborhood. For example, during a flu epidemic, the likelihood of a given complaint being related to the outbreak is increased. The effect of transitory shifts in probabilities is that the identical initial entry—"6-year-old, abdominal pain, on no current medications"—may produce a different sequence of tests at different times. Furthermore, system updating will also bring the original estimates of probabilities and costs closer to their actual values.

7. *Before any information for an individual patient is entered into the computer, diagnostic probabilities for this patient are considered equal to the current probabilities for the community at large.* Thus *before* any information is entered, viral upper respiratory infection is more likely to be the diagnosis of a random patient than is acute appendicitis. If the initial input included "abdominal pain," the diagnostic categories associated with various abdominal complaints undergo a significant increase in probability, while certain other diagnoses, such as middle ear infection, would be virtually extinguished from further consideration.

8. *The mathematical basis of the information system is Bayesian probability.* The selection for each "next best test" is based upon two factors—the cost of the test and the ability of the test to differentiate the diagnoses being considered. Each test result produces a calculated change in disease probabilities (by the use of Bayes theorem). Eventually a single diagnostic category is sufficiently likely that the cost of further testing outweighs the likelihood of improving the final decision. It is here that decision-making ceases and the disposition is printed out.

9. *The information system as described is feasible within current computer technology.* The information system for the neighborhood clinics would not be in the forefront of computer research and development, since the technology and logic required are *already available*. Furthermore, the richness of branching within the decision tree need not be very great, since both the diagnostic and treatment categories of the information system would be considerably reduced from those found in hospital medicine.

Good and Bad Features of the Plan

Good Features

1.   Many patients who either receive no medical care or inadequate, sporadic, depersonalized care can have access to an individual who is medically competent, will make house calls if necessary, and who can and will respond to their emotional problems.

2.   Physicians are relieved of the burden of screening trivial problems and treating minor problems, allowing them to see patients with major and life-threatening illnesses, for which they have been uniquely trained.

3.   The hospital emergency room and out-patient departments, which have become the sole source of care for many patients, and which are cost-ineffective to a high degree, could be relieved of 60% to 80% of their patient population.

4.   Once the neighborhood clinic system is developed, it can be duplicated easily.

Bad Features

1.   A new bureaucracy to supervise the neighborhood clinics and/or the neighborhood clinicians may appear.

2.   Local political fights over project control and such matters as the method of neighborhood clinician selection could torpedo the entire effort.

3.   The project has high visibility, which raises the unfortunate possibility of being *observed to death.*

4.   Since the project has high development costs (we estimate about 400 hours of multimedia instruction and about five man-years of information system development), the temptation to cut corners in neighborhood clinician training and information system comprehensiveness could lead to poor results and abandonment of the central principles.

Relationship of This Plan to Current Innovations

Various cities have already taken steps consistent with this plan, including regionalization of hospital services; increased neighborhood services (usually preventive in emphasis); the minor use of computer technology for scheduling and record-keeping; and increased use of non-physicians in clinical activities. A motive for all of these changes has been a more realistic allocation of dollars for urban health. This plan is a continuation of this trend, but with a discrete jump in which the physician is completely eliminated at the satellite station and *the full potential of computerized information systems is brought to bear.* We believe it does not require very much imagination to see how the elements in the system described in this paper might be applied to both training and service delivery in professional fields other than medicine—including education.

ON TECHNOLOGICAL ESCAPISM

James M. Beshers

By perceiving urban problems as essentially technological, one can move in an orderly fashion to the design and implementation of many pleasing solutions. The "alabaster cities" might be created in remote areas of the Far West, shining in uncontaminated air. Transportation, pollution, utilities, household conveniences, business and education might be implemented with great efficiency.

These dream cities, or utopias, may satisfy our fantasies, but do they really meet the pressing problems of today? Are they, at best, places for the privileged to run? Suburbs without cities as a final glory to civilization?

The temptation to proceed with such strictly technological solutions is increased by the availability of many engineers and scientists transferring from defense applications. The systems concepts and cost-benefit techniques of defense science are now widely proposed for urban problem-solving.

Here we shall argue that the statement of urban problems and their solution require explicit use of social system concepts. In particular, the notion of benefits must be made clear. Three forms of this argument will be developed.

First, I shall argue that social benefits will come from a shift in the

James M. Beshers is professor of sociology at Queens College and chairman of the Committee on Comparative Urban Studies, Graduate Center, City University of New York.

present systems, rather than the creation of wholly new systems. Such shifts may be designed in the light of strategic experiments, as might occur in the new cities programs. These experiments, however, may be inappropriately designed and executed; for example, a school system that is effective in suburban situations may fail in the inner city.

Second, I shall argue that particular mixes of technology and social factors are desirable and perhaps also necessary. The separation of technological factors from social factors is often implied by cost-benefit notions. This separation may lead, however, to ineffective solutions.

Third, I shall argue that innovation in social systems by direct manipulation of social processes is frequently desirable, and may be more pertinent than the indirect changes that come from technological shifts.

In order to define present urban problems it is necessary to develop social system models guided by social system concepts. I shall give examples of relevant models from my own work.*

For many purposes a core demographic model of cities and regions is essential. Such a model contains birth, death, migration and social mobility as social processes represented by stochastic probabilities. The population is classified by age, birth date and sex, as well as by race, occupation and other social characteristics (where the list of characteristics varies according to the particular problem under study). Such models can be used to forecast future distributions of the population in given areas. Especially interesting forecasts may be obtained if the transition probabilities are expressed as variables—the case of the non-stationary stochastic process.

The delivery of services, say health services, education services, and so on, may be greatly improved with forecasts of small area populations from demographic models. The detailed characteristics of the future population can be used to estimate demand for various

*My technical approach to model building is described in three books and a number of papers. The educational system is discussed in Models of the Educational Process: A Sociologist's Perspective, forthcoming in *On Equality of Educational Opportunity*, edited by Frederick Mosteller and Daniel P. Moynihan. More general approaches are given in *Urban Social Structure*, New York: Free Press, 1962; *Population Processes in Social Systems*, New York: Free Press, 1967; and *Computer Methods in the Analysis of Large Scale Social Systems* (Revised Edition), Cambridge, Mass.: MIT Press, 1968.

services at the local level. Clinics, schools and other facilities can be designed and administered.

Another general application of such demographic models is the simulation of the effects of policies or programs. Thus a particular transportation program may have effects on the migration probabilities that will produce new distributions of the population; housing policies also could be expected to modify migration probabilities. Similarly, education and job creation policies might modify social mobility probabilities. Various alternatives may be proposed and simulated.

For either the forecasting or the simulation application, the essential problem is to determine the transition probabilities, especially the functional form that determines how the probabilities change. This issue is one of social theory; no guidance comes from the natural sciences or engineering. Thus if the forecasting or simulation applications are desired, then social systems and social theory must be directly involved.

Now let us consider my first specific argument. Social system shifts, not wholly new systems, are the appropriate goal. This point is most easily seen if we note that, even if we create a wholly new environment, we will be placing in it people from our general population, with well developed prejudices, attitudes, weaknesses and other characteristics. There is a strong likelihood that these predispositions on the part of the people would dominate their relationship to the environment, as well as their relationships among each other.

It is also doubtful that wholly new environments, such as new cities, could do much more than offset the population growth in the U.S., and it is very unlikely that new cities would replace the functions of existing cities. Thus urban problems as presently defined would be only slightly affected by the new cities program.

Now let me turn to my second argument, namely that appropriate technology will often involve a complex mixture of new hardware and modified social processes. Here the best examples lie in communications and in information processing. In the field of education, much has been made of learning machines that serve as mechanical workbooks, yet the success of *Sesame Street* already indicates that educational television will be far more important. The social content of TV, as well as its vast diffusion, is continually modifying our present social systems.

Governmental decision processes may be dramatically influenced if the concept of the public hearing becomes more adequate. Already television has had quite an influence, but when coupled with effective computerized urban information systems the consequences of alternative policies might be more rapidly assessed. If the several public interests were represented by skilled advocates who could utilize the power of such computer based systems, then the television audience might share in evaluating the selection of alternative policies, rather than simply opposing a single "plan" as in the case of inner city highways.

More generally the conflicts among the several interest groups in the city will tend to shape the technological inputs. Adequate planning must take account of these conflict and power relations in much greater detail than was true in the past.

Let me turn to the third argument, namely that direct innovation in social processes may be more relevant than technological innovation. The simplest example would be the modification of the work day to spread peak commuter loads. Such modification would be an administrative action. Another example would be the t-groups, or sensitivity groups, that are intended to modify interpersonal relations.

These arguments above are intended to be suggestive. They can be summarized in the view that, until we adequately conceive of cities as social systems, we will not effectively design technological solutions to a broad range of current urban problems.

FITTING URBAN EDUCATIONAL REFORM TO THE WHOLE CLOTH OF SYNERGY

Raymond A. Ehrle

Many existing institutional, social and professional arrangements in urban education are structured so that the world is *artificially polarized* and *arbitrarily dichotomized* into "good guys" and "bad guys," "right thinkers" and "deviants," "teachers" and "administrators," "pupils" and "parents," etc. Such potential win-lose or lose-lose arrangements call for apparent self-seeking and defensive measures on the part of all group members involved.

As a result, each group becomes more closely knit and demands more loyalty and conformity from its members in order to be able to present a solid front. Each group also becomes more structured, organized and task oriented. On the other hand, they also begin to experience distortions in perception as they begin to see other groups as the "enemy." Hostility toward other groups increases while interaction and communication decrease. Even more perversely, if groups are *forced* to interact, each will listen more closely to its representative (who supports its position) and not to representatives of other groups. This is obviously a situation to be avoided or corrected, if possible.

Raymond A. Ehrle is director of marketing (Manpower Services) for Teledyne Packard Bell and professorial lecturer at George Washington University and American University, Washington, D.C.

Synergy, on the other hand, calls for the establishment of appropriate institutional and social arrangements which *facilitate cooperative and collaborative efforts* among various interested and concerned groups.

Within the existing school "system" five subsystems, or publics, some of which overlap, are identifiable. These are: parents, students, administrators, taxpayers and instructional staff. The current organizational and institutional arrangements are not synergistic, in that they result in the reward of some of these publics at the expense of others. Such arrangements work against the establishment of a wholly integrated and mutually beneficial educational system. They inevitably lead to win-lose group conflict.

Subsystem Objectives, Feedback and Defensive Efforts

In effect, each of these publics is a subsystem with data input, data processing and interpretation capabilities, data output and feedback components. Each has its own objectives based on the collective needs of the individual members. Each has been able to exert a negative influence on the operations of the other subsystems as well as on the development of a total educational system. Although each of the five subsystems is reasonably effective in meeting the needs of its members, each one is relatively ineffective in terms of collaborating to create a comprehensive educational system. This is true despite the fact that their internal communication and feedback mechanisms are operative and effective.

Parents receive feedback from their children, from the public school itself and from college admissions officers and potential employers. They occasionally, or frequently, express their opinion of the general educational "system" in disparaging terms. Taxpayers (who may or may not be parents) obtain feedback through progress reports around budget time as well as by reading newspaper features and editorials. They have recently come to express their disenchantment with the status quo through the rejection of new bond issues.

Administrators obtain feedback from parents, taxpayers, the teaching staff, the news media, college admissions officers and potential employers. They frequently suffer from low morale and take refuge in adopting bureaucratic coloration and defensive, depersonalized bureaucratic procedures.

The instructional staff obtains feedback from students, administrators, the world of potential employers and college admissions officers. Their low morale is demonstrated, for example, by a lack of professionalism and a felt necessity to join unions as a measure of personal protection.

Students have perhaps the weakest or most ambiguous kind of feedback arrangement. They are frequently unclear as to what the learning objectives of a course of study are; whether such objectives are valid or "relevant" to the real world as they see it; or, if valid, whether or not they are achieving their objectives. Students need short-cycle feedback to pace themselves, to see where they are going. They literally have to wait for years for feedback from college admissions officers and potential employers to really assess their goals, purposes and progress. Their uncertainty and ambivalence are demonstrated through "dropping out," "playing the game," or "acting out" in open dissension.

Need for a Synergistic System

The time is ready for the establishment of a more wholly integrated, coordinated and synergistic educational system in which the five subsystems can work positively together. In other words, the instructional arrangements must be such that cooperative and collaborative efforts within and between the five subsystems are facilitated in a win-win approach. Furthermore, the thesis of this writer is that *people are "good" and will act in ways that are not self-destructive or destructive of others, if given the chance. All persons and groups would be rewarded for certain kinds of behaviors, but only by facilitating other groups as they strive for their objectives.*

The development of such a system immediately involves key notions of: (a) defining learning objectives in behavioral terms, (b) considering the total educational enterprise as a whole made up of the five subsystems, (c) strengthening feedback channels among components of the enterprise as well as within each subsystem and (d) assuring that the system is provided the opportunity to be accountable to each of the subsystems and having each subsystem accountable to the overall system as well as to its membership.

The educational system must be built upon sets of behavioral objectives that can be assigned as learning tasks to individual students. (This, incidentally, does not deny the importance of humanistic or affective learning, either in or out of school.) These would be organized into learning packages, each dealing with a few closely related concepts. A short-cycle, closed-loop capability must be built in to provide constant feedback to the student regarding his progress.

The educational system would also develop a data bank that would allow researchers, curriculum developers and teachers to analyze individual performance, specific instructional items, tests, etc., as part of the evaluation and feedback process.

A good learning system should be self-corrective and cost-effective. Self-correction is contingent upon adequate feedback, while cost-effectiveness is related to accountability. Decentralization in educational management would make the educational bureaucracy more responsive to the human needs of its staff as well as its students. Additional benefits which would accrue include an increase in independence of thought and action at middle and lower administrative levels, the opportunity to bring staff members of courage and ability to the top through careful assignment and careering practices, and the setting-up of conditions whereby people would learn to assume responsibility.

Meeting Individual and Subsystem Needs

Since each subsystem is composed of people, it is possible to ascertain their intrinsic individual and collective needs. Each intrinsic need may be matched by a synergistic arrangement as well as by overt ways in which these needs can be met. For example, parents want quality education for their children. They also want to be able to either realistically *influence school policy* or *select educational alternatives* to achieve this end. At least two things are called for: (a) local control of boards of education to influence school policy *as necessary,* and (b) establishment of an educational voucher system to break the educational monopoly *if necessary.*

The adoption of these two contingencies, indeed, does pose a threat to the public school system if considered on a piecemeal basis. *Only if the entire system is overhauled to protect all subsystems will the sense of threat lessen.* The overriding virtue of meeting the needs of parents is an increased assurance, a "gut feeling" sense of credibility that their concerns for a quality education are being met.

Students, on the other hand, are concerned with the "what" and the "how." They are *concerned about "relevant" learning experiences* for tomorrow (as well as for yesterday and today) and with the opportunity to escape the lock-step system *and to learn at their own pace.* To achieve these dual purposes, a variety of synergistic approaches have been proposed and are being used in various degrees. These include: (a) Individually Prescribed Instruction (IPI), (b) Computer Assisted Instruction (CAI), (c) the use of "learning contracts" between teacher and student and (d) the development of directed experiential learning as an alternative to symbolic learning.

Widespread use of these approaches would indeed redefine teaching roles, affect the conduct of the student work day and even affect the architectural layout of the school. Students might learn more than their parents already know! In short, an adoption of these approaches will, indeed, create a threat to other subsystems in the schools unless concomitant changes are also made in them.

Although some might question this statement, it would appear that school administrators are primarily motivated by two things, namely: (a) an *opportunity to develop and manage a professionally sound quality educational system* and (b) an *opportunity to exercise authority commensurate with responsibility.* Some school and college administrators openly suffer from low morale and leave the field, while perhaps a larger proportion adapt to bureaucratic modes of coping to deal with problems not of their own making and over which they have little control. Although some have adjusted very well to a nonresponsive, ritualistic, depersonalized but relatively secure bureaucracy, most administrators would rather have community recognition and support, most tangibly reflected as monetary rewards for a good job well done.

Taxpayers, in the final analysis, want two things, *a "cost-effective" educational system* and *a "self-correcting" system,* insofar as possible. They are becoming aware that such is not the case at this time. For the taxpayer subsystem, both performance contracting and educational voucher systems offer promise as synergistic components. Again, these cannot stand alone as "the" answer, ignoring the needs and necessary components of the other subsystems. (See other chapters in this book for descriptions of educational vouchers and performance contracting.)

The teaching staff, by and large, would settle for recognition of a job well done and the general support of parents, the community and school administrators. Very often, they do not have this feeling, and show their lowered morale by joining unions to obtain "protection." If given a chance, they would prefer to have their performance recognized with rewards for excellence. Obviously, differentiated staffing—with differentiated roles and rewards—is the answer rather than further homogenization, role diffusion and equality of pay.

Again, however, differentiation within the educational staff subsystem must be carried out in the context of appropriate changes in the other subsystems of the educational enterprise.

Conclusion

The current malaise in American urban education can only be understood in terms of its evolution into a series of win-lose subsystems, each of which exists by imposing penalties on the others. The tragedy here is that this need not be, for people and groups will act in ways that are not self-destructive or destructive of others—if given the chance.

The five subsystems identified include parents, teachers, students, taxpayers and administrators. A more synergistic approach is called for whereby it becomes possible for each subsystem to meet its true objectives (some of which have been explicated) but not at the expense of the other subsystems involved. Various synergistic components, such as the use of educational vouchers and differentiated staffing, were briefly discussed—with a caveat against applying them in a piecemeal fashion, which might simply heighten intergroup conflict.